CLARENDON PLATO SERIES

General Editor: M. J. WOODS

PLATO
Phaedo

Translated with Notes

by

DAVID GALLOP

PROFESSOR OF PHILOSOPHY
TRENT UNIVERSITY, ONTARIO

CLARENDON PRESS · OXFORD
1975

Oxford University Press, Ely House, London W. 1

GLASGOW NEW YORK TORONTO MELBOURNE WELLINGTON
CAPE TOWN IBADAN NAIROBI DAR ES SALAAM LUSAKA ADDIS ABABA
DELHI BOMBAY CALCUTTA MADRAS KARACHI LAHORE DACCA
KUALA LUMPUR SINGAPORE HONG KONG TOKYO

CASEBOUND   ISBN 0 19 872047 5
PAPERBACK   ISBN 0 19 872049 1

© *Oxford University Press 1975*

*Printed in Great Britain by
Billing & Sons Limited, Guildford and London*

PREFACE

This book is designed for philosophical study of the *Phaedo*. Like other volumes in the present series, it is intended primarily for those who do not read Greek. The translation is based on J. Burnet's Oxford Classical Text (1900), except where indicated in the Notes, or Notes on the Text and Translation. Notes in the latter series are referred to by indices in the translation, and deal with linguistic and textual problems. They are inessential for grasp of the philosophical issues which occupy the main Notes.

The *Phaedo* is one of the most frequently translated, edited, and discussed of all Plato's dialogues. To take full account of the literature in English alone would need a book far larger than this one. As far as space allows, however, I have used existing studies as a spring-board for my own comments, and as a guide on problems that remain unsolved or lie beyond the scope of this work.

Earlier translations and editions have been referred to by author's name only. Abbreviations have been used for the titles of certain other books, and for most periodicals. A key to these will be found in the list of Works and Periodicals Cited. The Bibliography contains only a minimum of works necessary for detailed study.

The numbers and letters in the margin of the translation are the Stephanus page numbers and section markings used in most modern editions of Plato's works. The marginal line numbers, and the line numbers used for references in the Notes, are those of Burnet's text. They correspond closely, but not always exactly, with the division of lines in the translation. Cross-references of the form 'see on 64c2–9' are to the main Notes. Those of the form 'see note 27' are to the Notes on the Text and Translation. Parenthetical references in the form '(b3–c1)' are to places within the passage covered by the note in which they appear.

I have made frequent use of other translations, and have taken ideas from them wherever they served my purpose. This has been to render Plato's text as accurately and naturally as possible. When, as often, these criteria conflict, I have aimed for accuracy where philosophical questions are at stake. I have also tried, as far as possible, to avoid prejudging questions of interpretation in the translation itself. The intrusive 'he said', which is often awkward in translation, has frequently been omitted.

My cordial thanks are due to Mr. M. J. Woods, the General Editor of this series, for his advice and encouragement, and for the many improvements which his penetrating comments have led me to make. Professor T. M. Robinson kindly read a draft of the translation and made many valuable suggestions. I am indebted to members of the University of Toronto Ancient Philosophy seminar, whose discussions advanced my understanding of the dialogue; to Professors G. Vlastos and M. T. Thornton for correspondence; to Professor J. L. Ackrill and Mr. M. D. Reeve for helpful discussion; to Professor C. V. Boundas for advice on individual passages; and to many other friends and colleagues, who have contributed more often, and in more ways, than brief acknowledgements can convey.

The manuscript was prepared with the help of Mrs. Gillian Sparrow, for whose assiduous and careful typing I am most grateful, and Mr. K. E. Inwood, whose checking of the final draft saved me from many mistakes.

I am also grateful to Trent University for leaves of absence in 1970 and 1973—4, during which much of the book was written, and to the Canada Council and Nuffield Foundation for generous support. Finally, it is a pleasure to thank the Principal and Fellows of Brasenose College, Oxford, for their kindness in electing me to Senior Common Room membership in 1973—4, and for the hospitality of the College on several occasions while the work was in progress.

Trent University,   DAVID GALLOP
Peterborough,
Ontario

CONTENTS

PHAEDO

Echecrates. Were you there with Socrates yourself, Phaedo, on   **57**
the day he drank the poison in the prison, or did you hear of it from
someone else?

Phaedo. I was there myself, Echecrates.

Echecrates. Then what was it that he said before his death? And   **5**
how did he meet his end? I'd like to hear about it. You see, hardly
anyone from Phlius goes to stay at Athens nowadays, and no visitor
has come from there for a long time who could give us any definite   **b**
report of these events, beyond the fact that he died by drinking
poison; there was nothing more they could tell us.

Phaedo. Didn't you even learn, then, about how the trial went?   **58**

Echecrates. Yes, someone did report that to us, and we were
surprised that it was evidently long after it was over that he died.
Why was that, Phaedo?   **5**

Phaedo. It was chance in his case, Echecrates: it just chanced that
on the day before the trial the stern of the ship that Athenians send
to Delos had been wreathed.

Echecrates. What ship is that?

Phaedo. According to Athenian legend, it's the ship in which   **10**
Theseus once sailed to Crete, taking the famous 'seven pairs', when
he saved their lives and his own as well. It is said that at that time the   **b**
Athenians had made a vow to Apollo that if they were saved, they
would, in return, dispatch a mission to Delos every year; and this
they have sent annually ever since, down to this day, in honour of
the god. Once they've started the mission, it is their law that the city   **5**
shall be pure during that period, which means that the state shall put
no one to death, till the ship has reached Delos and returned; and
this sometimes takes a long time, when winds happen to hold them   **c**
back. The mission starts as soon as the priest of Apollo has wreathed
the stern of the ship; and, as I say, this chanced to have taken place
on the day before the trial. That's why Socrates spent a long time in
prison between his trial and death.   **5**

Echecrates. And what about the circumstances of the death itself,

1

Phaedo? What was it that was said and done, and which of his
intimates were there with him? Or would the authorities allow no
one to be present, so that he met his end isolated from his friends?

d   *Phaedo.* By no means: some were present, in fact quite a number.

Echecrates. Please do try, then, to give us as definite a report as
you can of the whole thing, unless you happen to be otherwise
engaged.

Phaedo. No, I am free, and I'll try to describe it for you; indeed
5   it's always the greatest of pleasures for me to recall Socrates, whether
speaking myself or listening to someone else.

Echecrates. Well, Phaedo, you certainly have an audience of the
same mind; so try to recount everything as minutely as you can.

e   *Phaedo.* Very well then. I myself was curiously affected while I
was there: it wasn't pity that visited me, as might have been expected
for someone present at the death of an intimate friend; because the
man seemed to me happy, Echecrates, both in his manner and his
words, so fearlessly and nobly was he meeting his end; and so I felt
5   assured that even while on his way to Hades he would not go without
divine providence, and that when he arrived there he would fare
59   well, if ever any man did. That's why I wasn't visited at all by the
pity that would seem natural for someone present at a scene of
sorrow, nor again by the pleasure from our being occupied, as usual,
with philosophy—because the discussion was, in fact, of that sort—
5   but a simply extraordinary feeling was upon me, a sort of strange
mixture of pleasure and pain combined, as I reflected that Socrates
was shortly going to die. All of us there were affected in much the
same way, now laughing, now in tears, one of us quite exceptionally
b   so, Apollodorus—I think you know the man and his manner.

Echecrates. Of course.

Phaedo. Well, he was completely overcome by this state; and I
myself was much upset, as were the others.

5   *Echecrates.* And just who were there, Phaedo?

Phaedo. Of the local people there was this Apollodorus, and
Critobulus and his father, and then there were Hermogenes, Epigenes,
Aeschines, and Antisthenes; Ctesippus of the Paeanian deme was
there too, and Menexenus and some other local people. Plato, I
10   believe, was sick.

Echecrates. Were there any visitors there?

Phaedo. Yes: Simmias of Thebes, and Cebes and Phaedondes; and   c
Euclides and Terpsion from Megara.

Echecrates. What about Aristippus and Cleombrotus? Were they
there?

Phaedo. No, they weren't; they were said to be in Aegina.

Echecrates. Was anyone else there?   5

Phaedo. I think those were about all.

Echecrates. Well then, what discussion do you say took place?

Phaedo. I'll try to describe everything for you from the beginning.
Regularly, you see, and especially on the preceding days, I myself   d
and Socrates' other companions had been in the habit of visiting
him; we would meet at daybreak at the court-house, where the trial
was held, as it was close to the prison. We used to wait each day
till the prison opened, talking with one another, as it didn't open   5
very early. When it did, we would go in to Socrates and generally
spent the day with him. On that particular day we'd met earlier
still; because when we left the prison the evening before, we learnt   e
that the ship had arrived from Delos. So we passed the word to one
another to come to our usual place as early as possible. When we
arrived, the door-keeper who usually admitted us came out and told
us to wait, and not to go in till he gave the word; 'because', he said,   5
'the Eleven are releasing Socrates, and giving orders that he's to die
today.' But after a short interval he came back and told us to go in.
On entering we found Socrates, just released, and Xanthippe—you   **60**
know her—holding his little boy and sitting beside him. When she saw
us, Xanthippe broke out and said just the kinds of thing that women
are given to saying: 'So this is the very last time, Socrates, that your   5
good friends will speak to you and you to them.' At which Socrates
looked at Crito and said: 'Crito, someone had better take her home.'

So she was taken away by some of Crito's people, calling out and
lamenting; Socrates, meanwhile, sat up on the bed, bent his leg, and   b
rubbed it down with his hand. As he rubbed it, he said: 'What an odd
thing it seems, friends, this state that men call "pleasant"; and how
curiously it's related to its supposed opposite, "painful": to think   5
that the pair of them refuse to visit a man together, yet if anybody

pursues one of them and catches it, he's always pretty well bound to catch the other as well, as if the two of them were attached to a
c   single head. I do believe that if Aesop had thought of them, he'd have made up a story telling how God wanted to reconcile them in their quarrelling, but when he couldn't he fastened their heads together, and that's why anybody visited by one of them is later
5   attended by the other as well. This is just what seems to be happening in my own case: there was discomfort in my leg because of the fetter, and now the pleasant seems to have come to succeed it.'

Here Cebes joined in and said: 'Goodness yes, Socrates, thanks for reminding me. Several people, you know, including Evenus just
d   the other day, have been asking me about the poems you've made up, putting the tales of Aesop into verse, and the hymn to Apollo: what had you in mind, they asked, in making them up after you'd come here, when you'd never made up anything before? So if you'd
5   like me to have an answer for Evenus when he asks me again—and I'm quite sure he will—tell me what I should say.'

'Tell him the truth, then, Cebes,' he said: 'I made them, not
e   because I wanted to compete with him or his verses—I knew that wouldn't be easy—but because I was trying to find out the meaning of certain dreams and fulfil a sacred duty, in case perhaps it was that kind of art they were ordering me to make. They were like this, you
5   see: often in my past life the same dream had visited me, now in one guise, now in another, but always saying the same thing: "Socrates," it said, "make art and practise it." Now in earlier times I used to assume that the dream was urging and telling me to do exactly what
61   I was doing: as people shout encouragement to runners, so the dream was telling me to do the very thing that I was doing, to make art, since philosophy is a very high art form, and that was what I was
5   making. But now that the trial was over and the festival of the god was preventing my death, I thought that in case it was art in the popular sense that the dream was commanding me to make, I ought not to disobey it, but should make it; as it was safer not to go off
b   before I'd fulfilled a sacred duty, by making verses and thus obeying the dream. And so I first made them for the god in whose honour the present feast was kept. Then, after addressing the god, I reflected that a poet should, if he were really going to be a poet, make tales

4

rather than true stories; and being no teller of tales myself, I there-   5
fore used some I had ready to hand; I knew the tales of Aesop by
heart, and I made verses from the first of these I came across. So
give Evenus this message, Cebes: say good-bye to him, and tell him,
if he's sensible, to come after me as quickly as he can. I'm off today,   c
it seems—by Athenians' orders.'
    'What a thing you're urging Evenus to do, Socrates!' said Simmias.
'I've come across the man often before now; and from what I've
seen of him, he'll hardly be at all willing to obey you.'   5
    'Why,' he said, 'isn't Evenus a philosopher?'
    'I believe so,' said Simmias.
    'Then Evenus will be willing, and so will everyone who engages
worthily in this business. Perhaps, though, he won't do violence to
himself: they say it's forbidden.' As he said this he lowered his legs   10
to the ground, and then remained sitting in that position for the rest   d
of the discussion.
    Cebes now asked him: 'How can you say this, Socrates? How can
it both be forbidden to do violence to oneself, and be the case
that the philosopher would be willing to follow the dying?'   5
    'Why Cebes, haven't you and Simmias heard about such things
through being with Philolaus?'
    'No, nothing definite, Socrates.'
    'Well, I myself can speak about them only from hearsay; but
what I happen to have heard I don't mind telling you. Indeed, maybe   10
it's specially fitting that someone about to make the journey to the   e
next world should inquire and speculate as to what we imagine that
journey to be like; after all, what else should one do during the time
till sundown?'
    'Well then, Socrates, on just what ground do they say it's for-   5
bidden to kill oneself? Because—to answer the question you were
just asking—I certainly did hear from Philolaus, when he was living
with us, and earlier from several others, that one ought not to do
that; but I've never heard anything definite about it from anyone.'
    'Well you must take heart,' he said; 'as maybe you will hear.   62
Perhaps, though, it will seem a matter for wonder to you if this
alone of all things is unqualified, and it never happens as other things
do sometimes and for some people, that it is better for a man to be

5 dead than alive; and for those for whom it is better to be dead, perhaps it seems a matter for wonder to you if for these men it is not holy to do good to themselves, but they must await another benefactor.'

Cebes chuckled at this. 'Hark at that, now!' he said, speaking in his own dialect.

b 'Well yes,' said Socrates, 'it would seem unreasonable, put that way; but perhaps there is, in fact, some reason for it. The reason given in mysteries on the subject, that we men are in some sort of prison,[1] and that one ought not to release oneself from it or run

5 away, seems to me a lofty idea and not easy to penetrate; but still, Cebes, this much seems to me well said: it is gods who care for us, and for the gods we men are among their belongings. Don't you think so?'

10 'I do,' said Cebes.

c 'Well, if one of your belongings were to kill itself, without your signifying that you wanted it to die, wouldn't you be vexed with it, and punish it, if you had any punishment at hand?'[2]

5 'Certainly.'

'So perhaps, in that case, it isn't unreasonable that one should not kill oneself until God sends some necessity, such as the one now before us.'

'Yes, that does seem fair,' said Cebes. 'But then what you were

10 saying just now—that philosophers should be willing to die lightly—

d that seems odd, if what we were just saying, that it is God who cares for us, and that we are his belongings, is well founded. Because it's unreasonable that the wisest of men should not be resentful at

5 quitting this service, where they're directed by the best directors there are—the gods; since a man of that sort, surely, doesn't believe he'll care for himself any better on becoming free. A stupid man would perhaps believe that: he would think he should escape from

e his master, and wouldn't reflect that a good master is not one to escape from, but to stay with as long as possible, and so his escape would be irrational; but a man of intelligence would surely always want to be with one better than himself. Yet in that case, Socrates, the

5 very opposite of what was said just now seems likely: it's the wise who should be resentful at dying, whereas the foolish should wel-

come it.'

When Socrates heard this he seemed to me pleased at Cebes'
persistence, and looking at us he said: 'There goes Cebes, always   63
hunting down arguments, and not at all willing to accept at once
what anyone may say.'

'Well yes,' said Simmias; 'but this time, Socrates, I think myself
there's something in what Cebes says: why, indeed, should truly   5
wise men want to escape from masters who are better than themselves, and be separated from them lightly? So I think it's at you
that Cebes is aiming his argument, because you take so lightly your
leaving both ourselves and the gods, who are good rulers by your
own admission.'

'What you both say is fair,' he said; 'as I take you to mean that I   b
should defend myself against these charges as if in a court of law.'

'Yes, exactly,' said Simmias.

'Very well then,' he said; 'let me try to defend myself more
convincingly before you than I did before the jury. Because if I   5
didn't believe, Simmias and Cebes, that I shall enter the presence,
first, of other gods both wise and good, and next of dead men better
than those in this world, then I should be wrong not to be resentful
at death; but as it is, be assured that I expect to join the company of
good men—although that point I shouldn't affirm with absolute   c
conviction; but that I shall enter the presence of gods who are very
good masters, be assured that if there's anything I should affirm on
such matters, it is that. So that's why I am not so resentful, but
rather am hopeful that there is something in store for those who've   5
died—in fact, as we've long been told, something far better for the
good than for the wicked.'

'Well then, Socrates,' said Simmias, 'do you mean to go off
keeping this thought to yourself, or would you share it with us too?
We have a common claim on this benefit as well, I think; and at the   d
same time your defence will be made, if you persuade us of what
you say.'

'All right, I'll try,' he said. 'But first let's find out what it is that
Crito here has been wanting to say, for some time past, I think.'

'Why Socrates,' said Crito, 'it's simply that the man who's going   5
to give you the poison has been telling me for some time that you

must be warned to talk as little as possible: he says people get
heated through talking too much,[3] and one must bring nothing of
e   that sort in contact with the poison; people doing that sort of thing
are sometimes obliged, otherwise, to drink twice or even three times.'
      'Never mind him,' said Socrates. 'Just let him prepare his stuff so
5   as to give two doses, or even three if need be.'
      'Yes, I pretty well knew it,' said Crito; 'but he's been giving me
trouble for some while.'

      'Let him be,' he said. 'Now then, with you for my jury I want to
give my defence, and show with what good reason, as it seems to me,
10   a man who has truly spent his life in philosophy feels confident when
64   about to die, and is hopeful that, when he has died, he will win
very great benefits in the other world. So I'll try, Simmias and
Cebes, to explain how this could be.
      'Other people may well be unaware that all who actually engage
5   in philosophy aright are practising nothing other than dying and
being dead.[4] Now if this is true, it would be odd indeed for them to
be eager in their whole life for nothing but this, and yet to be resentful when it comes, the very thing they'd long been eager for and
practised.'
      Simmias laughed at this and said: 'Goodness, Socrates, you've
b   made me laugh, even though I wasn't much inclined to laugh just
now. I imagine that most people, on hearing that, would think it
very well said of philosophers—and our own countrymen would
quite agree—that they are, indeed, verging on death, and that they, at
5   any rate, are well aware that this is what philosophers deserve to
undergo.'
      'Yes, and what they say would be true, Simmias, except for their
claim to be aware of it themselves; because they aren't aware in
what sense genuine philosophers are verging on death and deserving
c   of it, and what kind of death they deserve. Anyway, let's discuss it
among ourselves, disregarding them: do we suppose that death *is*
something?'
      'Certainly,' rejoined Simmias.
      'And that it is nothing but the separation of the soul from the
5   body? And that being dead is this: the body's having come to be

apart, separated from the soul, alone by itself, and the soul's being apart, alone by itself, separated from the body? Death can't be anything else but that, can it?'

'No, it's just that.'

'Now look, my friend, and see if maybe you agree with me on these points; because through them I think we'll improve our knowledge of what we're examining. Do you think it befits a philosophical man to be keen about the so-called pleasures of, for example, food and drink?'   10

d

'Not in the least, Socrates,' said Simmias.   5

'And what about those of sex?'

'Not at all.'

'And what about the other services to the body? Do you think such a man regards them as of any value? For instance, the possession of smart clothes and shoes, and the other bodily adornments—do you think he values them highly, or does he disdain them, except in so far as he's absolutely compelled to share in them?'   10

e

'I think the genuine philosopher disdains them.'

'Do you think in general, then, that such a man's concern is not for the body, but so far as he can stand aside from it, is directed towards the soul?'   5

'I do.'

'Then is it clear that, first, in such matters as these the philosopher differs from other men in releasing his soul, as far as possible, from its communion with the body?'   65

'It appears so.'

'And presumably, Simmias, it does seem to most men that someone who finds nothing of that sort pleasant, and takes no part in those things, doesn't deserve to live; rather, one who cares nothing for the pleasures that come by way of the body runs pretty close to being dead.'   5

'Yes, what you say is quite true.'

'And now, what about the actual gaining of wisdom? Is the body a hindrance or not, if one enlists it as a partner in the quest? This is the sort of thing I mean: do sight and hearing afford men any truth, or aren't even the poets always harping on such themes, telling us that we neither hear nor see anything accurately? And yet if these   10

b

9

5   of all the bodily senses are neither accurate nor clear, the others will
hardly be so; because they are, surely, all inferior to these. Don't
you think so?'

    'Certainly.'

    'So when does the soul attain the truth? Because plainly,
10   whenever it sets about examining anything in company with the
body, it is completely taken in by it.'

c   'That's true.'

    'So isn't it in reasoning, if anywhere at all, that any of the things
that *are* become manifest to it?'

    'Yes.'

5   'And it reasons best, presumably, whenever none of these things
bothers it, neither hearing nor sight nor pain, nor any pleasure
either, but whenever it comes to be alone by itself as far as possible,
disregarding the body, and whenever, having the least possible
communion and contact with it, it strives for that which is.'

10   'That is so.'

    'So there again the soul of the philosopher utterly disdains the
d   body and flees from it, seeking rather to come to be alone by itself?'

    'It seems so.'

    'Well now, what about things of this sort, Simmias? Do we say
5   that there is something *just*, or nothing?'[5]

    'Yes, we most certainly do!'

    'And again, something *beautiful*, and *good*?'

    'Of course.'

    'Now did you ever yet see any such things with your eyes?'
10   'Certainly not.'

    'Well did you grasp them with any other bodily sense-perception?[6]
And I'm talking about them all—about largeness, health, and strength,
for example—and, in short, about the Being of all other such things,
e   what each one actually is;[7] is it through the body that their truest
element[8] is viewed, or isn't it rather thus: whoever of us is prepared
to think most fully and minutely of each object of his inquiry, in
itself, will come closest to the knowledge of each?'

5   'Yes, certainly.'

    'Then would that be achieved most purely by the man who
approached each object with his intellect alone as far as possible,

neither adducing sight[9] in his thinking, nor dragging in any other
sense to accompany his reasoning; rather, using his intellect alone   66
by itself and unsullied, he would undertake the hunt for each of the
things that are, each alone by itself and unsullied; he would be
separated as far as possible from his eyes and ears, and virtually from
his whole body, on the ground that it confuses the soul, and doesn't   5
allow it to gain truth and wisdom when in partnership with it: isn't
it this man, Simmias, who will attain that which is, if anyone will?'
'What you say is abundantly true, Socrates,' said Simmias.   10
'For all these reasons, then, some such view as this must present   b
itself to genuine philosophers, so that they say such things to one
another as these: "There now, it looks as if some sort of track is
leading us, together with our reason, astray in our inquiry:[10] as long
as we possess the body, and our soul is contaminated by such an evil,   5
we'll surely never adequately gain what we desire—and that, we say,
is truth. Because the body affords us countless distractions, owing
to the nurture it must have; and again, if any illnesses befall it, they   c
hamper our pursuit of that which is. Besides, it fills us up with lusts
and desires, with fears and fantasies of every kind, and with any
amount of trash, so that really and truly we are, as the saying goes,
never able to think of anything at all because of it. Thus, it's nothing   5
but the body and its desires that brings wars and factions and fighting;
because it's over the gaining of wealth that all wars take place,
and we're compelled to gain wealth because of the body, enslaved   d
as we are to its service; so for all these reasons it leaves us no leisure
for philosophy. And the worst of it all is that if we do get any leisure
from it, and turn to some inquiry, once again it intrudes everywhere   5
in our researches, setting up a clamour and disturbance, and striking
terror, so that the truth can't be discerned because of it. Well now, it
really has been shown us that if we're ever going to know anything
purely, we must be rid of it, and must view the objects themselves   e
with the soul by itself; it's then, apparently, that the thing we desire
and whose lovers we claim to be, wisdom, will be ours—when we have
died, as the argument indicates, though not while we live. Because,
if we can know nothing purely in the body's company, then one of   5
two things must be true: either knowledge is nowhere to be gained,
or else it is for the dead; since then, but no sooner, will the soul be   67

alone by itself apart from the body. And therefore while we live, it
would seem that we shall be closest to knowledge in this way—if we
consort with the body as little as possible, and do not commune with
5   it, except in so far as we must, and do not infect ourselves with its
nature, but remain pure from it, until God himself shall release us;
and being thus pure, through separation from the body's folly, we
shall probably be in like company, and shall know through our
b   own selves all that is unsullied—and that, I dare say, is what the
truth is; because never will it be permissible for impure to touch
pure." Such are the things, I think, Simmias, that all who are rightly
called lovers of knowledge must say to one another, and must
5   believe. Don't you agree?'

'Emphatically, Socrates.'

'Well then, if that's true, my friend,' said Socrates, 'there's
plenty of hope for one who arrives where I'm going, that there, if
anywhere, he will adequately possess the object that's been our
10   great concern in life gone by; and thus the journey now appointed
c   for me may also be made with good hope by any other man who
regards his intellect as prepared, by having been, in a manner,
purified.'

'Yes indeed,' said Simmias.

5   'Then doesn't purification turn out to be just what's been mentioned for some while in our discussion[11]—the parting of the soul
from the body as far as possible, and the habituating of it to
assemble and gather itself together, away from every part of the
body, alone by itself, and to live, so far as it can, both in the present
d   and in the hereafter, released from the body, as from fetters?'

'Yes indeed.'

'And is it just this that is named "death"—a release and parting
5   of soul from body?'

'Indeed it is.'

'And it's especially those who practise philosophy aright, or
rather they alone, who are always eager to release it, as we say, and
the occupation of philosophers is just this, isn't it—a release and
10   parting of soul from body?'

'It seems so.'

'Then wouldn't it be absurd, as I said at the start, for a man

to prepare himself in his life to live as close as he can to being dead,   e
and then to be resentful when this comes to him?'

'It would be absurd, of course.'

'Truly then, Simmias, those who practise philosophy aright are
cultivating dying, and for them least of all men does being dead hold   5
any terror. Look at it like this: if they've set themselves at odds with
the body at every point, and desire to possess their soul alone by
itself, wouldn't it be quite illogical if they were afraid and resentful
when this came about—if, that is, they didn't go gladly to the place   68
where, on arrival, they may hope to attain what they longed for
throughout life, namely wisdom—and to be rid of the company of
that with which they'd set themselves at odds? Or again, many have
been willing to enter Hades of their own accord, in quest of human   5
loves, of wives and sons[12] who have died, led by this hope, that there
they would see and be united with those they desired; will anyone,
then, who truly longs for wisdom, and who firmly holds this same
hope, that nowhere but in Hades will he attain it in any way worth   b
mentioning, be resentful at dying; and will he not go there gladly?
One must suppose so, my friend, if he's truly a lover of wisdom;
since this will be his firm belief, that nowhere else but there will he
attain wisdom purely. Yet if that is so, wouldn't it, as I said just now,   5
be quite illogical if such a man were afraid of death?'

'Yes, quite illogical!'

'Then if you see a man resentful that he is going to die, isn't this
proof enough for you that he's no lover of wisdom after all, but   c
what we may call a lover of the body? And this same man turns out,
in some sense, to be a lover of riches and of prestige, either one of
these or both.'

'It's just as you say.'

'Well now, Simmias, isn't it also true that what is named "bravery"   5
belongs especially to people of the disposition we have described?'

'Most certainly.'

'And then temperance too, even what most people name
"temperance"—not being excited over one's desires, but being scorn-
ful of them and well-ordered—belongs, doesn't it, only to those who   10
utterly scorn the body and live in love of wisdom?'

'It must.'   d

13

'Yes, because if you care to consider the bravery and temperance of other men, you'll find it strange.'

'How so, Socrates?'

5   'You know, don't you, that all other men count death among great evils?'

'Very much so.'

'Is it, then, through being afraid of greater evils that the brave among them abide death, whenever they do so?'

10   'It is.'

'Then, it's through fearing and fear that all men except philosophers are brave; and yet it's surely illogical that anyone should be brave through fear and cowardice.'

e   'It certainly is.'

'And what about those of them who are well-ordered? Aren't they in this same state, temperate through a kind of intemperance? True, we say that's impossible; but still that state of simple-minded

5   temperance does turn out in their case to be like this: it's because they're afraid of being deprived of further pleasures, and desire them, that they abstain from some because they're overcome by

69   others. True, they call it "intemperance" to be ruled by pleasures, but still that's what happens to them: they overcome some pleasures because they're overcome by others. And this is the sort of thing that was just mentioned: after a fashion, they achieve temperance because of intemperance.'

5   'Yes, so it seems.'

'Yes, Simmias, my good friend;[13] since this may not be the right exchange with a view to goodness, the exchanging of pleasures for pleasures, pains for pains, and fear for fear, greater for lesser ones,

10   like coins; it may be, rather, that this alone is the right coin, for

b   which one should exchange all these things—wisdom; and the buying and selling of all things for that, or rather with that, may be real bravery, temperance, justice, and, in short, true goodness in company with wisdom, whether pleasures and fears and all else of that

5   sort be added or taken away; but as for their being parted from wisdom and exchanged for one another, goodness of that sort may be a kind of illusory facade, and fit for slaves indeed, and may have nothing healthy or true about it; whereas, truth to tell, temperance,

justice, and bravery may in fact be a kind of purification of all such   c
things, and wisdom itself a kind of purifying rite. So it really looks as
if those who established our initiations are no mean people, but
have in fact long been saying in riddles that whoever arrives in Hades   5
unadmitted to the rites, and uninitiated, shall lie in the slough, while
he who arrives there purified and initiated shall dwell with gods. For
truly there are, so say those concerned with the initiations, "many who
bear the wand, but few who are devotees". Now these latter, in my   d
view, are none other than those who have practised philosophy
aright. And it's to be among them that I myself have striven, in
every way I could, neglecting nothing during my life within my
power. Whether I have striven aright and we have achieved anything,   5
we shall, I think, know for certain, God willing, in a little while, on
arrival yonder.

'There's my defence, then, Simmias and Cebes, to show how
reasonable it is for me not to take it hard or be resentful at leaving   e
you and my masters here, since I believe that there also, no less than
here, I shall find good masters and companions; so if I'm any more
convincing in my defence to you than to the Athenian jury, it would
be well.'   5

When Socrates had said this, Cebes rejoined: 'The other things
you say, Socrates, I find excellent; but what you say about the soul
is the subject of much disbelief: men fear that when it's been separ-   70
ated from the body, it may no longer exist anywhere, but that on
the very day a man dies, it may be destroyed and perish, as soon as
it's separated from the body; and that as it goes out, it may be dispersed like breath or smoke, go flying off, and exist no longer any-   5
where at all. True, if it did exist somewhere, gathered together alone
by itself, and separated from those evils you were recounting just
now, there'd be plenty of hope, Socrates, and a fine hope it would
be, that what you say is true; but on just this point, perhaps, one   b
needs no little reassuring and convincing, that when the man has
died, his soul exists, and that it possesses some power and wisdom.'[14]

'That's true, Cebes,' said Socrates; 'but then what are we to do?   5
Would you like us to speculate[15] on these very questions, and see
whether this is likely to be the case or not?'

15

'For my part anyway,' said Cebes, 'I'd gladly hear whatever opinion you have about them.'

10 'Well,' said Socrates, 'I really don't think anyone listening now,
c even if he were a comic poet, would say that I'm talking idly, and arguing about things that don't concern me. If you agree, then, we should look into the matter.

'Let's consider it, perhaps, in this way: do the souls of men exist
5 in Hades when they have died, or do they not? Now there's an ancient doctrine, which we've recalled,[16] that they do exist in that world, entering it from this one, and that they re-enter this world and are born again from the dead; yet if this is so, if living people are born again from those who have died, surely our souls would have to
d exist in that world? Because they could hardly be born again, if they didn't exist;[17] so it would be sufficient evidence for the truth of these claims, if it really became plain that living people are born from the dead and from nowhere else; but if that isn't so, some other argu-
5 ment would be needed.'

'Certainly,' said Cebes.

'Well now, consider the matter, if you want to understand more readily, in connection not only with mankind, but with all animals and plants; and, in general, for all things subject to coming-to-be, let's
e see whether everything comes to be in this way: opposites come to be only from their opposites—in the case of all things that actually have an opposite—as, for example, the beautiful is opposite, of course, to the ugly, just to unjust, and so on in countless other cases. So let's consider this: is it necessary that whatever has an
5 opposite comes to be only from its opposite? For example, when a thing comes to be larger, it must, surely, come to be larger from being smaller before?'

'Yes.'

10 'And again, if it comes to be smaller, it will come to be smaller
71 later from being larger before?'

'That's so.'

'And that which is weaker comes to be, presumably, from a stronger, and that which is faster from a slower?'

5 'Certainly.'

'And again, if a thing comes to be worse, it's from a better, and

16

if more just, from a more unjust?'

'Of course.'

'Are we satisfied, then, that all things come to be in this way, opposite things from opposites?'   10

'Certainly.'

'Now again, do these things have a further feature of this sort: between the members of every pair of opposites, since they are two, aren't there two processes of coming-to-be, from one to the other,   b and back again from the latter to the former? Thus,[18] between a larger thing and a smaller, isn't there increase and decrease, so that in the one case we speak of "increasing" and in the other of "decreasing"?'

'Yes.'   5

'And similarly with separating and combining, cooling and heating, and all such; even if in some cases we don't use the names, still in actual fact mustn't the same principle everywhere hold good: they come to be from each other, and there's a process of coming-to-be of each into the other?'   10

'Certainly.'

'Well then, is there an opposite to living, as sleeping is opposite   c to being awake?'

'Certainly.'

'What is it?'

'Being dead.'   5

'Then these come to be from each other, if they are opposites; and between the pair of them, since they are two, the processes of coming-to-be are two?'

'Of course.'

'Now then,' said Socrates, 'I'll tell you one of the couples I was just mentioning, the couple itself and its processes; and you tell me   10 the other. My couple is sleeping and being awake: being awake comes to be from sleeping, and sleeping from being awake, and their   d processes are going to sleep and waking up. Is that sufficient for you or not?'

'Certainly.'

'Now it's for you to tell me in the same way about life and death.   5 You say, don't you, that being dead is opposite to living?'

17

'I do.'

'And that they come to be from each other?'

'Yes.'

10   'Then what is it that comes to be from that which is living?'

'That which is dead.'

'And what comes to be from that which is dead?'

'I must admit that it's that which is living.'

'Then it's from those that are dead, Cebes, that living things

15   and living people are born?'

e   'Apparently.'

'Then our souls do exist in Hades.'

'So it seems.'

'Now *one* of the relevant processes here is obvious, isn't it? For

5   dying is obvious enough, surely?'

'It certainly is.'

'What shall we do then? Shan't we assign the opposite process to balance it? Will nature be lame in this respect? Or must we supply

10   some process opposite to dying?'

'We surely must.'

'What will this be?'

'Coming to life again.'

'Then if there *is* such a thing as coming to life again, wouldn't

72   this, coming to life again, be a process from dead to living people.'

'Certainly.'

'In that way too, then, we're agreed that living people are born

5   from the dead no less than dead people from the living; and we thought that, if this were the case, it would be sufficient evidence that the souls of the dead must exist somewhere, whence they are born again.'

10   'I think, Socrates, that that must follow from our admissions.'

'Then look at it this way, Cebes, and you'll see, I think, that our admissions were not mistaken. If there were not perpetual recip-

b   rocity in coming to be, between one set of things and another, revolving in a circle, as it were—if, instead, coming-to-be were a linear process from one thing into its opposite only, without any bending back in the other direction or reversal, do you realize that all things

5   would ultimately have the same form: the same fate would overtake

them, and they would cease from coming to be?'

'What do you mean?'

'It's not at all hard to understand what I mean. If, for example, there were such a thing as going to sleep, but from sleeping there were no reverse process of waking up, you realize that everything would ultimately make Endymion seem a mere trifle: he'd be nowhere, because the same fate as his, sleeping, would have over- taken everything else. Again, if everything were combined, but not separated, then Anaxagoras' notion of "all things together" would soon be realized. And similarly, my dear Cebes, if all things that partake in life were to die, but when they'd died, the dead remained in that form, and didn't come back to life, wouldn't it be quite inevitable that everything would ultimately be dead, and nothing would live? Because if the living things came to be from the other things, but the living things were to die, what could possibly prevent everything from being completely spent in being dead?'

'Nothing whatever, in my view, Socrates,' said Cebes; 'what you say seems to be perfectly true.'

'Yes, it certainly is true, Cebes, as I see it; and we're not deceived in making just those admissions: there really is such a thing as coming to life again, living people *are* born from the dead, and the souls of the dead exist.'

'Yes, and besides, Socrates,' Cebes replied, 'there's also that theory you're always putting forward, that our learning is actually nothing but recollection; according to that too, if it's true, what we are now reminded of we must have learned at some former time. But that would be impossible, unless our souls existed somewhere before being born in this human form; so in this way too, it appears that the soul is something immortal.'

'Yes, what are the proofs of those points, Cebes?' put in Simmias. 'Remind me, as I don't recall them very well at the moment.'

'One excellent argument,'[19] said Cebes, 'is that when people are questioned, and if the questions are well put, they state the truth about everything for themselves—and yet unless knowledge and a correct account were present within them, they'd be unable to do this; thus, if one takes them to diagrams or anything else of that sort, one has there the plainest evidence that this is so.'

'But if that doesn't convince you, Simmias,' said Socrates, 'then
see whether maybe you agree if you look at it this way. Apparently
5   you doubt whether what is called "learning" is recollection?'

'I don't *doubt* it,' said Simmias; 'but I do need to undergo just
what the argument is about, to be "reminded". Actually, from the
way Cebes set about stating it, I do almost recall it and am nearly
convinced; but I'd like, none the less, to hear now how you set about
10 stating it yourself.'

c   'I'll put it this way. We agree, I take it, that if anyone is to be
reminded of a thing, he must have known that thing at some time
previously.'

'Certainly.'

'Then do we also agree on this point: that whenever knowledge
5   comes to be present in this sort of way, it is recollection? I mean in
some such way as this:[20] if someone, on seeing a thing, or hearing it,
or getting any other sense-perception of it, not only recognizes that
thing, but also thinks of something else, which is the object not of
the same knowledge but of another, don't we then rightly say that
d   he's been "reminded" of the object of which he has got the thought?'

'What do you mean?'

'Take the following examples: knowledge of a man, surely, is
other than that of a lyre?'

'Of course.'

5   'Well now, you know what happens to lovers, whenever they see
a lyre or cloak or anything else their loves are accustomed to use:
they recognize the lyre, and they get in their mind, don't they, the
form of the boy whose lyre it is? And that is recollection. Likewise,
someone seeing Simmias is often reminded of Cebes, and there'd
10 surely be countless other such cases.'

'Countless indeed!' said Simmias.

e   'Then is something of that sort a kind of recollection? More
especially, though, whenever it happens to someone in connection
with things he's since forgotten, through lapse of time or inattention?'

'Certainly.'

5   'Again now, is it possible, on seeing a horse depicted or a lyre
depicted, to be reminded of a man; and on seeing Simmias depicted,

to be reminded of Cebes?'

'Certainly.'

'And also, on seeing Simmias depicted, to be reminded of Simmias himself?'   10

'Yes, that's possible.'   74

'In all these cases, then, doesn't it turn out that there is recollection from similar things, but also from dissimilar things?'

'It does.'

'But whenever one is reminded of something from similar things,   5 mustn't one experience something further: mustn't one think whether or not the thing is lacking at all, in its similarity, in relation to what one is reminded of?'

'One must.'

'Then consider whether this is the case. We say, don't we, that there is something *equal*—I don't mean a log to a log, or a stone to a   10 stone, or anything else of that sort, but some further thing beyond all those, the equal itself: are we to say that there *is* something or nothing?'

'We most certainly are to say that there *is*,' said Simmias;   b 'unquestionably!'

'And do we know *what it is*?'[21]

'Certainly.'

'Where did we get the knowledge of it? Wasn't it from the things we were just mentioning: on seeing logs or stones or other   5 equal things, wasn't it from these that we thought of that object, it being different from them? Or doesn't it seem different to you? Look at it this way: don't equal stones and logs, the very same ones, sometimes seem equal to one, but not to another?'[22]

'Yes, certainly.'   10

'But now, did the equals themselves ever seem to you unequal, or   c equality inequality?'

'Never yet, Socrates.'

'Then those equals, and the equal itself, are not the same.'   5

'By no means, Socrates, in my view.'

'But still, it is from *those* equals, different as they are from *that* equal, that you have thought of and got the knowledge of it?'

'That's perfectly true.'   10

'It being either similar to them or dissimilar?'

'Certainly.'

'Anyway, it makes no difference; so long as[23] on seeing one thing,
d one does, from this sight, think of another, whether it be similar or
dissimilar, this must be recollection.'

'Certainly.'

'Well now, with regard to the instances in the logs, and, in general,
5 the equals we mentioned just now, are we affected in some way as
this: do they seem to us to be equal in the same way as *what it is*
itself?[24] Do they fall short of it at all in being like the equal, or not?'

'Very far short of it.'

'Then whenever anyone, on seeing a thing, thinks to himself, "this
10 thing that I now see seeks to be like another of the things that
e are, but falls short, and cannot be like that object: it is inferior", do
we agree that the man who thinks this must previously have known
the object he says it resembles but falls short of?'

5 'He must.'

'Now then, have we ourselves been affected in just this way, or
not, with regard to the equals and the equal itself?'

'Indeed we have.'

'Then we must previously have known the equal, before that time
75 when we first, on seeing the equals, thought that all of them were
striving to be like the equal but fell short of it.'

'That is so.'

5 'Yet we also agree on this: we haven't derived the thought of it,
nor could we do so, from anywhere but seeing or touching or some
other of the senses—I'm counting all these as the same.'

'Yes, they are the same, Socrates, for what the argument seeks
10 to show.'

'But of course it is *from* one's sense-perceptions that one must
b think that all the things in the sense-perceptions are striving for
what equal is,[25] yet are inferior to it; or how shall we put it?'

'Like that.'

'Then it must, surely, have been before we began to see and hear
5 and use the other senses that we got knowledge of the equal itself, of
what it is,[26] if we were going to refer the equals from our sense-
perceptions to it, supposing that[27] all things are doing their best to

be like it, but are inferior to it.'

'That must follow from what's been said before, Socrates.'

'Now we were seeing and hearing, and were possessed of our   10
other senses, weren't we, just as soon as we were born?'

'Certainly.'

'But we must, we're saying, have got our knowledge of the equal   c
before these?'

'Yes.'

'Then it seems that we must have got it before we were born.'   5

'It seems so.'

'Now if, having got it before birth, we were born in possession of
it, did we know, both before birth and as soon as we were born, not
only the equal, the larger and the smaller, but everything of that   10
sort? Because our present argument concerns the beautiful itself,
and the good itself, and just and holy, no less than the equal; in fact,   d
as I say, it concerns everything on which we set this seal, "*what it
is*",[28] in the questions we ask and in the answers we give. And so we
must have got pieces of knowledge[29] of all those things before birth.'   5

'That is so.'

'Moreover, if having got them, we did not on each occasion
forget them, we must always be born knowing, and must continue
to know throughout life: because this is knowing—to possess knowledge one has got of something, and not to have lost it; or isn't loss   10
of knowledge what we mean by "forgetting", Simmias?'

'Certainly it is, Socrates.'   e

'But on the other hand, I suppose that if, having got them before
birth, we lost them on being born, and later on, using the senses
about the things in question, we regain those pieces of knowledge
that we possessed at some former time, in that case wouldn't what
we call "learning" be the regaining of knowledge belonging to us?   5
And in saying that this was being reminded, shouldn't we be speaking
correctly?'

'Certainly.'

'Yes, because it did seem possible, on sensing an object, whether   76
by seeing or hearing or getting some other sense-perception of it, to
think from this of some other thing one had forgotten—either a
thing to which the object, though dissimilar to it, was related, or

else something to which it was similar; so, as I say, one of two
5 things is true: *either* all of us were born knowing those objects, and
we know them throughout life; *or* those we speak of as "learning"
are simply being reminded later on, and learning would be
recollection.'

'That's quite true, Socrates.'

'Then which do you choose, Simmias? That we are born knowing,
b or that we are later reminded of the things we'd gained knowledge
of before?'

'At the moment, Socrates, I can't make a choice.'

'Well, can you make one on the following point, and what do
5 you think about it? If a man knows things, can he give an
account of what he knows or not?'

'Of course he can, Socrates.'

'And do you think everyone can give an account of those
objects we were discussing just now?'

10 'I only wish they could,' said Simmias; 'but I'm afraid that, on
the contrary, this time tomorrow there may no longer be any man
who can do so properly.'

c 'You don't then, Simmias, think that everyone knows those
objects?'

'By no means.'

'Are they, then, reminded of what they once learned?'

5 'They must be.'

'When did our souls get the knowledge of those objects? Not, at
any rate, since we were born as human beings.'

'Indeed not.'

'Earlier, then.'

10 'Yes.'

'Then our souls did exist earlier, Simmias, before entering human
form, apart from bodies; and they possessed wisdom.'

'Unless maybe, Socrates, we get those pieces of knowledge at the
15 very moment of birth; that time still remains.'

d 'Very well, my friend; but then at what other time, may I ask,
do we lose them? We aren't born with them, as we agreed just now.
Do we then lose them at the very time at which we get them? Or have
you any other time to suggest?'

'None at all, Socrates. I didn't realize I was talking nonsense.'   5

'Then is our position as follows, Simmias? If the objects we're always harping on exist, a beautiful, and a good and all such Being, and if we refer all the things from our sense-perceptions to that Being, finding again what was formerly ours, and if we compare   e these things with that, then just as surely as those objects exist, so also must our soul exist before we are born. On the other hand, if they don't exist, this argument will have gone for nothing. Is this the position? Is it equally necessary that those objects exist, and   5 that our souls existed before birth, and if the former don't exist, then neither did the latter?'

'It's abundantly clear to me, Socrates,' said Simmias, 'that there's the same necessity in either case, and the argument takes opportune refuge in the view that our soul exists before birth, just as surely as   77 the Being of which you're now speaking. Because I myself find nothing so plain to me as that all such objects, beautiful and good and all the others you were speaking of just now, *are* in the fullest possible way; so in my view it's been adequately proved.'   5

'And what about Cebes?' said Socrates. 'We must convince Cebes too.'

'It's adequate for him, I think,' said Simmias; 'though he's the most obstinate of people when it comes to doubting arguments. But I think he's been sufficiently convinced that our soul existed before we were born. Whether it will still exist, however, after we've died,   b doesn't seem, even to me, to have been shown, Socrates; but the point Cebes made just now still stands—the popular fear that when a man dies, his soul may be dispersed at that time, and that that may   5 be the end of its existence. Because what's to prevent it from coming to be and being put together from some other source, and from existing before it enters a human body, yet when it has entered one, and again been separated from it, from then meeting its end, and being itself destroyed?'

'You're right, Simmias,' said Cebes. 'It seems that half, as it were,   c of what is needed has been shown—that our soul existed before we were born; it must also be shown that it will exist after we've died, no less than before we were born, if the proof is going to be complete.'   5

'That's been proved already, Simmias and Cebes,' said Socrates, 'if you will combine this argument with the one we agreed on earlier, to the effect that all that is living comes from that which is dead.

d Because if the soul does have previous existence, and if when it enters upon living and being born, it must come from no other source than death and being dead, surely it must also exist after it has died, given that it has to be born again? So your point has been

5 proved already. But even so, I think you and Simmias would like to thrash out this argument still further; you seem afraid, like children, that as the soul goes out from the body, the wind may literally blow

e it apart and disperse it, especially when someone happens not to die in calm weather but in a high wind.'

Cebes laughed at this, and said: 'Try to reassure us, Socrates, as if we were afraid; or rather, not as if we were afraid ourselves—but may-

5 be there's a child inside us, who has fears of that sort. Try to persuade him, then, to stop being afraid of death, as if it were a bogey-man.'

'Well, you must sing spells to him every day,' said Socrates, 'till you've charmed it out of him.'

78 'And where', he said, 'shall we find a charmer for such fears, Socrates, now that you're leaving us?'

'Greece is a large country, Cebes, which has good men in it, I suppose; and there are many foreign races too. You must ransack

5 all of them in search of such a charmer, sparing neither money nor trouble, because there's no object on which you could more opportunely spend your money. And you yourselves must search too, along with one another; you may not easily find anyone more capable of doing this than yourselves.'

10 'That shall certainly be done,' said Cebes; 'but let's go back to the

b point where we left off, if you've no objection.'

'Of course not; why should I?'

'Good.'

'Well then,' said Socrates, 'mustn't we ask ourselves something

5 like this: What kind of thing is liable to undergo this fate—namely, dispersal—and for what kind of thing should we fear lest it undergo it? And what kind of thing is not liable to it? And next, mustn't we

further ask to which of these two kinds soul belongs, and then feel
either confidence or fear for our own soul accordingly?'

'That's true.'   10

'Then is it true that what has been put together and is naturally   c
composite is liable to undergo this,[30] to break up at the point at
which it was put together; whereas if there be anything incomposite,
it alone is liable, if anything is, to escape this?'

'That's what I think,' said Cebes.   5

'Well now, aren't the things that are constant and unvarying most
likely to be the incomposite, whereas things that vary and are never
constant are likely to be composite?'

'I think so.'

'Then let's go back to those entities to which we turned in   10
our earlier argument. Is the Being itself, whose being we give an   d
account of in asking and answering questions, unvarying and constant, or does it vary? Does the equal itself, the beautiful itself,
what each thing is[31] itself, that which *is*,[32] ever admit of any change
whatever? Or does *what each of them is*, being uniform alone by   5
itself, remain unvarying and constant, and never admit of any kind
of alteration in any way or respect whatever?'

'It must be unvarying and constant, Socrates,' said Cebes.

'But what about the many beautiful things,[33] such as men or   10
horses or cloaks or anything else at all of that kind? Or equals, or all   e
things that bear the same name as those objects? Are they constant,
or are they just the opposite of those others, and practically never
constant at all, either in relation to themselves or to one another?'

'That is their condition,' said Cebes; 'they are never unvarying.'   5

'Now these things you could actually touch and see and sense   79
with the other senses, couldn't you, whereas those that are constant
you could lay hold of only by reasoning of the intellect; aren't such
things, rather, invisible and not seen?'

'What you say is perfectly true.'   5

'Then would you like us to posit two kinds of beings,[34] the one
kind seen, the other invisible?'

'Let's posit them.'

'And the invisible is always constant, whereas the seen is never
constant?'   10

'Let's posit that too.'

b   'Well, but we ourselves are part body and part soul, aren't we?'
'We are.'

'Then to which kind do we say that the body will be more
5   similar and more akin?'

'That's clear to anyone: obviously to the seen.'

'And what about the soul? Is it seen or invisible?'

'It's not seen by men, at any rate, Socrates.'

'But we meant, surely, things seen and not seen with reference
10   to human nature; or do you think we meant any other?'

'We meant human nature.'

'What do we say about soul, then? Is it seen or unseen?'

'It's not seen.'

'Then it's invisible?'

15   'Yes.'

'Then soul is more similar than body to the invisible, whereas
body is more similar to that which is seen.'

c   'That must be so, Socrates.'

'Now weren't we saying a while ago that whenever the soul uses
the body as a means to study anything, either by seeing or hearing
or any other sense—because to use the body as a means is to study
5   a thing through sense-perception—then it is dragged by the body
towards objects that are never constant; and it wanders about itself,
and is confused and dizzy, as if drunk, in virtue of contact with
things of a similar kind?'

'Certainly.'

d   'Whereas whenever it studies alone by itself, it departs yonder
towards that which is pure and always existent and immortal and
unvarying, and in virtue of its kinship with it, enters always into its
company, whenever it has come to be alone by itself, and whenever
5   it may do so; then it has ceased from its wandering and, when it is
about those objects, it is always constant and unvarying, because of
its contact with things of a similar kind; and this condition of it is
called "wisdom", is it not?'

'That's very well said and perfectly true, Socrates.'

'Once again, then, in the light of our earlier and present arguments,
e   to which kind do you think that soul is more similar and more akin?'

28

'Everyone, I think, Socrates, even the slowest learner, following
this line of inquiry, would agree that soul is totally and altogether
more similar to what is unvarying than to what is not.'   5
'And what about the body?'
'That is more like the latter.'
'Now look at it this way too: when soul and body are present
in the same thing, nature ordains that the one shall serve and be   80
ruled, whereas the other shall rule and be master; here again, which
do you think is similar to the divine and which to the mortal? Don't
you think the divine is naturally adapted for ruling and domin-
ation, whereas the mortal is adapted for being ruled and for service?'   5
'I do.'
'Which kind, then, does the soul resemble?'
'Obviously, Socrates, the soul resembles the divine, and the body
the mortal.'
'Consider, then, Cebes, if these are our conclusions from all that's   10
been said: soul is most similar to what is divine, immortal, intelli-   b
gible, uniform, indissoluble, unvarying, and constant in relation to
itself; whereas body, in its turn, is most similar to what is human,
mortal, multiform, non-intelligible, dissoluble, and never constant   5
in relation to itself. Have we anything to say against those statements, my dear Cebes, to show that they're false?'
'We haven't.'
'Well then, that being so, isn't body liable to be quickly dissolved,
whereas soul must be completely indissoluble, or something close   10
to it?'
'Of course.'   c
'Now you're aware that when a man has died, the part of him
that's seen, his body, which is situated in the seen world, the corpse
as we call it, although liable to be dissolved and fall apart and to
disintegrate, undergoes none of these things at once, but remains as   5
it is for a fairly long time—in fact for a very considerable time,[35] even
if someone dies with his body in beautiful condition, and in the
flower of youth; why, the body that is shrunken and embalmed, like
those who've been embalmed in Egypt, remains almost entire for an
immensely long time; and even should the body decay, some parts of   d
it, bones and sinews and all such things, are still practically immortal;

isn't that so?'
        'Yes.'
5   'Can it be, then, that the soul, the invisible part, which goes to
another place of that kind, noble, pure and invisible, to "Hades" in
the true sense of the word, into the presence of the good and wise
God—where, God willing, my own soul too must shortly enter—can
it be that this, which we've found to be a thing of such a kind and
10   nature, should on separation from the body at once be blown
e   apart and perish, as most men say? Far from it, my dear Cebes and
Simmias; rather, the truth is far more like this: suppose it is
separated in purity, while trailing nothing of the body with it,
since it had no avoidable commerce with it during life, but shunned
5   it; suppose too that it has been gathered together alone into itself,
since it always cultivated this—nothing else but the right practice of
81   philosophy, in fact, the cultivation of dying without complaint—
wouldn't this be the cultivation of death?'
        'It certainly would.'
        'If it is in that state, then, does it not depart to the invisible,
5   which is similar to it, the divine and immortal and wise; and on
arrival there, isn't its lot to be happy, released from its wandering
and folly, its fears and wild lusts, and other ills of the human
condition, and as is said of the initiated, does it not pass the rest of
10   time in very truth with gods? Are we to say this, Cebes, or something
else?'
        'This, most certainly!' said Cebes.
b   'Whereas, I imagine, if it is separated from the body when it has
been polluted and made impure, because it has always been with the
body, has served and loved it, and been so bewitched by it, by its
passions and pleasures, that it thinks nothing else real save what is
5   corporeal—what can be touched and seen, drunk and eaten, or used
for sexual enjoyment—yet it has been accustomed to hate and shun
and tremble before what is obscure to the eyes and invisible, but
c   intelligible and grasped by philosophy; do you think a soul in that
condition will separate unsullied, and alone by itself?'
        'By no means.'
        'Rather, I imagine, it will have been interspersed with a corporeal
5   element, ingrained in it by the body's company and intercourse,

through constant association and much training?'

'Certainly.'

'And one must suppose, my friend, that this element is ponderous, that it is heavy and earthy and is seen; and thus encumbered, such a soul is weighed down, and dragged back into the region of the seen,   10 through fear of the invisible and of Hades; and it roams among tombs and graves, so it is said, around which some shadowy phantoms of   d souls have actually been seen, such wraiths as souls of that kind afford, souls that have been released in no pure condition, but while partaking in the seen; and that is just why they are seen.'

'That's likely, Socrates.'   5

'It is indeed, Cebes; and they're likely to be the souls not of the good but of the wicked, that are compelled to wander about such places, paying the penalty for their former nurture, evil as it was. And they wander about until, owing to the desire of the corporeal element attendant upon them, they are once more imprisoned in a   e body; and they're likely to be imprisoned in whatever types of character they may have cultivated in their lifetime.'

'What types can you mean, Socrates?'

'Those who have cultivated gluttony, for example, and lechery,   5 and drunkenness, and have taken no pains to avoid them, are likely to enter the forms of donkeys and animals of that sort.   82 Don't you think so?'

'What you say is very likely.'

'Yes, and those who've preferred injustice, tyranny, and robbery will enter the forms of wolves and hawks and kites. Where else can we say that such souls will go?'   5

'Into such creatures, certainly,' said Cebes.

'And isn't the direction taken by the others as well obvious in each case, according to the affinities of their training?'

'Quite obvious, of course.'

'And aren't the happiest among these and the ones who enter the   10 best place, those who have practised popular and social goodness,   b "temperance" and "justice" so-called, developed from habit and training, but devoid of philosophy and intelligence?'

'In what way are these happiest?'

'Because they're likely to go back into a race of tame and social   5

31

creatures similar to their kind, bees perhaps, or wasps or ants; and to return to the human race again, and be born from those kinds as decent men.'

'That's likely.'

10   'But the company of gods may not rightly be joined by one who
c   has not practised philosophy and departed in absolute purity, by any but the lover of knowledge. It's for these reasons, Simmias and Cebes, my friends, that true philosophers abstain from all bodily desires, and stand firm without surrendering to them; it's not for any fear of
5   poverty or loss of estate, as with most men who are lovers of riches; nor again do they abstain through dread of dishonour or ill-repute attaching to wickedness, like lovers of power and prestige.'

'No, that would ill become them, Socrates,' said Cebes.

d   'Most certainly it would! And that, Cebes, is just why those who have any care for their own souls, and don't live fashioning the body,[36] disregard all those people; they do not walk in the same paths as those who, in their view, don't know where they are
5   going; but they themselves believe that their actions must not oppose philosophy, or the release and purifying rite it affords, and they are turned to follow it, in the direction in which it guides them.'

'How so, Socrates?'

'I'll tell you. Lovers of knowledge recognize that when philosophy
e   takes their soul in hand, it has been literally bound and glued to the body, and is forced to view the things that are as if through a prison, rather than alone by itself; and that it is wallowing in utter
5   ignorance. Now philosophy discerns the cunning of the prison, sees how it is effected through desire, so that the captive himself may
83   co-operate most of all in his imprisonment.[37] As I say, then, lovers of knowledge recognize that their soul is in that state when philo- sophy takes it in hand, gently reassures it and tries to release it, by showing that inquiry through the eyes is full of deceit, and deceitful
5   too is inquiry through the ears and other senses; and by persuading it to withdraw from these, so far as it need not use them, and by urging it to collect and gather itself together, and to trust none
b   other but itself, whenever, alone by itself, it thinks of any of the things that are, alone by *itself*; and not to regard as real what it observes by other means, and what varies in various things; that kind

of thing is sensible and seen, whereas the object of its own vision is
intelligible and invisible. It is, then, just because it believes it should   5
not oppose this release that the soul of the true philosopher abstains
from pleasures and desires and pains,[38] so far as it can, reckoning that
when one feels intense pleasure or fear, pain or desire, one incurs
harm from them not merely to the extent that might be supposed—   c
by being ill, for example, or spending money to satisfy one's desires—
but one incurs the greatest and most extreme of all evils, and does
not take it into account.'
        'And what is that, Socrates?' said Cebes.
        'It's that the soul of every man, when intensely pleased or   5
pained at something, is forced at the same time to suppose that
whatever most affects it in this way is most clear and most real,
when it is not so; and such objects especially are things seen,
aren't they?'
        'Certainly.'
        'Well, isn't it in this experience that soul is most thoroughly   d
bound fast by body?'
        'How so?'
        'Because each pleasure and pain fastens it to the body with a sort
of rivet, pins it there, and makes it corporeal, so that it takes for real   5
whatever the body declares to be so. Since by sharing opinions and
pleasures with the body, it is, I believe, forced to become of like
character and nurture to it, and to be incapable of entering Hades
in purity; but it must always exit contaminated by the body, and so   10
quickly fall back into another body, and grow in it as if sown there,   e
and so have no part in communion with the divine and pure and
uniform.'
        'What you say is perfectly true, Socrates,' said Cebes.
        'It's for these reasons, then, Cebes, that those who deserve to be   5
called "lovers of knowledge" are orderly and brave; it's not for the
reasons that count with most people;[39] or do you think it is?'
        'No, indeed I don't.'   84
        'Indeed not; but the soul of a philosophic man would reason as
we've said: it would not think that while philosophy should release
it, yet on being released, it should of itself surrender to pleasures
and pains, to bind it to the body once again, and should perform the   5

33

endless task of a Penelope working in reverse at a kind of web.[40]
Rather, securing rest from these feelings, by following reasoning and
being ever within it, and by beholding what is true and divine and
b   not the object of opinion, and being nurtured by it, it believes that it
must live thus for as long as it lives, and that when it has died, it will
enter that which is akin and of like nature to itself, and be rid of
5   human ills. With that kind of nurture, surely, Simmias and Cebes,
there's no danger of its fearing that on separation from the body it
may be rent apart, blown away by winds, go flying off, and exist
no longer anywhere at all.'

c   When Socrates had said this, there was silence for a long time.
To judge from his appearance, Socrates himself was absorbed in the
foregoing argument, and so were most of us; but Cebes and Simmias
went on talking to each other in a low voice.[41] When he noticed
5   them, Socrates asked: 'What is it? Can it be that you find something
lacking in what's been said? It certainly still leaves room for many
misgivings and objections, if, that is, one's going to examine it
adequately. If it's something else you're considering, never mind;
but if you have some difficulty about these matters, don't hesitate
d   to speak for yourselves and explain it, if you think what was said
could be improved in any way;[42] or again, enlist me too, if you think
you'll get out of your difficulty any better with my help.'
     Simmias replied: 'All right, Socrates, I'll tell you the truth. For
5   some time each of us has had difficulties, and has been prompting
and telling the other to question you, from eagerness to hear, but
hesitating to make trouble, in case you should find it unwelcome in
your present misfortune.'
     When Socrates heard this, he chuckled and said: 'Dear me,
Simmias! I'd certainly find it hard to convince other people that I
e   don't regard my present lot as a misfortune, when I can't convince
even you two, but you're afraid that I'm more ill-humoured now
than in my earlier life; you must, it seems, think I have a poorer
5   power of prophecy than the swans, who when they realize they must
85   die, then sing more fully and sweetly than they've ever sung before,
for joy that they are departing into the presence of the god whose
servants they are. Though indeed mankind, because of their own

fear of death, malign the swans, and say that they sing their farewell
song in distress, lamenting their death; they don't reflect that no   5
bird sings when it is hungry or cold or suffering any other distress,
not even the nightingale herself, nor the swallow, nor the hoopoe,
birds that are reputed to sing lamentations from distress. But, as I
see it, neither they nor the swans sing in distress, but rather, I believe,   b
because, belonging as they do to Apollo, they are prophetic birds
with foreknowledge of the blessings of Hades, and therefore sing
and rejoice more greatly on that day than ever before. Now I hold
that I myself am a fellow-servant of the swans, consecrated to the   5
same god, that I possess prophetic power from my master no less
than theirs, and that I'm departing this life with as good a cheer as
they do. No; so far as that goes, you should say and ask whatever
you wish, for as long as eleven Athenian gentlemen allow.'

'Thank you,' said Simmias; 'then I'll tell you my difficulty, and   10
Cebes here in his turn will say where he doesn't accept what's been   c
said. I think, Socrates, as perhaps you do too, that in these matters
certain knowledge is either impossible or very hard to come by in
this life; but that even so, not to test what is said about them in
every possible way, without leaving off till one has examined them   5
exhaustively from every aspect, shows a very feeble spirit; on these
questions one must achieve one of two things: either learn or find
out how things are; or, if that's impossible, then adopt the best and
least refutable of human doctrines, embarking on it as a kind of raft,   d
and risking the dangers of the voyage through life, unless one could
travel more safely and with less risk, on a securer conveyance
afforded by some divine doctrine. So now I shan't scruple to put
my question, since you tell me to, and then I shan't reproach myself   5
at a later time for failing to speak my mind now. In my view,
Socrates, when I examine what's been said, either alone or with
Cebes here, it doesn't seem altogether adequate.'   10

'Maybe your view is correct, my friend,' said Socrates; 'but tell   e
me, in what way inadequate?'

'I think in this way,' he said; 'one could surely use the same
argument about the attunement of a lyre and its strings, and say that
the attunement is something unseen and incorporeal and very lovely   5
and divine in the tuned lyre, while the lyre itself and its strings are   86

35

corporeal bodies and composite and earthy and akin to the mortal.
Now, if someone smashed the lyre, or severed and snapped its
5   strings, suppose it were maintained, by the same argument as yours,
that the attunement must still exist and not have perished—because
it would be inconceivable that when the strings had been snapped,
the lyre and the strings themselves, which are of mortal nature,
should still exist, and yet that the attunement, which has affinity
b   and kinship to the divine and the immortal, should have perished—
and perished before the mortal; rather, it might be said, the attunement itself must still exist somewhere, and the wood and the strings
5   would have to rot away before anything happened to it. And in point
of fact, Socrates, my own belief is that you're aware yourself that
something of this sort is what we actually take the soul to be: our
body is kept in tension, as it were, and held together by hot and
cold, dry and wet, and the like, and our soul is a blending and
c   attunement of these same things, when they're blended with each
other in due proportion. If, then, the soul proves to be some kind of
attunement, it's clear that when our body is unduly relaxed or
5   tautened by illnesses and other troubles, then the soul must perish
at once, no matter how divine it may be, just like other attunements,
those in musical notes and in all the products of craftsmen; whereas
the remains of each body will last for a long time, until they're
d   burnt up or rot away. Well, consider what we shall say in answer to
that argument, if anyone should claim that the soul, being a
blending of the bodily elements, is the first thing to perish in what
is called death.'

5   At this Socrates looked at us wide-eyed, as he often used to, and
said with a smile: 'Simmias' remarks are certainly fair. So if any of
you is more resourceful than I am, why doesn't he answer him?
Because he really seems to be coming to grips with the argument in
no mean fashion. However, before answering I think we should first
e   hear from Cebes here what further charge he has to bring against the
argument, so that in the intervening period we may be thinking what
to say; then, when we've heard them both, either we can agree with
them, if it seems they're at all in tune; or if not, we can enter a plea
5   for the argument at that point. Come on then, Cebes, tell us what's
been troubling you.'

'I certainly will,' said Cebes. 'You see, the argument seems to me
to remain where it was, and to be open to the same charge as we
made before. As to the existence of our soul even before it entered 87
its present form, I don't take back my admission that this has been
very neatly, and, if it's not presumptuous to say so, very adequately
proved; but I don't think the same about its still existing somewhere
when we've died. Not that I agree with Simmias' objection that soul 5
isn't stronger and longer-lived than body: because I think it far
superior in all those ways. "Why then", the argument would say,
"are you still in doubt, when you can see that the weaker part still
exists after the man has died? Don't you think the longer-lived part b
must still be preserved during that time?"

'Well, consider if there's anything in my reply to that; because it
seems that, like Simmias, I too need an image. What's being said, I
think, is very much as if someone should offer this argument about a
man—a weaver who has died in old age—to show that the man hasn't 5
perished but exists somewhere intact, and should produce as evidence
the fact that the cloak he had woven for himself, and worn, was
intact and had not perished; and if anyone doubted him, he should c
ask which class of thing is longer-lived, a man, or a cloak in constant
use and wear; and on being answered that a man is much longer-
lived, should think it had been proved that the man must therefore
surely be intact, seeing that something shorter-lived hadn't perished. 5
Yet in fact, Simmias, this isn't so: because you too must consider
what I'm saying. Everyone would object that this is a simple-minded
argument. Because this weaver, though he'd woven and worn out
many such cloaks, perished after all of them, despite their number, d
but still, presumably, before the last one; and yet for all that a man
is neither lesser nor weaker than a cloak.

'The relation of soul to body would, I think, admit of the same
comparison: anyone making the same points about them, that the
soul is long-lived, while the body is weaker and shorter-lived, would 5
in my view argue reasonably; true indeed, he might say, every soul
wears out many bodies, especially in a life of many years—because,
though the body may decay and perish while the man is still alive,
still the soul will always weave afresh what's being worn out; never- e
theless, when the soul does perish, it will have to be wearing its last

37

garment, and must perish before that one alone; and when the soul
5   has perished, then at last the body will reveal its natural weakness,
moulder away quickly, and be gone. So we've no right as yet to
88   trust this argument, and feel confident that our soul still exists
somewhere after we've died. Indeed, were one to grant the speaker
even more than what you say,[43] allowing him not only that our souls
existed in the time before we were born, but that nothing prevents
5   the souls of some, even after we've died, from still existing and
continuing to exist, and from being born and dying over and over
again—because soul is so strong by nature that it can endure repeated
births—even allowing all that, were one not to grant the further point
that it does not suffer in its many births, and does not end by
10   perishing completely in one of its deaths, and were one to say that
b   no one can know this death or detachment from the body which
brings perishing to the soul—since none of us can possibly perceive
it—well, if that's the case, then anyone who's confident in face of
5   death must be possessed of a foolish confidence, unless he can prove
that soul is completely immortal and imperishable; otherwise, anyone
about to die must always fear for his own soul, lest in its present
disjunction from the body it perish completely.'

c   All of us who heard them were disagreeably affected by their
words, as we afterwards told one another: we'd been completely
convinced by the earlier argument, yet now they seemed to disturb
us again, and make us doubtful not only about the arguments already
5   put forward but also about points yet to be raised, for fear that we
were incompetent judges of anything, or even that these things
might be inherently doubtful.

Echecrates. Goodness, Phaedo, you have my sympathy. Because
d   now that I've heard you, it occurs to me to say to myself something
like this: 'What argument shall we ever trust now? How thoroughly
convincing was the argument that Socrates gave, yet now it's fallen
into discredit.' This theory that our soul is a kind of attunement has
5   a strange hold on me, now as it always has done, so your statement
of it has served to remind me that I'd formerly held this view myself.
And I very much need some other argument that will convince me
once again, as if from the start, that the soul of one who has died

doesn't die with him. So do please tell me how Socrates pursued the
discussion. Did he become visibly troubled at all, as you say you   e
were, or did he come quietly to the argument's help? And was his
help adequate or deficient? Please relate everything to us, as minutely
as you can.

Phaedo. Well, Echecrates, often as I've admired Socrates, I never
found him more wonderful than when with him then. That he should   5
have had an answer to give isn't, perhaps, surprising; but what I   89
specially admired was, first, the pleasure, kindliness, and approval
with which he received the young men's argument; next his acute-
ness in perceiving how their speeches had affected us; and finally his
success in treating us, rallying us as if we were fleeing in defeat, and   5
encouraging us to follow him in examining the argument together.
Echecrates. In what way?

Phaedo. I'll tell you. I happened to be sitting to his right, on a
stool beside the bed, while he was a good way above me. Stroking   b
my head and gathering the hair on my neck—it was his way now and
again to make fun of my hair[44]—he said: 'So tomorrow perhaps,
Phaedo, you'll cut off those lovely locks.'   5

'I expect so, Socrates,' I replied.

'You won't, if you listen to me.'

'What then?' I asked.

'Today', he said, 'I'll cut mine and you yours—if, that is, the
argument dies on us and we can't revive it. For myself, if I were you   10
and the argument got away from me, I should swear an oath, like the   c
Argives, not to grow my hair again till I'd fought back and defeated
the argument of Simmias and Cebes.'

'But', I said, 'even Heracles is said to have been no match for two.'   5

'Then summon me as your Iolaus,' he said, 'while there's still
light.'

'All right,' I said, 'I summon you, not as if I were Heracles myself,
but rather as Iolaus summoning Heracles.'   10

'That will make no difference,' he said. 'But first let's take care
that a certain fate doesn't befall us.'

'What's that?' I asked.

'The fate of becoming "misologists", just as some become mis-   d
anthropists; because there's no greater evil that could befall anyone

than this—the hating of arguments. "Misology" and misanthropy
5   both arise from the same source. Misanthropy develops when,
without skill, one puts complete trust in somebody, thinking the
man absolutely true and sound and reliable, and then a little later
finds him bad and unreliable; and then this happens again with
another person; and when it happens to someone often, especially
e   at the hands of those he'd regard as his nearest and dearest friends,
he ends up, after repeated hard knocks, hating everyone, thinking
there's no soundness whatever in anyone at all. Have you never
noticed that happening?'

'I certainly have,' I said.

5   'Well, isn't it an ugly thing, and isn't it clear that such a man was
setting about handling human beings, without any skill in human
relations? Because if he handled them with skill, he'd surely have
90   recognized the truth, that extremely good and bad people are both
very few in number, and the majority lie in between.'

'What do you mean?' I asked.

'It's the same as with extremely small and large things: do you
5   think anything is rarer than finding an extremely large or extremely
small man, or dog, or anything else? Or again, one that's extremely
fast or slow, ugly or beautiful, pale or dark?[45] Haven't you noticed
that in all such cases extreme instances at either end are rare and few
in number, whereas intermediate ones are plentiful and common?'

10   'Certainly,' I said.

b   'Don't you think, then, that if a contest in badness were promoted,
there too those in the first class would be very few?'

'Probably,' I said.

'Yes, probably; though in that respect arguments aren't like men,
5   but I was following the lead you gave just now. The resemblance is
found, rather, when someone who lacks skill in arguments, trusts
some argument to be true, and then a little later it seems to him
false, sometimes when it is, and sometimes when it isn't, and then the
same thing happens with one argument after another—it is, as you
c   know, especially those who've spent all their time on antinomies,
who end up thinking they've become extremely wise: they alone
have discerned that there's nothing sound or secure whatever, either
in things or arguments; but that all the things that are are carried up

and down, just like things fluctuating in the Euripus, and never   5
remain at rest for any time.'

'What you say is perfectly true,' I said.

'Then, Phaedo, it would be a pitiful fate, if there were in fact
some true and secure argument, and one that could be discerned, yet   **d**
owing to association with arguments of the sort that seem now true
and now false, a man blamed neither himself nor his own lack of
skill, but finally relieved his distress by shifting the blame from
himself to arguments, and then finished out the rest of his life   5
hating and abusing arguments, and was deprived both of the truth
and of knowledge of the things that are.'[46]

'Goodness, that certainly would be pitiful,' I said.

'Then let's guard against this first, and let's not admit into our
soul the thought that there's probably nothing sound in arguments;   **e**
but let's far rather admit that we're not yet sound ourselves, but
must strive manfully to become sound—you and the others for the
sake of your whole future life, but I because of death itself; since   **91**
that very issue is one that I may not be facing as a philosopher
should, but rather as one bent on victory, like those quite devoid of
education. They too, when they dispute about something, care
nothing for the truth of the matter under discussion, but are eager
only that those present shall accept their own thesis. It seems to me   5
that on this occasion I shall differ from them only to this extent:
my concern will not be, except perhaps incidentally, that what I say
shall seem true to those present, but rather that it shall, as far as
possible, seem so to myself. Because I reckon, my dear friend—watch   **b**
how anxious I am to score—that if what I say proves true, it's surely
well to have been persuaded; whereas if there's nothing for a dead
man, still, at least during this very time before my death, I'll distress
those present less with lamentation, and this ignorance[47] of mine will 5
not persist—that would be a bad thing—but will in a little while
be ended.

'Thus prepared, Simmias and Cebes, I advance against the argument; but for your part, if you take my advice, you'll care little for
Socrates but much more for the truth: if I seem to you to say   **c**
anything true, agree with it; but if not, resist it with every argument
you can, taking care that in my zeal I don't deceive you and myself

5 alike, and go off like a bee leaving its sting behind.

'Well now, to proceed. First remind me of what you were saying, in case I prove not to have remembered. Simmias, I believe, is doubtful and afraid that the soul, though more divine and lovelier

d than the body, may still perish before it, being a kind of attunement. Whereas Cebes, I thought, agreed with me in this much, that soul is longer-lived than body; but he held that no one could be sure whether

5 the soul, after wearing out many bodies time and again, might not then perish itself, leaving its last body behind, and whether death might not be just this, the perishing of soul—since body, of course, is perishing incessantly and never stops. Aren't those the points, Simmias and Cebes, that we have to consider?'

e They both agreed that they were.

'Then do you reject all of the previous arguments, or only some of them?'

'Some of them,' they said, 'but not others.'

5 'Well what do you say, then, about the argument in which we said that learning was recollection, and that this being so, our souls must

92 exist somewhere else before being imprisoned in the body?'

'For my part,' said Cebes, 'I was wonderfully convinced by it at the time, and remain so now, as by no other argument.'

'And I'm of the same mind,' said Simmias; 'and I'd be very sur-

5 prised if I ever came to think otherwise about that.'

To this Socrates answered: 'But you'll have to think otherwise, my Theban friend, if you stick to this idea that attunement is a composite thing, and that soul is a kind of attunement composed of the bodily elements held in tension; because you surely won't allow

b yourself to say that an attunement existed as a composite, before the elements of which it was to be composed; or will you?'

'Certainly not, Socrates.'

'Then do you see that this is implied by your assertion, when you

5 say that the soul exists before entering human form and body, yet that it is a composite of things that don't yet exist? Surely your attunement isn't, in fact, the same kind of thing as that to which you liken it: rather, the lyre, and its strings and notes, come into

c being first, as yet untuned, whereas the attunement is put together last of all, and is the first to perish. So how's this theory of yours

42

going to harmonize with that one?'

'In no way,' said Simmias.

'Yet surely, if there's one theory that ought to be in harmony, it's   5
a theory about attunement.'

'So it ought,' said Simmias.

'Well, this one of yours isn't in harmony; but see which of the
theories you prefer: that learning is recollection, or that soul
is attunement.'   10

'The former, by a long way, Socrates. Because I acquired the
latter without any proof, but from a certain likelihood[48] and   d
plausibility about it, whence its appeal for most people;[49] but I'm
aware that arguments basing their proofs upon likelihoods are
impostors, and if one doesn't guard against them, they completely
deceive one, in geometry as well as in all other subjects. But the   5
argument about recollection and learning has come from a hypothesis
worthy of acceptance. Because it was, of course, asserted that our
soul existed even before it entered the body, just as surely as its
object exists—the Being, bearing the name of "*what it is*";[50] and this,
I'm convinced, I have accepted rightly and for adequate reason. So   e
it would seem, consequently, that I must allow neither myself nor
anyone else to say that soul is attunement.'

'Again now, look at it this way, Simmias. Do you think it befits
an attunement, or any other compound, to be in any state other   93
than that of the elements of which it's composed?'

'Certainly not.'

'Nor yet, I presume, to act, or be acted upon, in any way
differently from the way they may act or be acted upon?'   5

He assented.

'An attunement therefore should not properly direct the things
of which it's composed, but should follow them.'

He agreed.

'Then an attunement can't possibly undergo contrary movement
or utter sound or be opposed in any other way to its own parts.'

'It can't possibly.'   10

'Again now, isn't it natural for every attunement to be an attunement just as it's been tuned?'

'I don't understand.'

'Isn't it the case that if it's been tuned more and to a greater
b   extent,[51] assuming that to be possible,[52] it will be more an attunement and a greater one; whereas if less and to a smaller extent, it
will be a lesser and smaller one?'

'Certainly.'

'Well, is this the case with soul—that even in the least degree, one
5   soul is either to a greater extent and more than another, or to a
smaller extent and less, just itself—namely, a soul?'

'In no way whatever.'

'Well, but is one soul said to have intelligence and goodness and
to be good, while another is said to have folly and wickedness and
c   to be bad? And are we right in saying those things?'

'Quite right.'

'Then what will any of those who maintain that soul is attunement say these things are, existing in our souls—goodness and bad-
5   ness? Are they, in turn, a further attunement and non-attunement?
And is one soul, the good one, tuned, and does it have within
itself, being an attunement, a further attunement, whereas the
untuned one is just itself, and lacking a further attunement within
it?'

'I couldn't say myself,' said Simmias; 'but obviously anyone
10   maintaining the hypothesis would say something of that sort.'
d   'But it's already been agreed that no one soul is more or less a
soul than another; and this is the admission that no one attunement
is either more or to a greater extent, or less or to a smaller extent, an
attunement than another.[53] Isn't that so?'

5   'Certainly.'

'But that which is neither more nor less an attunement has been
neither more nor less tuned; is that so?'

'It is.'

'But does that which has been neither more nor less tuned
10   participate in attunement to a greater or to a smaller degree, or to
an equal degree?'

'To an equal degree.'

'But then, given that no one soul is either more or less itself,
e   namely a soul, than another, it hasn't been more or less tuned either?'

'That is so.'

'And this being its condition, surely it couldn't participate more
either in non-attunement or in attunement?'   5
'Indeed not.'
'And this again being its condition, could any one soul participate to a greater extent than another in badness or goodness,
assuming that badness is non-attunement, while goodness is attunement?'
'It couldn't.'   10
'Or rather, surely, following sound reasoning, Simmias, no soul   **94**
will participate in badness, assuming it is attunement; because
naturally an attunement, being completely itself, namely an attunement, could never participate in non-attunement.'
'No indeed.'   5
'Nor then, of course, could a soul, being completely a soul,
participate in badness.'
'How could it, in view of what's already been said?'
'By this argument, then, we find that all souls of all living things
will be equally good, assuming that it's the nature of souls to be
equally themselves, namely souls.'   10
'So it seems to me, Socrates.'
'Yes, and do you approve of this assertion, or think this would
happen to the argument, if the hypothesis that soul is attunement   **b**
were correct?'
'Not in the least.'
'Again now, would you say that of all the things in a man it is
anything but soul, especially if it's a wise one, that rules him?'[54] 5
'I wouldn't.'
'Does it comply with the bodily feelings or does it oppose them?
I mean, for example, when heat and thirst are in the body, by
pulling the opposite way, away from drinking, and away from
eating when it feels hunger; and surely in countless other ways we   10
see the soul opposing bodily feelings, don't we?'   **c**
'We certainly do.'
'And again, didn't we agree earlier that if it is attunement, it
would never utter notes opposed to the tensions, relaxations,   5
strikings, and any other affections of its components, but would
follow and never dominate them?'

'We did of course agree.'

'Well now, don't we find it, in fact, operating in just the opposite
10   way, dominating all those alleged sources of its existence, and
d   opposing them in almost everything throughout all of life, mastering
them in all kinds of ways, sometimes disciplining more harshly and
painfully with gymnastics and medicine, sometimes more mildly,
now threatening and now admonishing, conversing with our appetites
5   and passions and fears, as if with a separate thing? That, surely, is
the sort of thing Homer has represented in the *Odyssey*, where he
says that Odysseus:

> Striking his breast, reproved his heart with the words:
e   > "Endure, my heart; e'en worse thou didst once endure."

Do you think he'd have composed that, with the idea that the soul
was attunement, the sort of thing that could be led by the feelings of
the body rather than something that could lead and master them,
5   being itself far too divine a thing to rank as attunement?'

'Goodness no, Socrates, I don't!'

'In no way at all then, my friend, do we approve of the thesis
95   that soul is a kind of attunement; because it seems that we should
agree neither with the divine poet Homer nor with ourselves.'

'That is so.'

'Well then,' said Socrates, 'we seem to have placated the Theban
5   lady Harmonia moderately well; but now, how about the question
of Cadmus? How and with what argument, Cebes, shall we placate
him?'

'You'll find a way, I think,' said Cebes; 'at any rate this argument
of yours against attunement has surprised me beyond expectation.
Because when Simmias was speaking in his perplexity, I was very
b   much wondering if anyone would be able to handle his argument;
so it seemed to me quite remarkable that it immediately failed to
withstand the first assault of your own argument. Accordingly, I
shouldn't wonder if the argument of Cadmus suffered the same fate.'

5   'No big talking, my friend,' said Socrates, 'in case some evil eye
should turn the coming argument to rout. But that shall be God's
concern; for ourselves, let's come to close quarters, in Homeric
fashion, and try to see if, in fact, there's anything in what you say.

The sum and substance of what you're after is surely this: you want
it proved that our soul is imperishable and immortal, if a philo-   c
sophic man about to die, confidently believing that after death he'll
fare much better yonder than if he were ending a life lived differently, isn't to be possessed of a senseless and foolish confidence.
As for showing that the soul is something strong and god-like, and   5
existed even before we were born as men, nothing prevents all that,
you say, from indicating not immortality, but only that soul is
long-lived and existed somewhere for an immense length of time in
the past, and knew and did all kinds of things; even so, it was none
the more immortal for all that, but its very entry into a human body   d
was the beginning of its perishing, like an illness: it lives this life in
distress, and finally perishes in what is called death. And, you say, it
makes no difference, so far as our individual fears are concerned,
whether it enters a body once or many times: anyone who neither   5
knows nor can give proof that it's immortal should be afraid, unless
he has no sense.

'Something like this, Cebes, is what I think you're saying; and I'm   e
purposely reviewing it more than once, so that nothing may escape
us, and so that you may add or take away anything you wish.'

To this Cebes replied: 'No, there's nothing at present that I   5
want to take away or add; those are my very points.'

Here Socrates paused for a long time examining something in his
own mind. He then said: 'It's no trivial matter, this quest of yours,
Cebes: it calls for a thorough inquiry into the whole question of the
reason for coming-to-be and destruction.[55] So I will, if you like,   96
relate my own experiences on these matters: and then, if any of the
things I say seem helpful to you, you can use them for conviction on
the points you raise.'

'Well, I certainly should like that,' said Cebes.   5

'Then listen to my story. When I was young, Cebes, I was remark-
ably keen on the kind of wisdom known as natural science;[56] it
seemed to me splendid to know the reasons for each thing, why
each thing comes to be, why it perishes, and why it exists. And I   10
was always shifting back and forth, examining, for a start, questions b
like these: is it, as some said, whenever the hot and the cold give rise
to putrefâction, that living creatures develop? And is it blood that

5   we think with, or air, or fire? Or is it none of these, but the brain
that provides the senses of hearing and seeing and smelling, from
which memory and judgement come to be; and is it from memory
and judgement, when they've acquired stability, that knowledge
comes to be accordingly? Next, when I went on to examine the
c   destruction of these things, and what happens in the heavens and
the earth, I finally judged myself to have absolutely no gift for this
kind of inquiry. I'll tell you a good enough sign of this: there had
been things that I previously did know for sure, at least as I myself
5   and others thought; yet I was then so utterly blinded by this
inquiry, that I unlearned even those things I formerly supposed I
knew, including, amongst many other things, why it is that a human
being grows. That, I used earlier to suppose, was obvious to everyone:
d   it was because of eating and drinking; whenever, from food, flesh
came to accrue to flesh, and bone to bone, and similarly on the
same principle the appropriate matter came to accrue to each of the
other parts, it was then that the little bulk later came to be big; and
5   in this way the small human being comes to be large.[57] That was
what I supposed then: reasonably enough, don't you think?'

'I do,' said Cebes.

'Well, consider these further cases: I used to suppose it was an
adequate view, whenever a large man standing beside a small one
e   appeared to be larger just by a head; similarly with two horses. And,
to take cases even clearer than these, it seemed to me that ten was
greater than eight because of the accruing of two to the latter, and
that two cubits were larger than one cubit, because of their exceeding
the latter by half.'

5   'Well, what do you think about them now?' said Cebes.

'I can assure you that I'm far from supposing I know the reason
for any of these things, when I don't even accept from myself that
when you add one to one, it's either the one to which the addition
is made that's come to be two,[58] or the one that's been added *and*
97 the one to which it's been added, that have come to be two, because
of the addition of one to the other. Because I wonder if, when they
were apart from each other, each was one and they weren't two
then; whereas when they came close to each other, this then became
5   a reason for their coming to be two—the union in which they were

juxtaposed. Nor again can I any longer be persuaded, if you divide
one, that this has now become a reason for its coming to be two,
namely division; because if so, we have a reason opposite to the
previous one for its coming to be two; then it was their being brought   b
close to each other and added, one to the other; whereas now it's
their being drawn apart, and separated each from the other. Why, I
can't even persuade myself any longer that I know why it is that one .
comes to be; nor, in short, why anything else comes to be, or   5
perishes, or exists, following that method of inquiry. Instead I
rashly adopt a different method, a jumble of my own, and in no
way incline towards the other.

'One day, however, I heard someone reading from a book he said
was by Anaxagoras, according to which it is, in fact, Intelligence that   c
orders and is the reason for everything. Now this was a reason that
pleased me; it seemed to me, somehow, to be a good thing that
Intelligence should be the reason for everything. And I thought that,
if that's the case, then Intelligence in ordering all things must order   5
them and place each individual thing in the best way possible; so if
anyone wanted to find out the reason why each thing comes to be
or perishes or exists, this is what he must find out about it: how is it
best for that thing to exist, or to act or be acted upon in any way?[59]   d
On this theory, then, a man should consider nothing else, whether in
regard to himself or anything else, but the best, the highest good;
though the same man must also know the worse, as they are
objects of the same knowledge. Reckoning thus, I was pleased to   5
think I'd found, in Anaxagoras, an instructor to suit my own
intelligence in the reason for the things that are. And I thought he'd
inform me, first, whether the earth is flat or round, and when he'd
informed me, he'd go on to expound the reason why it must be so,   e
telling me what was better—better, that is, that it should be like this;
and if he said it was in the centre, he'd go on to expound the view
that a central position for it was better. If he could make these
things clear to me, I was prepared to hanker no more after any other   98
kind of reason. What's more, I was prepared to find out in just the
same way about the sun, the moon, and the stars, about their
relative velocity and turnings and the other things that happen to
them, and how it's better for each of them to act and be acted upon   5

just as they are. Because I never supposed that, having said they were ordered by Intelligence, he'd bring in any reason for them other than its being best for them to be just the way they are; and I

b supposed that in assigning the reason for each individual thing, and for things in general, he'd go on to expound what was best for the individual, and what was the common good for all; nor would I have sold these hopes for a large sum, but I made all haste to get

5 hold of the books and read them as quickly as I could, so that I might know as quickly as possible what was best and what was worse.

'Well, my friend, these marvellous hopes of mine were dashed; because, as I went on with my reading, I beheld a man making no use of his Intelligence at all, nor finding in it any reasons for

c the ordering of things, but imputing them to such things as air and aether and water and many other absurdities. In fact, he seemed to me to be in exactly the position of someone who said that all Socrates' actions were performed with his intelligence, and who then

5 tried to give the reasons for each of my actions by saying, first, that the reason why I'm now sitting here is that my body consists of bones and sinews, and the bones are hard and separated from each other by joints, whereas the sinews, which can be tightened and

d relaxed, surround the bones, together with the flesh and the skin that holds them together; so that when the bones are turned in their sockets, the sinews by stretching and tensing enable me somehow to bend my limbs at this moment, and that's the reason why I'm

5 sitting here bent in this way; or again, by mentioning other reasons of the same kind for my talking with you, imputing it to vocal sounds, air currents, auditory sensations, and countless other such

e things, yet neglecting to mention the true reasons: that Athenians judged it better to condemn me, and therefore I in my turn have judged it better to sit here, and thought it more just to stay

5 behind and submit to such penalty as they may ordain. Because, I

99 dare swear,[60] these sinews and bones would long since have been off in Megara or Boeotia, impelled by their judgement of what was best, had I not thought it more just and honourable not to escape and run away, but to submit to whatever penalty the city might impose.

5 But to call such things "reasons" is quite absurd. It would be quite true to say that without possessing such things as bones and sinews,

and whatever else I possess, I shouldn't be able to do what I judged
best; but to call these things the reasons for my actions, rather than
my choice of what is best, and that too though I act with intelligence,   b
would be a thoroughly loose way of talking. Fancy being unable to
distinguish two different things: the reason proper, and that without
which the reason could never be a reason! Yet it's this latter that
most people call a reason, appearing to me to be feeling it over blind-   5
fold,[61] as it were, and applying a wrong name to it. That's why one
man makes the earth stay in position by means of the heaven,
putting a whirl around it; while another presses down the air as a
base, as if with a flat kneading-trough.[62] Yet the power by which
they're now situated in the best way that they could be placed, this   c
they neither look for nor credit with any supernatural strength; but
they think they'll one day discover an Atlas stronger and more
immortal than this, who does more to hold everything together.
That it's the good or binding, that genuinely does bind and hold   5
things together, they don't believe at all. Now I should most gladly
have become anyone's pupil, to learn the truth about a reason of that
sort; but since I was deprived of this, proving unable either to find it
for myself or to learn it from anyone else, would you like me, Cebes,
to give you a display of how I've conducted my second voyage in   d
quest of the reason?'

'Yes, I'd like that immensely,' he said.

'Well then, it seemed to me next, since I'd wearied of studying
the things that are, that I must take care not to incur what happens   5
to people who observe and examine the sun during an eclipse; some
of them, you know, ruin their eyes, unless they examine its image
in water or something of that sort. I had a similar thought: I was   e
afraid I might be completely blinded in my soul, by looking at
objects with my eyes and trying to lay hold of them with each of my
senses. So I thought I should take refuge in theories, and study in   5
them the truth of the things that are. Perhaps my comparison is,
in a certain way, inept; as I don't at all admit that one who examines   **100**
in theories the things that are is any more studying them in images
than one who examines them in concrete. But anyhow, this was how
I proceeded: hypothesizing on each occasion the theory I judge
strongest, I put down as true whatever things seem to me to accord   5

with it, both about a reason and about everything else; and whatever
do not, I put down as not true. But I'd like to explain my meaning
more clearly; because L don't imagine you understand it as yet.'

'Not entirely, I must say!' said Cebes.

b   'Well, this is what I mean: it's nothing new, but what I've spoken
of incessantly in our earlier discussion as well as at other times. I'm
going to set about displaying to you the kind of reason I've been
5   dealing with; and I'll go back to those much harped-on entities, and
start from them, hypothesizing that a beautiful, itself by itself, is
something, and so are a good and a large and all the rest. If you grant
me that and agree that those things exist, I hope that from them I
shall display to you the reason, and find out that soul is immortal.'

c   'Well, you may certainly take that for granted,' said Cebes, 'so
you couldn't be too quick to conclude.'

'Then look at what comes next to those things, and see if you
think as I do. It seems to me that if anything else is beautiful besides
5   the beautiful itself, it is beautiful for no reason at all other than that
it participates in that beautiful; and the same goes for all of them.
Do you assent to a reason of that kind?'

'I do.'

'Then I no longer understand nor can I recognize those other wise
10   reasons; but if anyone gives me as the reason why a given thing is
d   beautiful either its having a blooming colour, or its shape, or
something else like that, I dismiss those other things—because all
those others confuse me—but in a plain, artless, and possibly simple-
minded way, I hold this close to myself: nothing else makes it
5   beautiful except that beautiful itself, whether by its presence or
communion or whatever the manner and nature of the relation may
be;[63] as I don't go so far as to affirm that, but only that it is by the
beautiful that all beautiful things are beautiful. Because that seems to
be the safest answer to give both to myself and to another, and if I
e   hang on to this, I believe I'll never fall: it's safe to answer both to
myself and to anyone else that it is by the beautiful that beautiful
things are beautiful; or don't you agree?'

'I do.'

5   'Similarly it's by largeness that large things are large, and larger
things larger, and by smallness that smaller things are smaller?'

'Yes.'

'Then you too wouldn't accept anyone's saying that one man was larger than another by a head, and that the smaller was smaller by that same thing; but you'd protest that you for your part will say **101** only that everything larger than something else is larger by nothing but largeness, and largeness is the reason for its being larger; and that the smaller is smaller by nothing but smallness, and smallness is the reason for its being smaller. You'd be afraid, I imagine, of meeting 5 the following contradiction:[64] if you say that someone is larger and smaller by a head, then, first, the larger will be larger and the smaller smaller by the same thing; and secondly, the head, by which the larger man is larger, is itself a small thing; and it's surely monstrous **b** that anyone should be large by something small; or wouldn't you be afraid of that?'

'Yes, I should,' said Cebes laughing.

'Then wouldn't you be afraid to say that ten is greater than eight by two, and that this is the reason for its exceeding, rather than 5 that it's by numerousness, and because of numerousness? Or that two cubits are larger than one cubit by half, rather than by largeness? Because, of course, there'd be the same fear.'

'Certainly,' he said.

'And again, wouldn't you beware of saying that when one is added to one, the addition is the reason for their coming to be two,[65] or when one is divided, that division is the reason? You'd **c** shout loudly that you know no other way in which each thing comes to be, except by participating in the peculiar Being[66] of any given thing in which it does participate; and in these cases you own no other reason for their coming to be two, save participation in 5 twoness: things that are going to be two must participate in that, and whatever is going to be one must participate in oneness. You'd dismiss those divisions and additions and other such subtleties, leaving them as answers to be given by people wiser than yourself; but you, scared of your own shadow, as the saying is, and of your **d** inexperience, would hang on to that safety of the hypothesis, and answer accordingly. But if anyone hung on to[67] the hypothesis itself, you would dismiss him, and you wouldn't answer till you should have examined its consequences, to see if, in your view, they

5   are in accord or discord with each other; and when you had to give
       an account of the hypothesis itself, you would give it in the same
       way, once again hypothesizing another hypothesis, whichever should
e   seem best of those above, till you came to something adequate; but
       you wouldn't jumble things as the contradiction-mongers do, by
       discussing the starting-point and its consequences at the same time,
       if, that is, you wanted to discover any of the things that are. For
       them, perhaps, this isn't a matter of the least thought or concern;
5   their wisdom enables them to mix everything up together, yet still
       be pleased with themselves; but you, if you really are a philosopher,
102   would, I imagine, do as I say.'
       'What you say is perfectly true,' said Simmias and Cebes together.
       Echecrates.   Goodness, Phaedo, there was reason to say that! It
       seems marvellous to me how clearly he put things, even for someone
5   of small intelligence.
       Phaedo.   Exactly, Echecrates. That was how it seemed to everyone
       there.
       Echecrates.   And to us who weren't there but are now hearing it.
       Tell us, though, what were the things that were said next?

10   *Phaedo.*   As I recall, when these points had been granted him, and
b   it was agreed that each of the forms *was* something, and that the
       other things, partaking in them, took the name of the forms them-
       selves, he next asked: 'If you say that that is so, then whenever you
       say that Simmias is larger than Socrates but smaller than Phaedo, you
5   mean then, don't you, that both things are in Simmias, largeness
       and smallness?'
       'I do.'
       'Well anyhow, do you agree that Simmias' overtopping of
       Socrates isn't expressed in those words according to the truth of the
c   matter? Because it isn't, surely, by nature that Simmias overtops
       him, by virtue, that is of his being Simmias, but by virtue of the
       largeness that he happens to have. Nor again does he overtop
       Socrates because Socrates is Socrates, but because of smallness that
       Socrates has in relation to his largeness?'
5   'True.'
       'Nor again is he overtopped by Phaedo in virtue of Phaedo's being

Phaedo, but because of largeness that Phaedo has in relation to
Simmias' smallness?'

'That is so.'

'So that's how Simmias takes the name of being both small and   10
large; it's because he's between the two of them, submitting his
smallness to the largeness of the one for it to overtop, and presenting   d
to the other his largeness which overtops the latter's smallness.'

At this he smiled, and added: 'That sounds as if I'm going to talk
like a book.[68] But anyway, things are surely as I say.'

He agreed.

'My reason for saying this is that I want you to think as I do.   5
Now it seems to me that not only is largeness itself never willing to
be large and small at the same time, but also that the largeness in us
never admits the small, nor is it willing to be overtopped. Rather,
one of two things must happen: either it must retreat and get out of
the way, when its opposite, the small, advances towards it; or else,   e
upon that opposite's advance, it must perish. But what it is not
willing to do is to abide and admit smallness, and thus be other
than what it was. Thus I, having admitted and abided smallness, am
still what I am, this same individual, only small; whereas the large in   5
us,[69] while being large, can't endure to be small. And similarly, the
small that's in us is not willing ever to come to be, or to be, large.
Nor will any other of the opposites, while still being what it was, at
the same time come to be, and be, its own opposite. If that befalls it,   **103**
either it goes away *or* it perishes.'

'I entirely agree,' said Cebes.

On hearing this, one of those present—I don't remember for sure
who it was—said: 'But look here, wasn't the very opposite of what's   5
now being said agreed in our earlier discussion: that the larger comes
to be from the smaller, and the smaller from the larger, and that
coming-to-be is, for opposites, just this—they come to be from their
opposites. Whereas now I think it's being said that this could never
happen.'   10

Socrates turned his head and listened. 'It's splendid of you to
have recalled that,' he said; 'but you don't realize the difference   b
between what's being said now and what was said then. It was said
then that one opposite *thing* comes to be from another opposite

thing; what we're saying now is that the opposite *itself* could never
5 come to be opposite to itself, whether it be the opposite in us or the
opposite in nature. Then, my friend, we were talking about things
that *have* opposites, calling them by the names they take from them;
whereas now we're talking about the opposites themselves, from
whose presence in them the things so called derive their names. It's
c these latter that we're saying would never be willing to admit coming-
to-be from each other.'

With this he looked towards Cebes and said: 'Cebes, you weren't
troubled, I suppose, by any of the things our friend here said,
were you?'

5 'No, not this time,' said Cebes; 'though I don't deny that many
things do trouble me.'

'We've agreed, then, unreservedly on this point: an opposite will
never be opposite to itself.'

'Completely.'

10 'Now please consider this further point, and see if you agree with
it. Is there something you call hot, and again cold?'

'There is.'

'Do you mean the same as snow and fire?'

d 'No, most certainly not.'

'Rather, the hot is something different from fire, and the cold is
something different from snow?'

'Yes.'

5 'But this I think you will agree: what is snow will never, on the
lines of what we were saying earlier, admit the hot and still be
what it was, namely snow, and also hot; but at the advance of the
hot, it will either get out of the way or perish.'

'Certainly.'

10 'And again fire, when cold advances, will either get out of the way
or perish; but it will never endure to admit the coldness, and still be
what it was, namely fire and also cold.'

e 'That's true.'

'The situation, then, in some cases of this kind, is as follows: not
only is the form itself entitled to its own name for all time; but
there's something else too, which is not the same as the form, but
5 which, whenever it exists, always has the character of that form.

Perhaps what I mean will be clearer in this further example: the odd
must, surely, always be given this name that we're now using,
mustn't it?'

'Certainly.'

'But is it the only thing there is—this is my question—or is there
something else, which is not the same as the odd, yet which one must **104**
also always call odd, as well as by its own name, because it is by
nature such that it can never be separated from the odd? I mean the
sort of thing that happens to threeness, and to many other
instances. Consider the case of threeness. Don't you think it must   5
always be called both by its own name and by that of the odd,
although the odd is not the same as threeness? They aren't the same,
yet threeness and fiveness and half the entire number series are by
nature, each of them, always odd, although they are not the same as   b
the odd. And again, two and four and the whole of the other row of
numbers, though not the same as the even, are still, each of them,
always even. Do you agree or not?'

'Of course.'   5

'Look closely then at what I want to show. It is this: apparently
it's not only the opposites we spoke of that don't admit each other.
This is also true of all things which, although not opposites to each
other, always have the opposites. These things too, it seems, don't
admit whatever form may be opposite to the one that's in them, but   10
when it attacks, *either* they perish *or* they get out of the way. Thus c
we shall say, shan't we, that three will sooner perish, will undergo
anything else whatever, sooner than abide coming to be even, while
remaining three?'

'Indeed we shall,' said Cebes.

'Moreover, twoness isn't opposite to threeness.'   5

'Indeed not.'

'Then not only do the forms that are opposites not abide each
other's attack; but there are, in addition, certain other things that
don't abide the opposites' attack.'

'Quite true.'   10

'Then would you like us, if we can, to define what kinds these are?'

'Certainly.'

'Would they, Cebes, be these: things that are compelled by what-   d

57

ever occupies them[70] to have not only its own form, but always the form of some opposite[71] as well?'

'What do you mean?'

5 'As we were saying just now. You recognize, no doubt, that whatever the form of three occupies must be not only three but also odd.'

'Certainly.'

'Then, we're saying, the form[72] opposite to the character that has

10 that effect could never go to a thing of that kind.'

'It couldn't.'

'But it was that of odd that had that effect?'

'Yes.'

'And opposite to this is that of the even?'

15 'Yes.'

e 'So that of the even will never come to three.'

'No, it won't.'

'Three, then, has no part in the even.'

'No part.'

5 'So threeness is uneven.'

'Yes.'

'So what I was saying we were to define, the kind of things which, while not opposite to a given thing, nevertheless don't admit it, the opposite in question[73]—as we've just seen that threeness, while not opposite to the even, nevertheless doesn't admit it, since it always

10 brings up its opposite, just as twoness brings up the opposite of the odd, and the fire brings up the opposite of the cold, and so on in a

105 great many other cases—well, see whether you would define them thus: it is not only the opposite that doesn't admit its opposite; there is also that which brings up an opposite into whatever it enters itself; and that thing, the very thing that brings it up, never admits

5 the quality opposed to the one that's brought up.[74] Recall it once more: there's no harm in hearing it several times. Five won't admit the form of the even, nor will ten, its double, admit that of the odd. This, of course, is itself also the opposite of something else; never-

b theless, it won't admit the form of the odd. Nor again will one-and-a half, and the rest of that series, the halves, admit the form of the whole; and the same applies to a third, and all that series. Do you follow and agree that that is so?'

'I agree most emphatically, and I do follow.'

'Then please repeat it from the start; and don't answer in the   5
exact terms of my question, but in imitation of my example. I say
this, because from what's now being said I see a different kind of
safeness beyond the answer I gave initially, the old safe one. Thus, if
you were to ask me what it is, by whose presence in a body, that
body will be hot,[75] I shan't give you the old safe, ignorant answer,   c
that it's *hotness*, but a subtler answer now available, that it's *fire*.
And again, if you ask what it is, by whose presence in a body, that
body will ail, I shan't say that it's *illness*, but *fever*. And again, if
asked what it is, by whose presence in a number, that number will   5
be odd, I shan't say *oddness*, but *oneness*; and so on. See whether
by now you have an adequate understanding of what I want.'

'Yes, quite adequate.'

'Answer then, and tell me what it is, by whose presence in a body,
that body will be living.'   10

'Soul.'

'And is this always so?'   d

'Of course.'

'Then soul, whatever it occupies, always comes to that thing
bringing life?'

'It comes indeed.'   5

'And is there an opposite to life, or is there none?'

'There is.'

'What is it?'

'Death.'

'Now soul will absolutely never admit the opposite of what it ●10
brings up, as has been agreed earlier?'

'Most emphatically,' said Cebes.

'Well now, what name did we give just now to what doesn't
admit the form of the even?'

'Un-even.'   15

'And to that which doesn't admit the just, and to whatever
doesn't admit the musical?'

'Un-musical, and un-just.'   e

'Well then, what do we call whatever doesn't admit death?'

'Im-mortal.'

'But soul doesn't admit death?'

5 'No.'

'Then soul is immortal.'

'It's immortal.'

'Very well. May we say that this much has been proved? Or how does it seem to you?'

'Yes, and very adequately proved, Socrates.'

10 'Now what about this, Cebes? If it were necessary for the un-
106 even to be imperishable, three would be imperishable, wouldn't it?'

'Of course.'

'Or again, if the un-hot were necessarily imperishable likewise, then whenever anyone brought hot against snow, the snow would
5 get out of the way, remaining intact and unmelted? Because it couldn't perish, nor again could it abide and admit the hotness.'

'True.'

'And in the same way, I imagine, if the un-coolable were imperishable, then whenever something cold attacked the fire, it could never
10 be put out nor could it perish, but it would depart and go away intact.'

'It would have to.'

b 'Then aren't we compelled to say the same thing about the im-mortal? If the immortal is also imperishable, it's impossible for soul, whenever death attacks it, to perish. Because it follows from what's been said before that it won't admit death, nor will it be
5 dead, just as we said that three will not be even, any more than the odd will be; and again that fire will not be cold, any more than the hotness in the fire will be. "But", someone might say, "what's to prevent the odd, instead of coming to be even, as we granted it
c didn't, when the even attacks, from perishing, and there coming to be even in its place?" Against one who said that, we could not contend that it doesn't perish; because the uneven is not imperishable. If that had been granted us, we could easily have contended
5 that when the even attacks, the odd and three depart and go away. And we could have contended similarly about fire and hot and the rest, couldn't we?'

'Certainly we could.'

'So now, about the immortal likewise: if it's granted us that it
must also be imperishable, then soul, besides being immortal, would   10
also be imperishable; but if not, another argument would be needed.'   d
    'But there's no need of one, on that score at least. Because it
could hardly be that anything else wouldn't admit destruction if the
immortal, being everlasting, is going to admit destruction.'
    'Well God anyway,' said Socrates, 'and the form of life itself, and   5
anything else immortal there may be, never perish, as would, I think,
be agreed by everyone.'
    'Why yes, to be sure; by all men and still more, I imagine, by gods.'
    'Then, given that the immortal is also indestructible,[76] wouldn't   e
soul, if it proves to be immortal, be imperishable as well?'
    'It absolutely must be imperishable.'
    'Then when death attacks a man, his mortal part, it seems, dies;   5
whereas the immortal part gets out of the way of death, departs, and
goes away intact and undestroyed.'
    'It appears so.'
    'Beyond all doubt then, Cebes, soul is immortal and imperishable,
and our souls really will exist in Hades.'   107
    'Well, Socrates, for my part I've no further objection, nor can I
doubt the arguments at any point. But if Simmias here or anyone
else has anything to say, he'd better not keep silent; as I know of no
future occasion to which anyone wanting to speak or hear about   5
such things could put it off.'
    'Well no,' said Simmias; 'nor have I any further ground for doubt
myself, as far as the arguments go; though in view of the size of the
subject under discussion, and having a low regard for human weakness,   b
I'm bound to retain some doubt in my mind about what's been said.'
    'Not only that, Simmias,' said Socrates; 'what you say is right, so
the initial hypotheses, even if they're acceptable to you people,   5
should still be examined more clearly: if you analyse them adequately, you will, I believe, follow the argument to the furthest
point to which man can follow it up; and if you get that clear,[77]
you'll seek nothing further.'
    'What you say is true.'   10

    'But this much it's fair to keep in mind, friends: if a soul *is*   c

immortal, then it needs care, not only for the sake of this time in which what we call "life" lasts, but for the whole of time; and if
5   anyone is going to neglect it, now the risk *would* seem fearful. Because if death were a separation from everything, it would be a godsend for the wicked, when they died, to be separated at once from the body and from their own wickedness along with the soul; but since,
d   in fact, it is evidently immortal, there would be no other refuge from ills or salvation for it, except to become as good and wise as possible. For the soul enters Hades taking nothing else but its education and nurture, which are, indeed, said to do the greatest
5   benefit or harm to the one who has died, at the very outset of his journey yonder.

'Now it is said that when each man has died, the spirit allotted to each while he was living proceeds to bring him to a certain place, where those gathered must submit to judgement, and then
e   journey to Hades with the guide appointed to conduct those in this world to the next; and when they have experienced there the things they must, and stayed there for the time required, another guide conveys them back here during many long cycles of time. So the journey is not as Aeschylus' Telephus describes it: he says it is a
108   simple path that leads to Hades, but to me it seems to be neither simple nor single. For then there would be no need of guides; since no one, surely, could lose the way anywhere, if there were only a single road. But in fact it probably has many forkings and branchings;
5   I speak from the evidence of the rites[78] and observances followed here. Now the wise and well-ordered soul follows along, and is not unfamiliar with what befalls it; but the soul in a state of desire for the body, as I said earlier, flutters around it for a long time, and around
b   the region of the seen,[79] and after much resistance and many sufferings it goes along, brought by force and against its will by the appointed spirit. And on arriving where the others have gone, if the soul is unpurified and has commited any such act as engaging in
5   wrongful killings, or performing such other deeds as may be akin to those and the work of kindred souls, everyone shuns and turns aside from it, and is unwilling to become its travelling companion or
c   guide; but it wanders by itself in a state of utter confusion, till certain periods of time have elapsed, and when these have passed,

it is taken perforce into the dwelling meet for it; but the soul that
has passed through life with purity and moderation finds gods for
travelling companions and guides, and each inhabits the region that   5
befits it.

'Now there are many wondrous regions in the earth, and the
earth itself is of neither the nature nor the size supposed by those
who usually describe it, as someone has convinced me.'

Here Simmias said: 'What do you mean by that, Socrates? I've   d
heard many things about the earth too, but not these that convince
you;[80] so I'd be glad to hear them.'

'Well, Simmias, I don't think the skill of Glaucus is needed to
relate what they are; although to prove them true does seem to me   5
too hard for the skill of Glaucus—I probably couldn't do it myself,
and besides, even if I knew how to, I think the life left me, Simmias,
doesn't suffice for the length of the argument. Still, nothing prevents
me from telling of what I've been convinced the earth is like in   e
shape, and of its regions.'

'Well, even that is enough,' said Simmias.

'First then, I've been convinced that if it is round and in the
centre of the heaven, it needs neither air nor any other such force to   5
prevent its falling, but the uniformity of the heaven in every direction **109**
with itself is enough to support it, together with the equilibrium of
the earth itself; because a thing in equilibrium placed in the middle
of something uniform will be unable to incline either more or less in   5
any direction, but being in a uniform state it will remain without
incline. So that's the first thing of which I've been convinced.'

'And rightly so,' said Simmias.

'And next, that it is of vast size, and that we who dwell between
the Phasis River and the Pillars of Heracles inhabit only a small part   b
of it, living around the sea like ants or frogs around a marsh, and
that there are many others living elsewhere in many such places.
For there are many hollows all over the earth, varying in their   5
shapes and sizes, into which water and mist and air have flowed
together; and the earth itself is set in the heaven, a pure thing in
pure surroundings, in which the stars are situated, and which most
of those who usually describe such things name "aether"; it's from this   c
that these elements are the dregs, and continually flow together into

the hollows of the earth. Now we ourselves are unaware that we
live in its hollows, and think we live above the earth—just as if
5   someone living at the bottom of the ocean were to think he lived
above the sea, and seeing the sun and the stars through the water,
were to imagine that the sea was heaven, and yet through slowness
d   and weakness had never reached the surface of the sea, nor emerged,
stuck his head up out of the sea into this region here, and seen how
much purer and fairer it really is than their world, nor had heard
5   this from anyone else who had seen it. Now this is just what has
happened to us: living in some hollow of the earth, we think we live
above it, and we call the air "heaven", as if this were heaven and the
stars moved through it; whereas the truth is just the same—because
e   of our weakness and slowness, we are unable to pass through to the
summit of the air; for were anyone to go to its surface, or gain wings
and fly aloft, he would stick his head up and see—just as here the
5   fishes of the sea stick their heads up and see the things here, so he
would see the things up there; and if his nature were able to bear
the vision, he would realize that this is the true heaven, the genuine
110 light, and the true earth. For this earth of ours, and its stones and all
the region here, are corrupted and eaten away, as are things in the
sea by the brine; nor does anything worth mentioning grow in the
5   sea, and practically nothing is perfect, but there are eroded rocks
and sand and unimaginable mud and mire, wherever there is earth
as well, and things are in no way worthy to be compared with the
beauties in our world. But those objects in their turn would be seen
to surpass the things in our world by a far greater measure still;
b   indeed, if it is proper to tell a tale, it's worth hearing, Simmias, what
the things upon the earth and beneath the heaven are actually like.'

    'Why yes, Socrates,' said Simmias, 'we'd be glad to hear this tale.'
5   'Well then, my friend, first of all the true earth, if one views it
from above, is said to look like those twelve-piece leather balls,
variegated, a patchwork of colours, of which our colours here are,
c   as it were, samples that painters use. There the whole earth is of such
colours, indeed of colours far brighter still and purer than these:
one portion is purple, marvellous for its beauty, another is golden,
and all that is white is whiter than chalk or snow; and the earth is
5   composed of the other colours likewise, indeed of colours more

numerous and beautiful than any we have seen. Even its very
hollows, full as they are of water and air, give an appearance of
colour, gleaming among the variety of the other colours, so that its   d
general appearance is of one continuous multi-coloured surface. This
being its nature, things that grow on it, trees and flowers and fruit,
grow in proportion; and again, the mountains contain stones likewise,   5
whose smoothness, transparency, and beauty of colour are in the
same proportion; it is from these that the little stones we value,
sardian stones, jaspers, emeralds, and all such, are pieces; but there,   e
every single one is like that, or even more beautiful still. This is
because the stones there are pure, and not corroded or corrupted,
like those here, by mildew and brine due to the elements that have
flowed together, bringing ugliness and disease to stones and earth,   5
and to plants and animals as well. But the true earth is adorned with
all these things, and with gold and silver also, and with the other   **111**
things of that kind as well. For they are plainly visible, being many
in number, large, and everywhere upon the earth; happy, therefore,
are they who behold the sight of it. Among many other living
things upon it there are men, some dwelling inland, some living by   5
the air, as we live by the sea, and some on islands surrounded by the
air and lying close to the mainland; and in a word, what the water
and the sea are to us for our needs, the air is to them; and what air is
for us, aether is for them. Their climate is such that they are free   b
from sickness and live a far longer time than people here, and they
surpass us in sight, hearing, wisdom, and all such faculties, by the
extent to which air surpasses water for its purity, and aether sur-   5
passes air. Moreover, they have groves and temples of gods, in which
gods are truly dwellers, and utterances and prophecies, and direct
awareness of the gods; and communion of that kind they experience
face to face. The sun and moon and stars are seen by them as they   c
really are, and their happiness in all else accords with this.

  'Such is the nature of the earth as a whole and its surroundings; but
in it there are many regions within the hollows it has all around it,[81] 5
some deeper and some more extended than the one in which we
dwell, some deeper but with a narrower opening than our own region,
and others that are shallower in depth but broader than this one. All   d
these are interconnected underground in every direction, by passages

5 both narrower and wider, and they have channels through which
abundant water flows from one into another, as into mixing bowls,
and continuous underground rivers of unimaginable size, with waters
hot and cold, and abundant fire and great rivers of fire, and many of
liquid mud, some purer and some more miry, like the rivers of mud
e in Sicily that flow ahead of the lava-stream, and the lava-stream
itself; with these each of the regions is filled, as the circling stream
happens to reach each one on each occasion. All of this is kept
moving back and forth by a kind of pulsation going on within the
5 earth; and the nature of this pulsation is something like this: one of
the openings in the earth happens to be especially large, and per-
112 forated right through the earth; it is this that Homer spoke of as:

A great way off, where lies the deepest pit beneath earth;

and it is this that he, and many other poets have elsewhere called
5 Tartarus. Now into this opening all the rivers flow together, and from
it they flow out again; and each acquires its character from the nature
b of the earth through which it flows. The reason why all the streams
flow out there, and flow in, is that this liquid has neither bottom
nor resting place. So it pulsates and surges back and forth, and the
air and the breath enveloping it do the same; because they follow
5 it, when it rushes towards those areas of the earth and again when it
returns to these; and just as in breathing the current of breath is
continuously exhaled and inhaled, so there the breath pulsating
together with the liquid causes terrible and unimaginable winds, as it
c passes in and out. Now when the water recedes into the so-called
"downward" region, it flows along the courses of those streams
through the earth[82] and fills them, as in the process of irrigation;
and when it leaves there again and rushes back here, then it fills
5 these ones here once more; these, when filled, flow through the
channels and through the earth, and reaching the regions into which
a way has been made for each, they make seas and lakes and rivers
d and springs; and then dipping again beneath the earth, some circling
longer and more numerous regions, and others fewer and shorter
ones, they discharge once more into Tartarus, some a long way and
others a little below where the irrigation began; but all flow in
5 below the point of outflow, some across from where they poured
out, and some in the same part; and there are some that go right

round in a circle, coiling once or even many times around the earth
like serpents, and then, after descending as far as possible, discharge
once more. It is possible to descend in either direction as far as the   e
middle but no further; because the part on either side slopes uphill
for both sets of streams.

'Now there are many large streams of every kind; but among their
number there happen to be four in particular, the largest of which,   5
flowing outermost and round in a circle, is the one called Oceanus;
across from this and flowing in the opposite direction is Acheron,
which flows through other desert regions, and in particular, flowing 113
underground, reaches the Acherusian Lake, where the souls of most
of those who have died arrive, and where, after they have stayed for
certain appointed periods, some longer, some shorter, they are sent
forth again into the generation of living things. The third river issues   5
between these two, and near the point of issue it pours into a huge
region all ablaze with fire, and forms a lake larger than our own sea,
boiling with water and mud; from there it proceeds in a circle,
turbid and muddy, and coiling about within the earth it reaches the   b
borders of the Acherusian Lake, amongst other places, but does not
mingle with its water; then, after repeated coiling underground, it
discharges lower down in Tartarus; this is the river they name
Pyriphlegethon, and it is from this that the lava-streams blast frag-   5
ments up at various points upon the earth. Across from this again
issues the fourth river, first into a region terrible and wild, it is said,
coloured bluish-grey all over, which they name the Stygian region,   c
and the river as it discharges forms a lake,[83] the Styx; when it has
poured in there, and gained terrible powers in the water, it dips
beneath the earth, coils round and proceeds in the opposite direction
to Pyriphlegethon, which it encounters in the Acherusian lake from   5
the opposite side; nor does the water of this river mingle with any
other, but it too goes round in a circle and discharges into Tartarus
opposite to Pyriphlegethon; and its name, according to the poets,
is Cocytus.

'Such, then, is their nature. Now when those who have died   d
arrive at the region to which the spirit conveys each one, they first
submit to judgement, both those who have lived honourable and
holy lives and those who have not. Those who are found to have

5   lived indifferently journey to Acheron, embark upon certain vessels
provided for them, and on these they reach the lake; there they
dwell, undergoing purgation by paying the penalty for their wrong-
doings, and are absolved, if any has committed any wrong, and they

e   secure reward for their good deeds, each according to his desert;
but all who are found to be incurable because of the magnitude of
their offences, through having committed many grave acts of
sacrilege, or many wrongful and illegal acts of killing, or any other

5   deeds that may be of that sort, are hurled by the appropriate
destiny into Tartarus, whence they nevermore emerge. Those, again,
who are found guilty of curable yet grave offences, such as an act

114 of violence in anger against a father or a mother, and have lived the
rest of their lives in penitence, or who have committed homicide in
some other such fashion, must fall into Tartarus; and when they
have fallen and stayed there for a year, the surge casts them forth,

5   the homicides by way of Cocytus, and those who have assaulted
father or mother by way of Pyriphlegethon; then, as they are carried
along and draw level with the Acherusian lake, they cry out and call,
some to those they killed, others to those they injured; calling upon

b   them, they beg and beseech them to allow them to come forth into
the lake and to receive them; and if they persuade them, they come
forth and cease from their woes; but if not, they are carried back
into Tartarus, and from there again into the rivers, and they do not

5   cease from these sufferings till they persuade those they have
wronged; for this is the penalty imposed upon them by their
judges. But as for those who are found to have lived exceptionally
holy lives, it is they who are freed and delivered from these regions
within the earth, as from prisons, and who attain to the pure

c   dwelling above, and make their dwelling above ground. And among
their number, those who have been adequately purified by philosophy live bodiless for the whole of time to come, and attain to
dwelling places fairer even than these, which it is not easy to

5   reveal, nor is the time sufficient at present. But it is for the sake of
just the things we have related, Simmias, that one must do everything possible to have part in goodness and wisdom during life; for
fair is the prize and great the hope.

d   'Now to insist that these things are just as I've related them

would not be fitting for a man of intelligence; but that either this
or something like it is true about our souls and their dwellings,
given that the soul evidently is immortal, this, I think, *is* fitting and   5
worth risking, for one who believes that it is so—for a noble risk
it is—so one should repeat such things to oneself like a spell; which is
just why I've so prolonged the tale. For these reasons, then, any
man should have confidence for his own soul, who during his life   e
has rejected the pleasures of the body and its adornments as alien,
thinking they do more harm than good, but has devoted himself to
the pleasures of learning, and has decked his soul with no alien   5
adornment, but with its own, with temperance and justice, bravery, **115**
liberality, and truth, thus awaiting the journey he will make to
Hades, whenever destiny shall summon him.[84] Now as for you,
Simmias and Cebes and the rest, you will make your several journeys
at some future time, but for myself, "e'en now", as a tragic hero
might say, "destiny doth summon me"; and it's just about time I   5
made for the bath: it really seems better to take a bath before
drinking the poison, and not to give the women the trouble of
washing a dead body.'

When he'd spoken, Crito said: 'Very well, Socrates: what instruc-   b
tions have you for these others or for me, about your children or
about anything else? What could we do, that would be of most
service to you?'

'What I'm always telling you, Crito,' said he, 'and nothing very   5
new: if you take care for yourselves, your actions will be of service
to me and mine, and to yourselves too, whatever they may be, even
if you make no promises now; but if you take no care for yourselves,
and are unwilling to pursue your lives along the tracks, as it were,
marked by our present and earlier discussions, then even if you   10
make many firm promises at this time, you'll do no good at all.'   c

'Then we'll strive to do as you say,' he said; 'but in what fashion
are we to bury you?'

'However you wish,' said he; 'provided you catch me, that is,
and I don't get away from you.' And with this he laughed quietly,   5
looked towards us and said: 'Friends, I can't persuade Crito that I
am Socrates here, the one who is now conversing and arranging each

of the things being discussed; but he imagines I'm that dead body

d he'll see in a little while, so he goes and asks how he's to bury me! But as for the great case I've been arguing all this time, that when I drink the poison, I shall no longer remain with you, but shall go off and depart for some happy state of the blessed, this, I think, I'm

5 putting to him in vain, while comforting you and myself alike. So please stand surety for me with Crito, the opposite surety to that which he stood for me with the judges: his guarantee was that I *would* stay behind, whereas you must guarantee that, when I die, I shall *not* stay behind, but shall go off and depart; then Crito will

e bear it more easily, and when he sees the burning or interment of my body, he won't be distressed for me, as if I were suffering dreadful things, and won't say at the funeral that it is Socrates they are laying out or bearing to the grave or interring. Because you can be sure, my

5 dear Crito, that misuse of words is not only troublesome in itself, but actually has a bad effect on the soul. Rather, you should have confidence, and say you are burying my body; and bury it however

116 you please, and think most proper.'

After saying this, he rose and went into a room to take a bath, and Crito followed him but told us to wait. So we waited, talking among ourselves about what had been said and reviewing it, and then

5 again dwelling on how great a misfortune had befallen us, literally thinking of it as if we were deprived of a father and would lead the rest of our life as orphans. After he'd bathed and his children had

b been brought to him—he had two little sons and one big one—and those women of his household had come, he talked with them in Crito's presence, and gave certain directions as to his wishes; he then

5 told the women and children to leave, and himself returned to us.

By now it was close to sunset, as he'd spent a long time inside. So he came and sat down, fresh from his bath, and there wasn't much talk after that. Then the prison official came in, stepped up to

c him and said: 'Socrates, I shan't reproach you as I reproach others for being angry with me and cursing, whenever by order of the rulers I direct them to drink the poison. In your time here I've

5 known you for the most generous and gentlest and best of men who have ever come to this place; and now especially, I feel sure it isn't with me that you're angry, but with others, because you know who

are responsible. Well now, you know the message I've come to
bring: good-bye, then, and try to bear the inevitable as easily as you   d
can.' And with this he turned away in tears, and went off.

Socrates looked up at him and said: 'Good-bye to you too, and
we'll do as you say.' And to us he added: 'What a civil man he is!   5
Throughout my time here he's been to see me, and sometimes
talked with me, and been the best of fellows; and now how generous
of him to weep for me! But come on, Crito, let's obey him: let
someone bring in the poison, if it has been prepared; if not, let the
man prepare it.'

Crito said: 'But Socrates, I think the sun is still on the mountains   e
and hasn't yet gone down. And besides, I know of others who've
taken the draught long after the order had been given them, and after
dining well and drinking plenty, and even in some cases enjoying
themselves with those they fancied. Be in no hurry, then: there's   5
still time left.'

Socrates said: 'It's reasonable for those you speak of to do those
things—because they think they gain by doing them; for myself, it's
reasonable not to do them; because I think I'll gain nothing by
taking the draught a little later: I'll only earn my own ridicule by   117
clinging to life, and being sparing when there's nothing more left.
Go on now; do as I ask, and nothing else.'

Hearing this, Crito nodded to the boy who was standing nearby.
The boy went out, and after spending a long time away he returned,   5
bringing the man who was going to administer the poison, and was
carrying it ready-pounded in a cup. When he saw the man, Socrates
said: 'Well, my friend, you're an expert in these things: what must
one do?'

'Simply drink it,' he said, 'and walk about till a heaviness comes
over your legs; then lie down, and it will act of itself.' And with this   b
he held out the cup to Socrates.

He took it perfectly calmly, Echecrates, without a tremor, or any
change of colour or countenance; but looking up at the man, and
fixing him with his customary stare, he said: 'What do you say to   5
pouring someone a libation from this drink? Is it allowed or not?'

'We only prepare as much as we judge the proper dose, Socrates,'
he said.

c   'I understand,' he said; 'but at least one may pray to the gods, and so one should, that the removal from this world to the next will be a happy one; that is my own prayer: so may it be.' With these words he pressed the cup to his lips, and drank it off with good humour and without the least distaste.

5   Till then most of us had been fairly well able to restrain our tears; but when we saw he was drinking, that he'd actually drunk it, we could do so no longer. In my own case, the tears came pouring out in spite of myself, so that I covered my face and wept for myself— not for him, no, but for my own misfortune in being deprived of

d   such a man for a companion. Even before me, Crito had moved away, when he was unable to restrain his tears. And Apollodorus, who even earlier had been continuously in tears, now burst forth

5   into such a storm of weeping and grieving, that he made everyone present break down except Socrates himself.

    But Socrates said: 'What a way to behave, my strange friends! Why, it was mainly for this reason that I sent the women away, so

e   that they shouldn't make this sort of trouble; in fact, I've heard one should die in silence. Come now, calm yourselves and have strength.'

    When we heard this, we were ashamed and checked our tears. He walked about, and when he said that his legs felt heavy he lay down

5   on his back—as the man told him—and then the man, this one who'd given him the poison, felt him, and after an interval examined his feet and legs; he then pinched his foot hard and asked if he could feel it,

118   and Socrates said not. After that he felt his shins once more; and moving upwards in this way, he showed us that he was becoming cold and numb. He[85] went on feeling him, and said that when the coldness reached his heart, he would be gone.

5   By this time the coldness was somewhere in the region of his abdomen, when he uncovered his face—it had been covered over— and spoke; and this was in fact his last utterance: 'Crito,' he said, 'we owe a cock to Asclepius: please pay the debt, and don't neglect it.'

10   'It shall be done,' said Crito; 'have you anything else to say?'

    To this question he made no answer, but after a short interval he stirred, and when the man uncovered him his eyes were fixed; when he saw this, Crito closed his mouth and his eyes.

And that, Echecrates, was the end of our companion, a man   15
who, among those of his time we knew, was—so we should say—the
best, the wisest too, and the most just.

NOTES

The events dramatized in the *Phaedo* took place in 399 B.C., when Plato was in his twenties. The dialogue portrays the execution of Socrates, which followed his conviction by an Athenian court on charges of 'impiety' and 'corrupting the young'. It thus forms a sequel to the episodes from his trial and imprisonment presented in the *Apology* and *Crito*.

Plato's version of his master's death is a philosophical memoir rather than a biographical record. The death scene is made the occasion of a philosophical discussion which can hardly be authentic. But the discussion is perfectly matched to the events in which it is framed. Thought and action are interfused throughout in the manner typical of Plato's maturity as a philosopher-dramatist. The date of composition is uncertain, but the work is usually assigned to Plato's 'middle period'. It was probably written more than a decade after the events it purports to depict.

In these notes the name 'Socrates' will generally refer to the dramatic personage, not to the historical figure, and without prejudice to the question of how far the views under discussion were Plato's own. It is not unreasonable to attribute to him the general position and main theses of 'Socrates' in this work. But he need not be taken to endorse every argument he puts into Socrates' mouth. The work is not an exposition of his doctrines, but a meditation upon the issues it raises, and a stimulus to the reader to explore them for himself.

1. PROLOGUE
(57a1–59c7)

The opening conversation between Phaedo and Echecrates takes place at Phlius, a small town in the Peloponnese. It was a centre of Pythagorean philosophy, of which Echecrates was an adherent, and which colours the thought of much of the dialogue. Of Phaedo of Elis, who tells the story, little is known. Possibly it was he who gave the original account of Socrates' death to Plato himself. There will be two interludes later (88c8–89a8, 102a3–9), which revert briefly to the present scene, reminding us that the main dialogue is narrated.

57a1–b3. 'How did he meet his end?': the primary meaning of the verb in this question (a6) is 'to end'. Hence it commonly means 'end one's life'. Here, as at 58c9 and 58e4, the imperfect tense suggests that the question concerns Socrates' whole conduct of his death, and not merely the terminal event. Cf. 58c6–'the circumstances of the death itself'. The dialogue will examine the concept of death in the context of this particular death.

Another common word for 'die' appears at 57b2–'he died by drinking poison'. It is sometimes used as a passive form of the verb for 'kill', and thus could, here and at 58a5, mean 'he was put to death'. Both verbs recur often in the dialogue, but they have not been distinguished elsewhere in the translation, and have generally been rendered 'die'. See also note 41 and on 71d5–e3.

58a6–c5. In explaining the deferment of Socrates' execution as due to the festival of Apollo, Phaedo touches on two important religious themes: (1) human service to the gods, and (2) purification.

(1) Socrates himself will be represented throughout as the true servant of Apollo (60d2, 61b2–3, 85b4–5). He thus embodies the principle enunciated later that to be ruled is mortal, to rule divine (80a, cf.94e4–5).

(2) The concept of purification pervades the whole dialogue, and strengthens the Pythagorean associations suggested by its characterization and setting. See, e.g., 65e6, 66d–e, 67a–c, 69c, 80d–e, 82c–d, 114c1–3. It is ironical that Athens's concern for her 'purity' should have delayed Socrates' death. His execution was to afford the release of soul from body in which his own 'purification' would be perfected.

'Chance' and its cognate verb occur together at 58a6 and perhaps mean more than mere coincidence. They may contain a hint of supernatural intervention. Cf.58e5–6 and see Loriaux, 17, 38–9.

59a1–b4. Phaedo's account of the 'strange mixture of pleasure and pain' (a5–7) he felt at Socrates' death has sometimes been felt to conflict with the latter's statement at 60b6 that pleasure and pain will not visit a man together. There is, in fact, no reason why a speaker in the prologue should not be contradicted by a different speaker in the narrated dialogue. However, Socrates' words need not be taken to conflict with what is said here, since he may be denying not that pleasure and pain can coexist, but only that they can 'arise' at the same time. See on 60b1–c7.

59b5–c4. Plato is mentioned by name only three times in the dialogues: twice in the *Apology* (34a1, 38b6) his presence at Socrates' trial is noted; here it is recorded that he was absent at Socrates' death. Thus, although Phaedo's account of the death scene

75

is marked as first hand (57a1—4), Plato indicates that he did not witness it himself. For the other persons named here, see Hackforth, 30—1.

2. SOCRATES IN PRISON
(59c8—69e5)

Socrates' friends visit and converse with him in prison. This section forms a prelude to the main discussion.

2.1 Opening Conversation (59c8—63e7)

The conversation soon leads to a discussion of suicide. Here an apparent contradiction develops: the true philosopher should welcome death, yet he may not kill himself. The paradox is not resolved by supposing that men are possessions of the gods.

59e6—60a1. 'The Eleven are releasing Socrates' (e6): 'the Eleven' were the Athenian prison authorities responsible for state executions. Cf.85b9 and 116b8. The release of Socrates from his chains (a1) prefigures the release of his soul from its bodily prison. The notion of death as a 'release' occurs often. See note 1, and cf.65a1, 67a6, , 67d1—10, 82e1—83a3, 83d1—2, 84a2—5.

60b1—c7. 'Its supposed opposite, "painful" ' (b4—5): this translation assumes that the phrase 'the painful' indicates reference to the *word* 'painful', making it parallel to 'this state that men call "pleasant" ' (60b4). Socrates may be hinting that so-called 'pleasant' things are miscalled, though he does not speak analogously of 'so-called pains'. His reflections on pleasure and pain are sometimes held to contain the germ of the theory, developed at length in the *Republic* (583b—585a), *Timaeus* (64c, ff.), and *Philebus* (31d—32b), that many so-called 'pleasures' of the body are no more than relief from pain, and are therefore in some sense 'false'. Cf. the 'so-called pleasures' of 64d3, and the related, although logically distinct, doctrine of 83c5—e3.
    Several questions arise: (1) Are pleasure and pain 'opposites'? (2) In what sense can they not visit at the same time? (3) Why are they nevertheless held to be inseparably connected?
    (1) The opposition between pleasure and pain is expressed only in non-committal terms: the painful is referred to as 'the supposed opposite' of pleasant. On this point the *Phaedo's* position falls between those of the *Gorgias* and the *Republic*. In the *Gorgias* (495e—497d) it is not said that pleasure and pain are opposites, and

it may even be implied (495e6–7) that they are not. In the *Republic* (583c3–4) it is firmly asserted that they are. The present remarks are sometimes held to prepare for the treatment of opposites that lies ahead (70d–72e, 102b–106e). However, pleasure and pain are noticeably absent from the opposites mentioned later, and the law that opposites come to be from opposites (70e–71a) cannot be plausibly applied to them—see (3) below.

(2) Does Socrates mean merely (a) that pleasure and pain cannot 'arise' at the same time, or (b) that they cannot coexist in a single subject at all? (b) would indeed follow from the doctrine that pleasure and pain are opposites, combined with the principle that no pair of opposites can belong to a given subject in the same respect at the same time (*Republic* 436b). However, this principle is not expressly stated in the *Phaedo*. Moreover, the view that pleasure and pain cannot coexist in a single subject would run counter to the case of Phaedo's mingled pleasure and pain in face of Socrates' death (59a). (a), on the other hand, would be well supported by the case of Socrates' leg. The pain caused by the fetter would have to have preceded the pleasure felt upon its removal. More generally, the pleasure of relief must depend upon antecedent pain. Even though pleasure and pain may coexist, it remains true that they cannot 'arise' at the same time.

(3) The alleged inseparability of pleasure from pain seems a curious moral for Socrates to draw from the state of his leg. Neither possible application of it fits the example.

(a) To say that anyone who pursues and catches pain is virtually bound to catch pleasure would be neither relevant nor true. Pain is not a normal object of pursuit at all, and Socrates did not, of course, 'pursue' the pain in his leg. Nor is pain bound to be followed by pleasure: the pleasure Socrates now feels is not a necessary sequel to the pain, but contingent upon the removal of the fetter. It is true that the pleasure of relief depends upon antecedent pain; and from such texts as *Republic* 583c10–d11 it is tempting to interpret Socrates similarly here. However, on a strict reading he seems committed to the quite different, and less defensible, proposition that pain must generally be *succeeded* by pleasure.

(b) The more plausible application would be that anyone who pursues and catches pleasure is virtually bound to catch pain. This avoids some of the difficulties of (a), but is also objectionable. It does not fit the present example, since Socrates is not pursuing pleasure. Moreover, the suggestion would have to be, once again, not merely that the pleasure in his leg depended upon a previous pain, but that such pleasure must nearly always be followed by pain. Yet there is no likelihood that the pleasure he now feels in his leg will be followed

by pain. Pleasure and pain are not experienced in continuous alternation. This will be recognized in the *Republic*, where a distinction
is drawn between pleasure and pain, and a state of 'rest', which is
neither pleasant nor painful. The mere absence of one opposite, it is
there argued, is not to be mistaken for the presence of the other
(584a4–6).
    See, further, E. R. Dodds, ed. *Gorgias* 495e2–497d8.

60c8–61c1. The translation 'putting into verse' has been adopted
at 60d1 rather than 'setting to music' (Burnet). Verses are nowhere
expressly mentioned, but Socrates' words at 61b3–4 suggest that he
made poetry out of Aesop's tales rather than 'music' in the modern
sense. This would be consistent with the command of his dream to
'make art and practise it'. 'Art' has been used for the Greek word
from which 'music' is derived, which means 'activity presided over
by the Muses'. See Hackforth, 37.
    Socrates' denial that he is a 'teller of tales' (61b5) is rather oddly
belied by 60c1–5. At 61e2 he will propose to 'inquire and speculate'
regarding the afterlife. The word translated 'speculate' means,
literally, 'tell tales'. The phrase expresses the spirit of the whole
dialogue, argument and tale-telling being interwoven throughout.
Cf.70b6 and see note 15.
    The translation 'dream' has been used at 60e2–61b1, despite the
oddity in English of saying that a dream, as distinct from a dream-
figure, speaks, gives orders, and is obeyed. The Greeks did not
distinguish sharply between the content of a dream and the dream
itself. When, as often, the dream-figure is a human being or a god,
the dream itself can be credited with the words or actions that a real
agent might utter or perform.
    It may seem curious at 60e4–6 that 'the same dream' should
have different visual manifestations. Whatever the necessary conditions of 'sameness' in dreams may be, it seems natural to count
similarity of visual content among them. But perhaps Socrates
means that the dream figure was Apollo himself, and that the god
has often appeared to him in different forms. The translation 'now
in one guise, now in another' assumes this interpretation.
    For the Greek view of dream experience see E. R. Dodds, *G.I.*,
Ch.4. For Plato's treatment of dreams see D. Gallop, *E.A.G.P.*
187–201.

61d3–e9. Philolaus was a Pythagorean who survived the expul-
sion of the sect from southern Italy in the mid-fifth century B.C. and
settled in Thebes. If his teaching on suicide was along the lines that
Socrates suggests at 62b–c, it can hardly be reconciled with the

account of the soul that his disciple, Simmias, will give later. See on
86b5—d4 (p.148).

62a2—7. The grammar and logic of this intractable sentence are
much disputed. The present translation requires deletion of the
comma in Burnet's text after 'as other things do' (a4), and insertion
of a comma after 'for some people'. For the translation 'to be dead'
(a5), see note 4. For a review of many proposed solutions see
Loriaux, 50—9.

Full discussion of the sentence is impossible here. The meaning
will depend upon (1) the implications of the repeated phrase
'perhaps it (will) seem(s) a matter for wonder to you' (a2, a5—6) for
the truth-value of the two 'if' clauses (hereafter P and Q) that
follow it; and upon (2) the content of P and Q themselves.

(1) Note that Socrates is anticipating Cebes' reaction to the view
of suicide he has been putting forward. He is imagining an objection
Cebes might well make, pending any satisfactory rationale for the
prohibition of suicide. 'Perhaps', he is suggesting, 'you will (some
day) hear something (to satisfy you). But (meanwhile) it will perhaps
seem a matter for wonder to you if P; and perhaps it seems a matter
for wonder to you if Q.' The wording 'a matter for wonder if'
preserves an ambiguity in the Greek construction between (a) 'it
(will) seem(s) surprising to you *that* P (or Q) *should be* the case',
(b) 'it (will) seem(s) questionable to you *whether* P (or Q) *is* the
case', and (c) 'it (will) seem(s) surprising to you *if* P (or Q) *is* the
case'. For the ambiguity in 'wonder if' see 97a2. Cf. also 95a9—b4,
where the first 'wonder if' is clearly interrogative, and the second
conditional. Matters are further complicated by the question whether
Cebes is supposed to wonder about P and Q as two separate propositions, or as one compound proposition to the effect that 'P and
yet Q' or 'Despite P, nevertheless Q'.

Of the three variants just noted, only (a) carries any implication
that Socrates for his part regards P or Q (or both) as true. (b) would
imply merely that Cebes doubts whether they are true. (c) would
suggest that he believes them to be probably false. But neither with
(b) nor with (c) need Socrates be committed to them. It seems
preferable, in fact, to regard him as uncommitted, at least with
respect to Q. For the view of suicide under discussion, which is
embodied in Q, is not his own (61c10, e5). He is repeating it only at
second hand (61d9—10). Not until 62b2 does he express any support
for it, and he finally endorses it only in qualified terms (62c6).
While it may be assumed, therefore, that P or Q (or both) would be
questioned by Cebes, it is not clear that Socrates, let alone Plato,
would maintain them without reservation. Cf. *Laws* 873c—d, and

see next note.

(2) What are P and Q? The latter (a5–7) presents no problem. Clearly, it is that 'for these men (sc. those for whom it is better to be dead), it is not holy to do good to themselves, but they must await another benefactor'. Cebes will find it paradoxical that those who would be better off dead may not dispatch themselves, but must wait for someone else. It would seem 'unreasonable' (cf.62b1–2) to prohibit suicide in cases where it is in the agent's own interest. This is, indeed, the basic point in the whole speech. For it is precisely the apparent contradiction between a veto upon suicide and the belief that death may sometimes be for a person's own good that Socrates will now try to resolve.

The content of P, however, is highly obscure, and it is here (a2–5) that the heart of the difficulty lies. The meaning turns partly upon the referent of 'this' in 'if this alone of all things is unqualified' (P1); partly upon the relationship of that phrase to 'and it never happens to man as other things do' (P2); and partly upon the connection between P2 and 'sometimes and for some people it is better to be dead than alive' (P3). Five solutions will be considered.

(i) 'This' in P1 refers to the doctrine that *death is preferable to life*. On this view, defended by Bluck (151–3), it will surprise Cebes that despite the universal applicability of this doctrine to man, suicide should nevertheless be forbidden. 'You will be surprised that although (P1) this (sc. death is preferable to life) is alone of all things true without exception, and (P2) it never happens for man, as do other things (sc. whose preferability depends upon circumstances), that (P3) it is only sometimes and for some people that it is better to be dead than alive, *nevertheless* (Q) suicide is forbidden.'

This interpretation places immense strain upon the text. To say 'it never happens that it is only sometimes and for some people that it is better to be dead than alive' seems an intolerably clumsy way of expressing the idea that it is always better to be dead than alive; and it requires a gratuitous 'only', unwarranted in the text. Moreover, neither in the *Phaedo* nor elsewhere is it held that death is always better than life. Nor could this plausibly be supposed as a basis for questioning the prohibition of suicide. It is a recurrent thought in Plato that some people, those who are incurably sick in body or soul, would be better off dead (e.g. *Laches* 195c–d, *Gorgias* 511e–512a, *Republic* 409e–410a), but not that everyone would be. In the *Phaedo* it is only philosophers, and not mankind in general, for whom death is said to be pleasurable to life (cf.61c8–9).

(ii) 'This' in P1 refers to the supposition that *life is preferable to death*. This view, adopted with variations by Burnet, Hackforth, and Verdenius, interprets Cebes as challenging the idea that (P) life is unconditionally preferable to death; and then, granted that this idea is mistaken, as being surprised that (Q) suicide should nevertheless be forbidden. 'Perhaps it will seem questionable to you whether (P) this (sc. life is preferable to death) is alone of all things simple (i.e. admits of no distinctions according to circumstances), and (P2) it never happens as other things do, that for man (P3) it is better on some occasions and for some people to be dead than alive; and perhaps it surprises you that (Q) for those who would be better dead, suicide should nevertheless be forbidden.'

The chief difficulty here is that 'this' in P1 would have to refer to a completely unstated doctrine. The supposition that life is always preferable to death might, indeed, be naturally represented as a vulgar error, rejection of which would justify Cebes' surprise at the absolute prohibition of suicide. However, it is not at all easy to supply this doctrine out of the blue. Burnet says that 'this' in P1 is 'really anticipatory and only acquires a definite meaning as the sentence proceeds'. But could it 'anticipate' something that is nowhere expressly said?

The solutions still to be considered share a common starting point: they all take 'this' in P1 to refer to the *prohibition of suicide*, which is surely its most natural referent in the context–cf.61e8 'one ought not to do that', and 62c9, where 'that' clearly refers to the same prohibition.

(iii) With Loriaux's translation (199), the meaning will be: 'You will perhaps be surprised at the idea that (P1) this doctrine (sc. the prohibition of suicide) is alone of all things (sc. doctrines) absolute, and that (P2) it never happens for man, as other things do on some occasions and for some people, that (P3) it is better to be dead than alive. And (Q) if there are some for whom death would be preferable, you are no doubt surprised that for them suicide is forbidden.' Cebes is here viewed as expressing surprise at P1 and P2+P3. He takes both of them to be Socrates' opinion, and disputes P1 because he rejects P2+P3. This line of thought is then developed more explicitly in Q.

This reading has the advantage of giving point to the words 'on some occasions and for some people'. They are here taken with 'as other things do', to mean 'as in other domains, where one distinguishes circumstances and people'. However, the interpretation takes P2+P3 in an unnatural way. For it seems unlikely that Cebes should impute to Socrates, even as part of an objection, the view that there is never anyone for whom death is better than life. Socrates has already virtually rejected such a view in saying that philosophers will wish for death (61c8–9, d4–5). Nor could it reasonably be ascribed to him on the strength of anything he has said about the wrongness of suicide.

(iv) L. Tarán (*A.J.P.* 1966, 326–36) has advocated taking P1 and P2 closely together, and P3 after a semicolon as a new main clause. On his reading, 'this' in P1 refers to the prohibition of suicide, and it is *this prohibition* that is being contrasted with all others: 'It will perhaps seem surprising to you that (P1) this (sc. the prohibition of suicide) is alone of all things (sc. all prohibitions) unqualified (i.e. unaffected by the addition of good and bad), and (P2) never applies to man in the way the others (sc. other prohibitions) do; (P3) there are times when and people for whom it is better to be dead than alive; but (Q) for those for whom it is better to be dead, you are surprised if for these very men it is not holy etc.' Here P1+P2 are represented as true for Socrates but as surprising to Cebes. Socrates then asserts P3 outright, and finally gives it to Cebes as (Q) a basis for questioning the absolute character of the prohibition of suicide.

Tarán's punctuation leaves P3 without a connective particle. But his solution is attractive. It simplifies the grammar and makes sound logical sense. Alternatively, if his punctuation is not accepted, the sentence may be taken as in the present translation and construed as follows:

(v) 'It will perhaps seem questionable to you whether (P1) this (sc. the prohibition of suicide) is alone of all things (sc. doctrines) unqualified, and whether (P2) it never happens, as other things do on some occasions and for some people, that (P3) it is better for man to be dead than alive; and (Q) for those for whom it is better to be dead, it perhaps seems surprising to you if for these men it is not holy etc.' P1 and P2+P3 are here put forward as doctrines that Cebes might doubt ('wonder whether'), without any implication that Socrates holds them to be true. Q is likewise translated so as to leave Socrates uncommitted. Good sense is obtained by reading the sentence purely as an expression of the doubts in Cebes' mind: 'Is suicide alone', he may ask, 'unlike everything else, to be absolutely prohibited without regard to circumstances? Are there never times when, and people for whom, it is better to be dead than alive? And is it forbidden for such people to do themselves a good turn?' These doubts, expressed in indirect speech by another person, would yield the sentence in the text.

This interpretation requires the sense 'questionable' for the first occurrence of the word translated 'a matter for wonder'. The force may be, more exactly, 'Perhaps it will seem to you that one must ask in astonishment whether . . .' See H. Reynen, *Hermes* 1968, 41–6.

It may be useful to summarize the above solutions in symbolic form. If *D* = 'a man better dead than living', *K* = 'a man permitted to kill himself', T = 'true for', F = 'false for', ? = 'possibly', S = 'Socrates', and C = 'Cebes', then:

(i)	P1	$(x)(Dx)$	TS, TC
	P2+P3	$\sim(\exists x)(\sim Dx)$	TS, TC
	Q	$(\exists x)(Dx.\sim Kx)$	TS, FC
(ii)	P1	$(x)(\sim Dx)$	FS, FC
	P2+P3	$(\exists x)(Dx)$	TS, TC
	Q	$(\exists x)(Dx.\sim Kx)$	TS, FC
(iii)	P1	$(x)(\sim Kx)$	TS, FC
	P2+P3	$\sim(\exists x)(Dx)$	TS,* FC *as alleged by Cebes
	Q	$(\exists x)(Dx.\sim Kx)$	
(iv)	P1+P2	$(x)(\sim Kx)$	TS, FC
	P3	$(\exists x)(Dx)$	TS, TC
	Q	$(\exists x)(Dx.\sim Kx)$	TS, FC
(v)	P1	$(x)(\sim Kx)$	?TS, ?FC
	P2+P3	$\sim(\exists x)(Dx)$	FS, FC
	Q	$(\exists x)(Dx.\sim Kx)$	?TS, ?FC

The above symbolism is too simple to express the variety of possible relationships between P and Q and their components. It cannot, for example, handle 'P, nevertheless Q'. Moreover, an exact interpretation should indicate not only the truth-values of P and Q, but the speakers' beliefs and attitudes regarding them, which are inadequately represented here. However, the symbolization shows the scale of the problem, and the range of solutions now in the field.

62b1–c8. Socrates suggests two possible grounds for the prohibition of suicide: (1) we are placed in a 'prison' (or 'garrison') from which we should not run away (b2–6); (2) we are the possessions of the gods, and therefore may not dispose of our own lives (b6–c8). These suggestions are not sharply distinct, but they will be considered separately here.

(i) The meaning will depend upon the translation at 62b4. If 'prison' is correct (see note 1), Socrates is probably referring to the Orphic doctrine that life is an imprisonment of the soul within the body. Cf. *Cratylus* 400c and *Gorgias* 493a. The consequent analogy between suicide and escape from prison recalls the theme of the *Crito*. Cf. also 98e3–5. However, the central argument of the *Crito* against escaping from gaol would be ineffective against suicide. In that dialogue Socrates derives his obligation to obey the Laws of Athens from the benefits of citizenship he has enjoyed (50d–e, 51c). But life in itself confers no benefits analogous to these. He argues that he has implicitly contracted to obey the Laws, by spending his life in Athens when he might have emigrated (51d–e, 52d–53a). But there could be no comparable 'emigration' from life, and hence no analogous opportunity to opt out of the 'contract'–except through suicide itself.

It might perhaps be held that, on the *Crito* view, suicide would be wrong, if expressly forbidden by law. This is just how it is treated by Aristotle (*Nicomachean Ethics* 1138a9–13): it is illegal and therefore an offence against the state. However, no such argument is advanced here, nor would it show why suicide is 'forbidden' in the relevant sense. For this phrase (61c10, d4, e5) strongly suggests a religious prohibition (cf. 'not holy', 62a6). To condemn suicide merely on account of its illegality would simply be to disregard the religious and moral questions it raises. For if suicide is sinful or morally wrong, presumably it is so whether it is legal or not.

The alternative translation at 62b4, 'garrison', would place suicide in a different light. It would then be viewed as desertion of a military post, and might be thought culpable as dereliction of duty or as cowardice. The latter notion appears in the *Laws* (873c7), in Aristotle (op.cit. 1116a12–14), and often in later literature. Clearly, however, many acts of self-destruction are not liable to the charge of cowardice. It is plainly inapplicable to altruistic self-sacrifice, to self-destruction on behalf of a worthy cause, and to the taking of one's own life to avoid morally worse alternatives. Even if 'suicide' were defined so as to exclude these cases, it would often remain debatable whether a charge of 'cowardice' was deserved. The word is itself a term of moral reproach. To apply it to conduct of any given kind is not to show why that conduct is morally wrong, but only to claim in a more specific way that it is so. Cebes' question why suicide is impermissible would not be answered, therefore, by branding it as 'cowardice', but would only be reopened in a more specific form.

(2) The reasoning at 62b6–c8 prefigures the Christian orthodoxy that life is given, and may therefore be taken away, only by God. Cf.67a6–'until God himself shall release us'. The doctrine raises radical difficulties for the relation between human action and the divine will. If all things are arranged by a cosmic Intelligence, as Socrates will later suggest (97c–d), then human actions, including suicides, would seem no more capable of counteracting its designs than anything else. If all men die in God's good time, how can suicide be condemned as a usurpation of His prerogative? On this view of the divine will, as Hume says: 'When I fall upon my own sword . . . I receive my death equally from the hands of the Deity as if it had proceeded from a lion, a precipice, or a fever' (*Essay on Suicide*). On the other hand, if acts of suicide are conceived as

successful contraventions of the divine will, how are they to be distinguished from other voluntary actions affecting the natural order of events, including those aimed at preserving human life? 'If I turn aside a stone which is falling upon my head, I disturb the course of nature, and I invade the peculiar province of the Almighty by lengthening out my life beyond the period which by the general laws of matter and motion he had assigned it' (Hume, ibid.). Since virtually any action might in this way be regarded as contravening the divine will, there would still be need to determine which kinds of action were impermissible, and whether suicide should be counted among them.

Socrates is not maintaining an absolute veto upon suicide. On the contrary, with the words 'until God sends some necessity, such as the one now before us' (c7–8), he implies that his own death will be self-inflicted. In his case, at least, self-destruction would be not merely permissible, but a religious duty. That such acts, when required by the state, were viewed by Plato as exceptions to the general rule is clear from the provisions for treatment of suicides in the *Laws* (873c–d). Indeed, a still broader range of exceptions is there envisaged, since a suicide is subject to punitive burial only if 'no state has required it of him, no stress of cruel and inevitable calamity driven him to the act, and he has been involved in no desperate and intolerable disgrace'. This is a far cry from the 'condemnation of suicide in every circumstance and form' for which Geddes (201) admires the present passage, but which is not to be found in it. Socrates is not denouncing suicide at large; he is trying to explain why the philosopher's desire for death would not justify him in procuring it for himself. See previous note.

'Kill' at 62c2 and 62c7 could possibly be interpreted, with Loriaux (69), to mean 'try to kill', on the ground that punishment proper could be inflicted only upon something still living. However, the words 'if you had any punishment at hand' (c3–4) are perhaps meant to concede that for a successful suicide no punishment would be practicable. Moreover, posthumous 'punishments', such as dishonouring the corpse, were sometimes imposed. No distinctive penalties in the afterlife are specified in the closing myth, although culpable acts of suicide would no doubt have been included among 'wrongful acts of killing' (113e, cf. *Republic* 615c), and punished accordingly.

On the whole subject see J. M. Rist, *Stoic Philosophy* (Cambridge, 1969), Ch.13, and, for a broader study, A. Alvarez, *The Savage God* (London, 1971).

2.2 Socrates' Defence (63e8—69e5)

This section contains a passionate apologia for the philosophic life. It resolves the contradiction with which Socrates had been faced. The philosopher's whole life is a preparation for death. He should therefore welcome death when it comes.

64c2—9. The translation 'death *is* something' (c2) preserves the Greek idiom. Less literally: 'there is such a thing as death'. Socrates means, non-technically, that 'death occurs' or 'there is death'. A 'Form' of Death will be needed later (105d9) but Socrates can hardly be referring to it here.

In defining death at 64c4—5 as 'the separation of the soul from the body', he seems to be treating it as the 'event' in which their separation is effected—cf.67d4, d9—10, and *Gorgias* 524b. At 64c5—8, however, it is treated no longer as an 'event', but as the 'state' of 'being dead', the separated condition of soul and body. Cf.66e6—67a2. See also note 4 and on 71d5—e3. It is to that 'state' that Socrates seems to refer when he asks at 64c8: 'Death can't be anything else but that, can it?'

Several difficulties arise here. (1) In what sense 'is there' such a thing as death? People die. But do they exist when dead? Or are 'the dead' simply those who no longer exist at all? Socrates avoids these questions by assuming that a living being is a body conjoined with a soul, and by defining death as the separation of one from the other. For a person to be dead is for his soul to be separated from his body and vice versa. This leaves it unclear what is the proper subject of the predicate 'dead'. Is it only *the man* who is to be called 'dead' when soul and body are parted, or may 'dead' be predicated of soul and body separately? See on 105e10—107a1 (p.221). Socrates will generally avoid speaking of 'dead souls'—although the soul is twice said to 'die' (77d4, 84b2)—perhaps because this would produce a conflict with the conclusion of the dialogue, that the soul is 'deathless': 'it won't admit death, nor will it be dead' (106b3—4). He will speak, rather, of 'the souls of the dead' (72a7, 72d9). But the question now arises whether 'the souls of the dead' exist.

(2) By defining death as he does, Socrates seems to prejudge this question in favour of the soul's survival. Hackforth (44, n.1) tries to defend him against this objection: 'all that Socrates here wants is an admission that we can properly think and speak of soul "apart" from body; whether soul continues to exist when thus apart is the question at issue.' However, 'being dead' is taken to include 'the soul's being apart, alone by itself, separated from the body'. From this definition, conjoined with the admission that there is such a thing as death (c2),

it follows that the soul does exist apart from the body. If it did not, there would be no such thing as death, in the sense given to the word at 64c5–8. It therefore seems hard to acquit Socrates of pre-judging the issue at this point. See also on 70c4–8 (p.106), 71a12–b5.

(3) A definition of death in terms of the relation between soul and body provides, it need hardly be said, no useful criterion for determining when a person is dead. But even if this medical question is judged irrelevant, the definition gives a questionable account of the concept. For it provides that the body has 'come to be apart, separated from the soul, alone by itself'. But the body's *post mortem* existence is not, in fact, a necessary condition for death, whether death be viewed as an event or as a state. The bodies of those long dead do not exist. And after certain kinds of death the body may not remain 'alone by itself' at all. Nor, in saying that a person is dead, need any reference be made to the existence or state of his body.

(4) The definition of death poses some difficulty for the inter-pretation of 'deathless', as that term will later be applied to the soul. If 'death' means 'the soul's being separated from the body', how can the soul be 'deathless' in that sense? So far from denying that it is separated from the body, Socrates affirms precisely this. For the word 'deathless' or 'immortal' see on 72e7–73a3, 95b5–e6, 105d13–e9. As applied to the soul it must mean the capacity to persist through separation from the body. The soul survives the transition from attachment to the body to a state of detachment from it. It survives, we might say, the 'event' of death into the 'state' of death. In this sense it could be held 'deathless' in a manner consistent with the present definition. It is, however, a further question whether the term 'death' is itself used consistently with this definition throughout the dialogue. See on 71d5–e3, 91d2–9, 105e10–107a1 (p.221), and cf.88a1–b8, 95b8–e1, 106b2–4, 106e5–7.

(5) Behind the above difficulties lies a more fundamental one. Is the view that living beings are a composite of body and soul tenable? The assumption that an independent entity, 'the soul', animates the body is implicit throughout the discussion, and is made explicit at 105c9–d5 (cf.79b1–2). Yet for many readers the question of the soul's immortality is pre-empted by that of its existence. Socrates' conception of it will later be challenged by Simmias, with the counter-hypothesis that the soul is an 'attunement' of bodily elements (85e–86d). By refuting that alternative (91e–95a), Socrates clears the way for his own view. More positive support for the assumption can be found in other sections of the dialogue. See on 76c11–13 and 105e10–107a1 (p.220). A philosophical reading of the dialogue should examine the basis for it. See next note.

64e4–65a3. Socrates now pursues the implications of the soul-body dichotomy for the philosopher's life: his attention will be turned away from the body as far as possible, and 'towards the soul'. The traditional 'soul' has been used throughout for *psychē*. But the dialogue contains no explicit account or consistent usage of this term, and it therefore remains unclear exactly what it is whose immortality Socrates is seeking to prove. No short account can do justice to this huge subject. All that can be attempted is an outline of some aspects of it that are especially relevant to the *Phaedo*.

(1) The soul is that element in us whose good condition constitutes our true well-being. Its 'care' is therefore paramount, and overrides all other human concerns. This teaching, familiar from other Platonic dialogues, is elaborated in the *Phaedo* in two ways. First, the body is seen as a constant hindrance to the care of the soul, its demands incessantly conflicting with the soul's interests (66b–d). Hence the repeated stress upon 'purifying' the soul (67a–c, 69c), 'releasing' it from the body as far as possible (67c–d), and 'admonishing' or 'punishing' the body (94b–d). Hence, also, the stern disparagement of bodily pleasures and material possessions (64d–65a). Nowhere else in Plato is asceticism so uncompromisingly extolled. Secondly, the nurture of the soul is viewed as of vital importance, not only for this life but for the life to come. This gospel, proclaimed with unequalled eloquence, imbues the dialogue with its distinctive ethos of religious fervour and earnest moral concern. See especially 63b5–9, 69d2–e2, 80d5–84b8, 90d9–91a1, 107c1–5, 108a6–c5, 114d1–115a3.

(2) The soul is 'the true self', 'the real person'. Hence in caring for his soul, the philosopher is caring for 'himself'. In this vein Socrates will urge his friends to take care of 'themselves' (115b5–c1). After his death they should not speak of burying 'him', but rather 'his body' (115c4–116a1). 'Socrates' is to be distinguished from his body, and is thus implicitly identified with his soul. The use of 'our souls' for 'us' will be critical for the argument at certain points. See on 70c4–8 (p.105). An argument for identifying the person with his soul is presented in the (possibly spurious) *Alcibiades* I (129a–130e).

(3) The soul is often equivalent to 'intellect' or 'reason', a 'thinking faculty' or 'cognitive principle' by which the quest for wisdom is pursued. In this quest, the soul is referred to as 'attaining the truth' (65b9), as 'reasoning' (65c2–5), 'getting knowledge' (76c6), and 'possessing wisdom' (76c12–13). It seeks 'vision' or 'grasp' of its objects, analogous to the seeing or touching of material things. It is an organ of intellectual sight or touch, or a 'subject' by which the truth is apprehended. At 67c3 'soul' is

replaced by 'intellect', as if that term were a natural variant for it. Cf.65e7, 66a2, 79a3, and see on 65c2–4.

(4) The soul also functions as 'the rational self' in opposition to emotions and bodily desires. This opposition is not between 'reason' and some other 'part' of the soul, but simply between soul and body. No distinction is drawn in the *Phaedo* between 'reason', 'spirit', and 'appetite', which Plato treats elsewhere as separate 'parts' of the soul–see *Republic* 435a–441c and *Phaedrus* 246a–b, 253c–e. Phenomena viewed in those dialogues as 'mental conflicts' are described in the *Phaedo* as struggles between soul and body: the soul opposes 'the bodily feelings' (94b7–c1, c9–e6), which include not only hunger and thirst (94b8–10), but also passions and fears (94d5). In opposing them, the soul thus performs the role played in the *Republic* (439c2–d8, 441b2–c2) by the 'reasoning element' only.

(5) In several passages the soul is treated as the subject not only of rational thought but of a wide range of conscious states. Thus Socrates can speak of 'the pleasures that come by way of the body' (65a7), and of hearing or sight, pleasure or pain, as 'bothering' the soul (65c5–9). Later (79c2–8), the soul is said to be 'confused and dizzy' when it studies things through the senses, to be 'intensely pleased or pained' (83c5–6), and to 'share opinions and pleasures with the body' (83d7). Pleasure and pain are viewed not merely as changes in the body, but as psychic states (cf. *Philebus* 33d2–e1, 35c3–d7, 55b3). In such places the soul is depicted as an inner recipient or 'owner' of sense impressions and feelings–or as what will, in a later era, be called 'the mind'. Cf. *Theaetetus* 184b–186a.

(6) The soul is often conceived as a 'life-principle', or 'animating agent', bringing life to the body which it occupies. This idea, although largely absent from the English 'soul', is close to the root sense of *psychē*, which is cognate with a verb meaning 'to breathe'. It underlies the definition of death already given at 64c, and will appear in both the first and the final arguments for immortality (72a11–d5, 105c9–d5). This view of the soul is not restricted to human beings but applies to all living things. Cf.70d7–9. Note also that since the universe as a whole is regarded by Plato as a living thing (cf. *Timaeus* 30d, 92c), soul as life-principle may be conceived as animating not only individual organisms, but also the universe itself. For the etymology of *psychē* see *Cratylus* 399d–400b.

(7) One feature of 'soul' is easily obscured in translation. The word may be used not only of individuals, but also in a generic sense to connote a kind of 'stuff', just as 'body' may be used to mean not only individual bodies but also 'matter'. See on 70c8–d6 and 80c2–d7. It is not always clear whether 'soul-stuff' or 'the individual soul' is meant. The distinction is critical for immortality. For the idea that

'soul is immortal', merely in the sense that there exists a permanent quantum of 'soul-stuff', would no more imply the immortality of individual souls than the notion of a permanent quantum of matter implies the immortality of individual bodies. Clearly, the latter notion is compatible with the view that no individual body is immortal, and that there may be continual variation in the total number of bodies existing at any given time. Might not the same hold true of souls? At *Republic* 611a it is argued that the total number of souls must be 'always the same'. This would imply, assuming that no soul can be shared by several organisms, a fixed limit to the number of things that could be simultaneously living.

The foregoing notions of soul are immensely varied. They range, on a descending scale, from the intellectual and spiritual functions of a small class of human beings to that which is shared by living things in general. This variation poses several problems. First, it may be asked whether arguments appealing to such widely divergent concepts of soul could establish the immortality of the same thing. The notions of soul as 'intellect' and soul as 'life-principle' will, between them, largely monopolize the coming arguments. But these 'souls' can hardly be identified. Soul as intellect is said to be 'similar to what is unvarying' in virtue of its kinship with the changeless objects which it knows (80b2–3); whereas soul as life-principle is an agent of change in living bodies, and will, through its association with the body, be subject to change itself (e.g. 79c2–8, 81b1–c6, 83d4–e3).

Secondly, it remains uncertain which psychical characteristics are supposed in the *Phaedo* to survive death, and whether any others could, consistently with its arguments, be supposed to do so. Much of the argument suggests survival of the intellect or rational self only; and it may be asked whether this would be sufficient for, or even compatible with, the faith in 'personal' survival which Socrates affirms. If, for example, such features as memory or emotion are required for personal immortality, but are, at least implicitly, excluded from survival by the philosophical arguments, then personal survival not only goes unproven in the *Phaedo* but is actually ruled out.

Finally, the wide range of notions of 'soul' gives rise to a series of images of the soul-body relationship that can hardly be reconciled with one another. We may ask, for example, how the soul can at once 'bring life' to the body (105c–d), 'rule and be master' of the body (80a, 94b–d), and yet be a 'prisoner' within the body, co-operating in its own captivity (82e–83a). The dialogue contains no single, logically coherent 'doctrine' that might answer such questions. As E. R. Dodds has said (*G.I.* 179), 'the Classical Age inherited a

whole series of inconsistent pictures of the "soul" or "self".' Several
of these are amalgamated, no doubt consciously, in Plato's thought.
But the more clearly they are distinguished, the more usefully the
philosophical arguments can be explored.
    See, further, E. R. Dodds, op.cit., Ch.7, and T. M. Robinson,
P.P., Ch.2.

65b1–7. Plato's language for sense experience is often hard to
interpret. The words translated 'sight' and 'hearing' at 65b2 may
mean either, as here, the *senses* of sight and hearing, or, as at 74d1
and 98d7, visual and auditory *sensations*. Both words recur at
65c6, where they seem best taken in the latter sense. For the meaning
of 'sight' at 65e8, where the text is uncertain, see note 9.
    The generic word for 'perception' is similarly ambiguous between
'sense' and 'sensation'. At 65b5 the phrase translated 'the bodily
senses' means, literally, 'the senses around the body', suggesting that
they are thought of as having bodily location. 'Sense' has been used
in the translation also at 75b11, 79a2, 79c4, 79c5, 83a5, 96b5–6,
and 99e4. At 65d11 'sense-perception' has been used, since the phrase
'those that come by way of the body' suggests that sensations are
meant. This translation has been used also at 73c7 and 76a2. The
meaning is uncertain at 66a1, 75a7, 75a11, 75b1, 75b6, 75e3, and
76d9. See also on 74c7–d3 and note 6.
    The senses are continually disparaged—cf.65c5–10, 65e6–66a6,
79c2–8, 83a4–7, 99e1–4. Yet just how they are 'neither accurate
nor clear' (b5) is never properly explained. Can Socrates be thinking
of misjudgements of size due to distance, or of refraction or other
sources of visual error? His talk of the soul being 'taken in by the
body' (65b11, cf.83a4–5) might suggest this. Cf. *Protagoras* 356c5–
357a2, *Republic* 602c–e. Such 'deceit', however, occurs against a
background of perceptual judgements that are generally correct.
Moreover, the senses themselves play an indispensable part in
measurement, and thus in the correction of error. Mistaken judgements of size or shape would therefore fail to illustrate the theme
that 'we neither hear nor see anything accurately' (b3–4), unless,
indeed, the poets are to be credited with some version of the modern
'argument from illusion', to show that we never perceive physical
objects as they really are.
    Socrates' quarrel with the senses appears more radical. It is not
merely that they misrepresent the physical world, but that they
never present anything else. They hamper the soul's access to the
real objects of its understanding, the 'Forms', that will be introduced
at 65d4–5 below. They give no indication that there are any such
objects, and strongly suggest that there are not. Clear philosophic

understanding can therefore be achieved only when normal sensory awareness is suspended.

At 65b3, if any specific poets are meant, the reference may be to Epicharmus' line 'intelligence sees; intelligence hears; the others are deaf and blind' (DK 23 B 12).

65c2–4. 'The things that *are*': here, as often, Plato uses the present participle of the verb 'to be' with the definite article, to denote the object of the soul's understanding. The singular phrase has generally been translated 'that which is', and the plural 'the things that are'.

The Greek verb 'to be' has both (1) an 'incomplete' use, in which it requires a complement, expressed or understood, and (2) a 'complete' or 'absolute' use, in which it stands by itself. In use (1) the verb may express identity of subject with complement, or it may predicate the complement of the subject. In some contexts it is not certain which of these is meant. Nor is it clear whether any such distinction was recognized by Plato when this dialogue was written. Not until the much later *Sophist* is any systematic clarification of 'being' attempted. The distinction between the 'is' of identity and that of predication sometimes affects the interpretation of a phrase (see on 75c7–d6, p.131), or the assessment of an argument (see on 93d1–5, p.162).

In use (2), which survives only vestigially in English, the verb commonly means either 'to be true' or 'to exist'. It has often been rendered in one or other of these ways. In the present passage, however, it is not clear whether 'the things that are' are thought of as 'truths' or 'existents'. They are said to become clear to the soul in its reasoning. This might suggest that, as Burnet holds (note on 65c2–4), 'truths' are meant. Yet Socrates will shortly go on to speak of 'the hunt for each of the things that are' (66a3) in connection with 'Forms', which are introduced in terms suggestive of existents (see next note). It should be borne in mind that Plato constantly treats thought processes as analogous to perceptual ones. Sight and touch are his standard models for intellectual discovery and understanding. Such understanding, even when expressed as vision or grasp of 'objects', may well be thought of as including the apprehension of truths. If so, a sharp dichotomy between 'truths' and 'existents' need not be drawn at this point. Cf. C. H. Kahn (*V.B.A.G.* 457): 'If we recognise some interaction between the old use of the participle to refer to facts or events and the new use to designate whatever things there are in the world, this will help us to understand the persistent Greek refusal to make any sharp distinction between states of affairs or facts with a propositional structure, on the one hand, and individual objects or entities on the other. For the Greeks, both types count as "beings".'

Sometimes 'the things that are' clearly refers to Forms (78d4, 83b2), sometimes clearly not (79a6, 97d7, 99d5). More often the reference is indefinite: cf.65c9, 66a8, 66c2, 74d10, 82e3–4, 90c4, 90d6, 99e6, 100a2, 101e3, 103e9.

65d4–e5. The so-called 'Theory of Forms' is introduced at this point. As this theory is of central importance in Plato's thought, and is more prominent in this work than in any dialogue usually regarded as of earlier date, a general note on the Forms may be useful here. The following account will be based mainly upon the *Phaedo*, and will be limited to (1) the terminology of the Theory, (2) its philosophical basis, and (3) its relationship with the proofs of immortality.

(1) Two of Plato's commonest semi-technical terms for Forms are *eidos* (102b1, 103e3, 104c7, 106d6) and *idea* (104b9, 104d2, 104d6, 104d9, 104e1, 105d13). Both derive from a common root which appears in the Greek verb 'to see', and they are thus connected with the visual appearance of a thing. Ordinarily, they connote 'shape' or 'figure', and also 'sort' or 'species'. These associations are preserved in the conventional translation 'form', which has been adopted for both words in their Form-referring use. A third word, *morphē*, also normally meaning 'shape', has been translated 'character' (103e5, 104d10). As used for Forms, the three words seem interchangeable. See note 72.

The English 'idea' is an exact transliteration of one of the above words. But its associations are misleading. The Forms are in no sense 'psychological' or 'subjective' entities. They are not thoughts or concepts, existing only 'in the mind' of a thinker. Nor are they mind-dependent objects. They may be thought of *by* the mind, 'viewed with the soul' (66e1–2, and see previous note), but they do not depend upon being thought of for their existence. Just as physical objects exist independently of eye and vision, so Forms exist independently of mind and thought.

Individual Forms are typically designated by a neuter singular adjective, occasionally standing alone, but more often with the definite article or the pronoun 'itself', or with both. Such expressions have been translated as literally as possible. Thus, phrases such as 'the equal', 'the beautiful itself', have generally been retained. For the present passage, however, see note 5, and on 74a9–b1, 100b1–c8. Abstract nouns are frequently used for Forms, and have been translated by the corresponding English abstracts, e.g., 'health', 'largeness', 'strength' (65d12–13). For the special problem posed by

Forms for numbers, see on 101b9–c9.

Individual Forms are referred to in these Notes as, e.g., 'the Form Equal', 'the Form Beautiful', 'the Form of Three', or as 'Equality', 'Beauty', etc. The variable F is sometimes used to stand for the adjectival component—'the Form F', 'the F', 'the F itself', 'F-ness'. Note that phrases of the form 'the F' are liable to be ambiguous. They need not refer to a Form, but may simply mean 'that which is F', i.e. a thing characterized as F. See on 70e4–71a11 (p.108), 103a4–c9. It is sometimes uncertain whether a Form is being referred to or not. Typographical distinctions for Forms of any kind have therefore usually been avoided in the translation.

Forms are designated by several other expressions. 'That which is' and 'the things that are' are sometimes, although not always, so used—see previous note. Plato also uses *ousia*, an abstract noun ordinarily meaning 'property' or 'estate'. This has been translated 'Being', to distinguish it from the present participle 'being', on which it is formed—see note 7. Sometimes a Form F is referred to as 'the F in nature'. See on 103a4–c9. In several places an exceptionally puzzling expression for Forms is used: literally 'what F is', or perhaps 'what is F', or 'the F which is'—with or without the emphatic 'itself'. Sometimes F is omitted, leaving only 'what it is'. The phrase is still in need of elucidation. Cf.65d13–e1, 74b2, 74d6, 75b1–2, 75b5–6, 75d2, 78d3–5, 92d9. See on 75c7–d6 (p.130), and notes 7, 21, 24–6, 28, 31, 50.

(2) Platonic Forms are conceived as timeless and non-spatial objects, immutable entities set over against the changing world of sensible things, a realm of 'things that are' transcending the 'things that come to be'. They are the realities of which sensible objects are mere appearances or 'phenomena'. Each Form is unique, a single 'one' set over its 'many' sensible instances. Each is a perfect original, of which sensible things are imperfect copies. Forms are invisible to the eye, but 'intelligible'—accessible to 'intelligence', the mental organ that 'sees' them. In terms of a contrast that Plato draws in the *Republic* between 'knowledge' and 'opinion', they are the only objects of true 'knowledge'. See on 84a2–b8.

Plato writes of Forms, such as Equality, Largeness and Health, as if they existed 'alone by themselves', in splendid isolation from the familiar world of equal sticks, large men and healthy children. It is this 'separation' of Forms from sensible objects that distinguishes the fully-fledged version of the Theory found in the *Phaedo*. Nowhere is the contrast between Forms and sensible things drawn more sharply than here. The soul-body dualism already postulated (64e–65a) is one aspect of the same dichotomy. In effect, Plato adapts metaphysical dualism to his present purpose by equating the domain of Forms with the 'next world' of religious faith. Thus the Forms not only afford the ground for believing in the immortality of the soul; they are also its destination.

They are sometimes spoken of in terms suggestive of direct acquaintance or even mystical experience. See, e.g., 79d1—7, 84a8—b4. Since it is also suggested that such direct acquaintance is unattainable during this life (66e2—67b2), it might be supposed that their existence has to be accepted purely on faith. The Theory is, indeed, everywhere assumed rather than proved. Nevertheless, it is not adopted arbitrarily or merely to buttress the case for immortality. Rather, it offers a solution to a number of philosophical difficulties, which will now be considered.

(a) The Theory has its origin in Socratic inquiries into value concepts such as 'just', 'beautiful', 'holy', and 'good'. Plato depicts these in several earlier dialogues, whose prime question is 'What is F?', where 'F' stands for a value term in common use that is felt to require clarification. No such inquiries occur in the *Phaedo*, but they are familiar to the speakers, and the Theory is explicitly connected with them. Cf.75d1—3 and 78d1—2, where the 'questions and answers' mentioned evidently concern the essential nature of each of the concepts referred to, the attempt to specify what each of them is. This enterprise is envisaged in the *Republic* as a prospective science called 'dialectic', which would aim, in ethical and metaphysical matters, for the objectivity and rigour achieved in mathematics. It would also aim to secure the foundations of the mathematical sciences themselves.

The programme requires Forms to be posited as objects of scientific knowledge. They provide the sciences with a subject-matter about which their statements are made, and of which these statements hold true. 'The true' is not clearly distinguishable in Greek from 'the real', nor 'that which is the case' from 'that which exists'. See previous note and on 66b1—c5. The requirement that what is known must 'be true' thus gives rise to the view that the objects of knowledge must be 'realities' or 'existents'. And, since the truths attained in mathematics and dialectic are timeless or eternal, the 'realities' are credited with this feature as well. The Forms thus serve as timeless realities discovered in mathematics and dialectic. Their existence is a necessary condition for there being scientific knowledge at all.

(b) For certain mathematical concepts, such as squareness, circularity, and equality, the Forms are treated as ideal exemplars of properties that are never perfectly embodied in physical objects. No piece of wood is perfectly square, no stone is perfectly circular, no two sticks are exactly equal. The perfect Square or Circle, or

Absolute Equality, may thus be thought of as a standard, to which objects in the sensible world approximate but of which they fall short. The Form serves as a paradigm for such properties. Indeed 'paradigm' derives from a word Plato sometimes uses for Forms in this role. It connotes an individual used as a pattern, sample, or model for a given property, to determine whether or how far other individuals possess it. Just as the length or weight of a thing is determined by appealing, ultimately, to the standard metre or pound, so—according to the Theory—there is an implicit appeal to the Form F when an individual is judged to be F.

This idea is fairly naturally extended to concepts of value. No man or society is perfectly just or good. Yet to say that individuals fall short of perfect justice or goodness is to suggest that these ideals exist independently of any particular man or society, and may be more or less closely approached by them. Moreover, since the ascription of these properties is often uncertain or controversial, the Form is supposed, once again, to provide a paradigm or measure against which individuals can be assessed. In the *Republic* Plato portrays the perfectly just man and society with this express purpose.

There is, however, a crucial difference between Platonic paradigms and the standards used in weighing or measuring physical objects. The standard metre is itself a sensible item, whereas a Form is not. It is an important feature of the Theory that no sensible item can provide an ultimate standard against which others may be measured. Sensible Fs are inherently defective, and must therefore fail to be 'really' F. Only a non-sensible F can be properly so called. The Form cannot be identified with any of its sensible instances. The various grounds for this claim will be discussed below. See on 74b7−c6.

(c) The Forms posited in the *Phaedo* are mainly those for the quantitative and value concepts studied in mathematics and dialectic. But the Theory has a further dimension: it offers a general account of predication and naming. Forms are the designata of common adjectives and nouns predicated of individual subjects. Thus at 102b2 (cf.78e2, 102c10, 103b7) it will be said that things called 'large', 'small' and 'beautiful' are 'named after' the relevant Forms. The prime bearer of the name 'F' is the Form F. It is the one thing common to each of the many Fs, the single feature F-ness shared by its many instances, the meaning of their common name. In this capacity, it functions as what later came to be called a 'universal'.

In the *Republic* (596a) Forms are said to be posited for each plurality of things 'to which we apply the same name'. This formula is so broad that it has sometimes been doubted whether Plato would seriously have posited Forms for every item it covers. Forms for artificial objects, for example, seldom appear. Such Forms as Shuttle (*Cratylus* 389b), Bed, and Table (*Republic* 596b) are introduced only for special purposes, and may have played no part in the Theory in its original form. Yet, clearly, a far wider range of Forms is demanded by a theory of 'universals' than by the concerns of mathematics and dialectic. This implication is faced in the *Parmenides* (130c—d), where misgivings are expressed over extending the Theory to such classes as Hair, Mud, and Dirt.

It should be noted that the 'universal' role of Forms is distinct from their scientific and paradigmatic roles. Immense difficulty is incurred if these roles are conflated by treating all Forms alike as postulates of a single, comprehensive 'theory'. Some of the resulting problems will be considered further below. See on 74d4—8 and 102a10—d4.

(3) The Theory of Forms and the belief in immortality were called by F. M. Cornford the 'twin pillars' of Platonic philosophy. But the metaphor misrepresents the logical relationship between them. For the doctrine of immortality is logically dependent upon the Theory. All of the major arguments except the first are based upon it. This dependence is made explicit at 76e—77a, 92d—e and 100b. The Theory is clearly fundamental.

It is, however, nowhere defended, but is simply accepted without argument by all parties (65d6, 74b1, 78d8—9, 92d6—e2, 100c1—2, 102a10—b1). Its status is well described in Simmias' words at 85c8— d1: it is 'the best and least refutable of human doctrines'. These words, though they do not, as uttered by Simmias, refer to the Theory, are so closely echoed by Socrates later that they may be taken to express his own position. Cf.99c6—100a8 and see on 84d4— 85d10. The Theory is 'the theory he judges to be strongest', adopted provisionally and for the sake of argument. It offers the most plausible solution he can find to the problems outlined above.

Socrates will urge that the validation of a first principle should not be mixed up with the testing of its consequences (101e1—3). Similarly, criticism of arguments based upon the Theory should be distinguished from criticism of the Theory itself. The arguments for immortality must remain inconclusive without a defence of the Theory, as Socrates recognizes at 107b4—6. But the Theory is, in this dialogue, subordinated to the discussion of immortality and cannot be further investigated here.

A lucid exposition of the Theory of Forms is given in G. Ryle's article 'Plato', in the *Encyclopaedia of Philosophy*, ed. P. Edwards (New York, 1967) vi. 320—4.

66b1—c5. For the text and translation at 66b4 see note 10. The words translated 'that, we say, is truth' (66b7) mean, more literally, 'we say the true to be that', the referent of 'that' being 'what we desire'. Cf.67b1. 'The true' combines a neuter singular adjective with the definite article, not to designate an individual Form, but to characterize the Form world in general. Many other adjectives are so used. Cf., e.g., 79d2, 80b1–2, 81a5, 83e2, 84a8. 'The *A*' in such passages does not mean 'the Form *A*' but 'that (domain) which is *A*', where '*A*' is an attribute of Forms as such–'pure', 'divine', 'immortal' and the like.

The adjective translated 'true' can also mean 'real', as well as 'genuine' or 'truthful'. It has an attributive use, in which 'true *X*' means 'genuine *X*' or '*X* properly so called'–e.g. 'true goodness' (69b3). Plato commonly uses 'the truly *X*' in this sense–e.g. 'genuine philosophers' (64b9). Note also that 'true' or 'real' admits of degrees–cf., e.g., 65e1–2, 83c7. See note 8, and on 83b2–3.

'True' has generally been used, and 'truth' for the abstract noun. But 'real' has seemed necessary at 81b4, 83b3, 83c7, and 83d6. Like the verb 'to be' (see on 65c2–4), 'the true' embraces that which exists as well as that which is the case. Since the Platonic Form world is 'the real', and knowledge of it affords 'the truth', the two senses of the word naturally converge in references to it. 'Truth' in this sense is perhaps meant at 65b9, 66a6, 66d7, 67b1, and 99e6. Sometimes the meaning seems more general, as at 91c1–2, 102b9, and 115a1. At 65b2 'truth' approaches 'veracity', and at 89d6 'true' approaches 'truthful'. See also on 89d1–4 and 90b4–91c5.

The saying referred to at 66c4–5 is unknown. For the verb there translated 'think' cf.96b4. It is cognate with one of the nouns for 'wisdom' discussed at 69a6–c3, and is thus linked with apprehension of the Forms.

68a3–b7. The analogy between wisdom and human loved ones demands that the literal meaning of 'philosopher' be brought out at 68b2–3. He is a 'lover of wisdom', contrasted with other kinds of 'lover' at 68c1–2 (cf.82b10–c8). Philosophy is thought of as the quest for wisdom, not the attainment of it. See 66e2–67a1, and note 12. Cf. also *Symposium* 204a–c.

At 68a4–5 there may be a reference to Jocasta or Evadne, whose suicides occur in Euripides' *Supplices* (985ff.) and *Phoenissae* (1455ff.). Evadne's was committed for the sake of reunion with her husband.

68b8–69a5. This passage develops a contrast between the genuine goodness of the philosopher and the spurious goodness of other men. Non-philosophers withstand evils only for fear of worse alternatives, or forgo some pleasures only to secure others. Their so-called 'bravery' and 'temperance' are thus no more than an intelligent hedonism.

The hedonistic position is elaborated more fully, perhaps ironically, in the *Protagoras* (351b–360e), where a calculus of pleasures and pains is expounded in terms similar to those used here. Its role in the *Protagoras*, and the extent of Plato's commitment to it in that dialogue, which is probably earlier than the *Phaedo*, are much disputed. However, the view proclaimed in it by Socrates is essentially similar to the one he is made to disparage here. In other dialogues the thesis that 'good' is equivalent to, or definable in terms of, 'pleasure' is generally rejected. See *Gorgias* 495e–500a, *Republic* 505c–d, *Philebus* 20c–21d, 53c–55c.

Socrates deals here with 'bravery' and 'temperance' only. No parallel argument is given for 'justice', despite its inclusion at 69b1–c3 and 82a11–b3. These qualities, together with wisdom, make up the quartet of 'cardinal virtues', as they later came to be called. They are analysed more fully in the *Republic* (427e–444e), where the central concept is justice. The *Phaedo*, concerned as it is with the distinctive nature of philosophers, assigns a special role to wisdom. Bravery and temperance are explored in the *Laches* and *Charmides* respectively.

At 68c6 the translation 'people of the disposition we have described' slightly expands the text, so as to make clear that it refers to philosophers, and not to the non-philosophers who have just been mentioned (c1–3). 'Bravery' could not be meant to apply to the latter, for it must be parallel to 'temperance', which is ascribed at 68c10 to philosophers only. 'What is named "bravery" ' (c5) is best taken, with Burnet, to be paralleled at 68c8 by 'what most people name "temperance" '. In respect of both qualities, a distinction is being drawn between 'so-called' and genuine goodness, which Socrates will proceed to sharpen at 69a6–c3. Cf.82b1–2. Here, as often, 'what they call *X*' suggests that in ordinary usage the term '*X*' is misapplied. See on 107c1–d2.

Note that Socrates does not, as might be expected, simply ascribe 'so-called' goodness to the ordinary man, while reserving true goodness for philosophers. What he suggests is that 'bravery' and 'temperance', even as commonly understood, apply especially to philosophers, or to them alone. He is questioning the non-philosophers' title not only to 'true bravery' and 'true temperance', but also to 'bravery' and 'temperance' so-called. A weaker claim is made for 'bravery' than for 'temperance': the former is attributed to philosophers 'especially' (c6), the latter to them 'only' (c10). In arguing that philosophers deserve the title of 'so-called' bravery and temperance, Socrates does not, of course, mean to deny 'true' bravery and temperance to them. See 69b2, c1–2, and Hackforth, 57.

The arguments about (1) bravery and (2) temperance are rather different. In both cases, however, it is claimed that the qualities are 'strange' (d2–3) or 'illogical' (d12–13, cf.e3): non-philosophers are 'brave through cowardice', 'temperate through intemperance'. They are thus *F* by reason of *G*-ness, where *F* and *G* are opposites. This is paradoxical, and also—it may be noticed—conflicts with the account given later (100c–e) of the 'reasons' by which a subject can be characterized by one member of a pair of opposites.

(1) For 'bravery' the argument runs as follows (68d5–e1): (A) non-philosophers count death a great evil (d5–6); hence, (B) 'brave' ones abide death through being afraid of greater evils (d8–9); hence (C) they are 'brave' through fearing and fear (d11–12); yet (D) it is illogical that anyone should be brave through fear and cowardice (d12–13).

The argument hinges partly upon an assumed equivalence between 'brave' and 'fearless', 'cowardly' and 'fearful'. Philosophers are 'brave' in this popular sense, since, unlike other men, they do not regard death as an evil, and are therefore 'fearless' of it. The noun translated 'being afraid' in (B) differs from that used in (C) and (D) for 'fear'. The latter is cognate with the verb for 'fearing' in (C) and also with the noun translated 'cowardice' in (D). This facilitates the dubious slide in (D) from 'brave through fear' to the full-blown paradox 'brave through cowardice'.

The move from (A) to (B) assumes (i) that men faced with a choice between evils will take the one they regard as lesser; and (ii) that what they regard as evil they also fear. For these assumptions see *Protagoras* 358d–e. It is worth noting that they could be used to represent *any* agent who chooses what he considers a lesser evil as doing so from 'fear' of a greater one, and therefore as acting 'from cowardice'. Even philosophers may be motivated by a desire to avoid consequences which they regard as evil, and which they therefore 'fear' to incur—see, e.g., 83b5–c3. If so, they too might be represented, along the lines of the present argument, as acting 'from cowardice'.

Conversely, it could be shown that non-philosophers may perform cowardly actions 'from bravery': those who shun death do so through being 'fearless' of the alternatives. They are 'fearful through fearlessness', hence 'cowardly through bravery'. In this way it might be argued that the 'cowardice' of non-philosophers is no less paradoxical than their 'bravery'. Yet Socrates does not speak of 'so-called cowardice'. Nor is it anywhere suggested that the terms for bad qualities, like those for good ones, might be systematically misapplied.

(2) The word rendered 'temperate' is notoriously difficult to translate. It can mean either (a) 'sensible' or (b) 'self-controlled' in the sphere of bodily pleasures. Its opposite in the latter sense, here translated 'intemperate', means literally 'unchastened'. 'Temperance' in sense (b) signifies moderation rather than abstinence, control rather than elimination of the desires. It is only the 'true temperance' of the philosopher that entails a purifying or total purging of the emotions (69c1).

The argument at 68e2—69a5 runs thus: (A) 'well-ordered' non-philosophers, being afraid of being deprived of certain pleasures, and desiring them (e5—6), (B) abstain from some pleasures, being overcome by others (e6—7); yet (C) 'to be ruled by pleasures' they call 'intemperance' (e7—69a1); therefore (D) they overcome some pleasures, being overcome by others (69a2); hence, (E) they achieve temperance, after a fashion, as a result of 'intemperance' (a3—4).

The participles in (A), (B), and (D), 'being afraid' (e5), 'desiring' (e6), 'being overcome' (e7, a2) have all been translated with causal force. This is essential to support the claim that temperance is achieved 'because of' intemperance. The agent abstains from certain pleasures only 'because' he desires others, e.g. those of health or saving money.

'Well-ordered' non-philosophers are so called in (A) as a variant for 'temperate'. They are characterized in (B) as 'abstaining from pleasures', and thus in (D) as 'overcoming pleasures'. In (C) 'intemperance' is equated with 'being overcome by pleasures (e7—a1). Thus, a man who restrains himself for reasons of health or economy can be represented as temperate 'because of intemperance', since he is 'overcome' by the pleasures of health or saving money (cf.82c5—8, 83c1—2). Yet the meaning of 'intemperance' has here been artificially stretched, as Socrates recognizes with the phrase 'a kind of intemperance' (e3), and by adding the qualification 'after a fashion' at 69a3. By a parallel extension of 'temperance', it might be argued that a drunkard is 'intemperate because of temperance'. For he is overcome by the pleasures of the bottle, through having overcome those of a healthy liver and bank-balance. This is parallel to the difficulty raised about bravery in (1) above.

There is a parallel problem here also in keeping Socrates' argument from impinging upon the philosopher. He too, it might be objected, is gratifying one kind of desire only through yielding to another, his passionate desire for truth and wisdom (66e, 68a—b). He too, therefore, overcomes some pleasures through being overcome by others. At 114d8—115a1 Socrates will speak of one who rejects bodily pleasures and devotes himself to those of learning, adorning his soul with temperance, justice, and bravery. It might be asked what distinguishes the virtues of such a man from those of an enlightened hedonist? This raises the question of the role of wisdom in relation to the other virtues, and of the ethical position of the *Phaedo* more generally. See next note.

69a6–c3. This eloquent but difficult sentence forms the climax of Socrates' defence of the philosophic life. For the text and grammar see note 13. The key concepts are those of wisdom, goodness, and pleasure. The relations between these call for some comment.

Two words are usually translated 'wisdom': *sophia* and *phronēsis*. The former ordinarily means 'skill', 'knowledge', 'learning', or (in a pejorative sense) 'cleverness', 'subtlety' (96a7, 101e5). The latter normally means 'practical judgement', 'prudence', or 'good sense'. In Plato's usage, however, the words are not sharply differentiated. Here, and generally in this dialogue, *phronēsis* is a solemn term for the condition of the soul for which the philosopher yearns (66e3, 68a2, 68a7, 68b4), attainable only in communion with the Forms (79d1–7). It has been translated 'wisdom' throughout. See note 14.

The word translated 'goodness' at 69a7, 69b3 and 69b7 (*aretē*) can connote non-human as well as human goodness. Hence the inadequacy of the traditional translation 'virtue', which is mainly confined to good qualities in human beings, and a limited range even of these. 'Virtue' has a convenient plural, however, and is sometimes useful as a generic term. It stands for the 'whole' of which bravery, temperance, justice, and wisdom are elsewhere treated as 'parts'. Each of them is *a* virtue, and also part of virtue as a whole. See *Protagoras* 329c–330a and *Meno* 73e–74b. For the virtues generally see F. E. Sparshott, *Monist* 1970, 40–65.

What is the relation between wisdom and virtue? Are they identical, or is the former a means to the latter? If they are identical, is the whole being equated with one of its parts? Or is one of the parts supposed to be a necessary and sufficient condition for each of the others, and thus for virtue as a whole? If wisdom is a means to virtue, regarded as something distinct from it, why is it represented (a6–10) as the sole object of value? And how can it be 'sold' (b2) without being given up? These questions turn upon the interpretation of the 'money' metaphors at 69a6–b6 and of 'purification' at 69c1–3. See Bluck, 154–6, Hackforth, 191–3, J. V. Luce, *C.Q.* 1944, 60–4, and P. W. Gooch, *J.H.P.* 1974, 153–9.

In treating wisdom as the only 'right coin' (a9–10), Plato assigns to it an intrinsic worth that he denies to pleasure. The latter is supplanted by wisdom as the sole standard of value. In this context 'pleasure' is implicitly restricted to that of the body (cf.83b–d). The distinctions Plato will draw in other dialogues between different kinds of pleasure (see on 60b1–c7) enable this stark and misleading opposition between wisdom and pleasure to be moderated. At *Republic* 505b–d rival accounts of 'the good' in terms of wisdom or pleasure alone are both rejected. Cf. *Philebus* 20e–21e. The opposition between them is evidently artificial, since there can be pleasure in the pursuit of wisdom itself–cf.59a3.

On a sufficiently broad interpretation of 'pleasure', it might be argued that the philosopher pursues it as much as anyone else. He too seeks to maximize his own pleasure, now and hereafter. His practice of virtue in this life, it might also be said, is motivated ultimately by self-interest in the next. See, e.g., 107c1–d5, 114c6– 8. But the spirit of the present passage, and of the dialogue as a whole, is against this interpretation. The philosopher is not merely one whose prudential judgements take account of the afterlife. He seeks wisdom and virtue for their own sakes, and not merely as a means to eternal reward. They are, in some sense, their own reward. See on 81d6–82d8 and 107c1–d2.

3. THE CASE FOR IMMORTALITY
(69e6–107b10)

Cebes' objection that the soul may not survive death leads to the series of arguments that form the core of the dialogue. Each of these will be labelled for convenient reference, and they will be separately analysed in the following notes. But it is important to observe the connections between them. Plato does not offer a set of discrete, self-contained proofs of immortality, but a developing sequence of arguments, objections, and counter-arguments. As the dialogue unfolds, the earlier arguments are criticized, refined, or superseded, until Socrates' belief in immortality is finally vindicated. It is in this process that the intellectual power of the work is largely to be found.

The closely integrated arguments of the *Phaedo* contrast sharply with the solitary, and quite different, proofs of immortality in the *Republic* (608c–611a) and *Phaedrus* (245c–246a).

3.1 The Cyclical Argument (69e6–72e1)

Socrates begins by appealing to the principle that opposites come from opposites, and positing cyclical processes between every pair of opposites.

69e6–70c3. The popular idea that the soul may be dispersed at death rests on a misunderstanding of its *nature*. Later Socrates will return to this idea (77d5–e2), and will argue that the soul is not the kind of thing that can be 'blown away by winds' (84b4–7). In the Cyclical Argument he is concerned, rather, with the possibility of its separate *existence*. The other half of what Cebes requires, 'that it possesses some power and wisdom' (70b3–4), will be supplied by the Recollection Argument (72e–78b). For the relation between these arguments see on 77a6–d5. For the translation 'wisdom' see note 14.

Socrates' denial that he is 'talking idly' (70c1–2) may be an allusion to Aristophanes' caricature of him in the *Clouds*. For the gibe cf. *Republic* 489a, *Gorgias* 485d–e. As if in answer to charges of 'irrelevance', the close connection between the present inquiry and Socrates' own situation is stressed again and again (76b10–12, 78a1–2, 80d7–8, 84c6–85b9, 89b, 91a–c, 98c–99a).

The Cyclical Argument has defects that have often enough been pointed out. It is better construed as an opening dialectical move than as an argument to which Plato was seriously committed. But it deserves more credit for ingenuity and subtlety than it is usually given. It serves to introduce some of the concepts that will be of central interest, and gives fertile ground for philosophical argument. See, e.g., J. Wolfe, *Dialogue* 1966, 237–8, J. Wolfe and P. W. Gooch, *I.A.C.P.* ii. 239–44, 251–4, and C. J. F. Williams, *Philosophy* 1969, 217–30.

70c4–8. To appraise the argument it is essential to keep in mind the different functions of the verb translated 'come to be' or 'be born'. This verb (*gignesthai*), which is quite unconnected with Greek words for either 'come' or 'be', may be used both with a complement, meaning (1) 'become', and absolutely, meaning either (2) 'come into being' or (3) 'be born'. In uses (1) and (2) it has generally been rendered 'come to be'. The distinction between these is not, indeed, clear-cut, since a subject's coming to possess a property may also be thought of as that property's coming to exist in the subject. Thus '*x* comes to be *F*' may also be expressed as '*F* comes to be (in *x*)'. The grammar of sentences containing 'come to be' is not always clear—cf.97a–b, 101c, and see notes 58 and 65. In the present argument, when opposites are said to 'come to be' from each other (70e5–6, 71a9–10), it is meant that things come to be characterized by one member of a pair of opposites from having previously been characterized by the other. See 103b1–c2. Note also that the Greek verb is liable to be misleading in translation. (i) It may be thought that the things in question are 'generated' from distinct sources, as eggs 'come' from hens, or offspring from their parents. In this sense it would not, of course, be true that the living 'come to be from the dead'. Nor would the claim that 'opposites come to be from opposites' have any plausibility as a general principle at all. But this is not Plato's meaning. (ii) The word 'come' may suggest a local point of departure 'from' which the things in question 'arrive'. The argument can, indeed, be represented as exploiting this idea, Hades being thought of as the 'place' where souls begin their journey. But the verb under discussion carries no connotations of the kind suggested by the English 'come'.

The distinction between uses (2) and (3) is also critical for the argument. As applied to the soul, the verb is not generally used as in (2), since the soul is not, on Socrates' view of it, subject to 'coming into being'. Rather, the verb is used to mean that the soul 'is born'. In this use it is frequently linked with talk of the soul's 'entering' the body (cf., e.g., 77d1–2, 95c5–d2). It means, in fact, 'become incarnate'. Thus, in the next few lines (70c8–d2) Socrates will argue that our souls 'could hardly be born again, if they didn't exist'. The translation 'be born' is clearly demanded here. For it could not be argued that 'our souls could hardly *come into being* again, if they did not exist'.

Note, however, that 'being born' permits inference to an earlier, discarnate existence, only if it is *the soul*, as distinct from the living thing, that is said to 'be born'. For it is plausible to hold that, for a living thing, its birth, or (where this is distinct) its conception, *is* its coming into being. An inference from birth or conception to an earlier existence would then be as unwarranted as an inference from its coming into being to an earlier existence. It is only if 'be born' is predicated of the soul, and taken to mean 'be born into a body' or 'become incarnate' that the required inference to an earlier existence can be drawn.

The actual subject of 'be born' varies. Often Socrates will speak simply of 'our' being born (e.g. 76a9, 76e4, 76e6, 77a1, 77a10–b1, 77c2). But at critical points (70c8–d1, 72a6–8) he will speak, rather, of 'our souls' being born. At 73a1–2 the verb is used explicitly to mean 'become incarnate'. Later (83d10–e1) the soul will be said to 'fall back into another body, and grow in it as if sown there'. It is 'bound' or 'imprisoned' in the body (82e2–83a1, 83d1–5, 84a5, 92a1, cf.67d1–10). These metaphors sustain a distinction, vital for the argument, between the soul and the living thing that it animates. Yet this use of 'the soul' as subject of 'be born' is logically suspect. For it insinuates a view of 'birth' in which the soul's discarnate existence is already covertly assumed. And since that is precisely what the argument purports to prove, the very concept of incarnation can be seen to beg the essential question.

This central objection to the Cyclical Argument may be restated. Life and existence, it may reasonably be held, both begin for a living thing at birth or conception. Yet the argument treats the predicate 'alive' as if it stood for an attribute capable of being acquired by an antecedently existing subject, and 'birth' as if it were something undergone by such a subject, rather than the coming into being of something that did not previously exist. A wedge is forced between 'being born' and 'coming into being' by predicating the former of a supposedly independent subject—'the soul'. Yet whether there *is* any such subject is just what has to be shown.

Much the same applies to the predicate 'dead'. 'That which is dead', says Socrates, 'comes to be from that which is living' (71d10–11, 72a5–6). This is, in a way, undeniable. Yet it fails to prove the posthumous existence of that which is dead. For if 'death' consists precisely in a living thing's ceasing to exist, then when someone passes from being alive to being dead, he will not, in the latter state, enjoy discarnate existence, but will have ceased to exist altogether. 'Socrates is dead' does not, on this view, ascribe a property to a persisting subject, but says merely that someone, who once lived and existed, no longer does so. Here again, a wedge might be driven between 'being dead' and 'ceasing to exist' by treating Socrates' soul as a separate subject, distinct from Socrates himself, and alternating between incarnate and discarnate states. But this would be, once again, to assume what has to be proved. See also on 64c2–9.

70c8–d6. Reference is made at 70d1 to 'our souls', i.e. the souls of individual human beings. It is not merely 'soul' in a generic sense whose survival is at issue. Nor, again, is it merely a 'universal' or 'cosmic' soul, into which individuals might somehow be 'absorbed' at death. Throughout the dialogue the speakers are concerned with the fate of their own souls (e.g. 63c1–5, 69d7–e2, 88b6–8, 95d4–e1, 115d2–4), and conclusions are continually drawn in terms of those (e.g. 71e2, 76c11, 107a1, 114d8). See also on 64e4–65a3 (p.89–90).

Hackforth points out (59, n.2) that if the *first* part of the 'ancient doctrine'—'that they do exist in that world entering it from this one'—were included as a premiss of the argument, Socrates would be taking for granted the existence of the soul in the other world after death, which is exactly what he has to prove. He thinks, however, that the argument actually rests only upon the *second* part of the 'ancient doctrine'—'that they re-enter this world and are born again from the dead'. It is true that after 'if this is so' (c8), only the second part of the doctrine is taken up again in the words 'if living people are born again from those who have died' (c8–9). Perhaps, however, the ancient doctrine should be read not as stating the premisses of an argument, but rather as formulating *in toto* what still has to be proved, that the soul passes alternately from incarnate to discarnate existence.

It is important to note that the proof of our souls' existence in Hades rests upon their being 'born again from *the dead*'. 'The dead' are those who 'have died', and who have therefore already lived. Every incarnation is thus a *re*incarnation. The shift of tense from 'the dead' (70c8, d4) to 'those who have died' (70c5, c9) suggests this—see Loriaux, 122—6. The soul could not be 'born again', it is assumed, unless it persisted in Hades between incarnations. Cf.77d3—4. Here, once again (see previous note), it is apparent that 'be born' must be taken as predicated of the soul, and not of the living things. For a living thing can be born, in the literal sense, only once.

70d7—e4. The argument is here extended to plants and animals as well as human beings. The scope of 'all things subject to coming-to-be' (d9) is not very clear. It could be interpreted broadly to include all things subject to any kind of change. That it is not limited to the genesis of living things becomes apparent when Socrates starts talking (70e1—6) about the coming-to-be of opposites. For some of the properties mentioned are not peculiar to organisms or even to physical objects.

The noun here translated 'coming-to-be' (*genesis*) corresponds to the verb discussed above (see on 70c4—8), and shares its ambiguity. 'Coming-to-be' is a key concept, and will be more fully explored later—see on 95e7—96a5 (p.170). In the present argument the noun will be used several times from 71a13 onwards for a *process* of change between each of a pair of opposite states. It has there been translated 'process of coming-to-be' or simply 'process'.

The concept of an 'opposite', though critical for the argument both here and later (102b—106e), is never defined, but is illustrated with the pairs 'beautiful' and 'ugly', 'just' and 'unjust'. These pairs are contrary rather than contradictory opposites. They may not both be truthfully asserted of a given subject at the same time, but they may both be truthfully denied. With such pairs inferences cannot be made from the denial of one member to the affirmation of the other. Cf. *Symposium* 201e—202b, *Sophist* 257b. Plato notices at 90a that such properties may lie upon a *range*. The denial of a predicate at one end of the range does not license the affirmation of a predicate at the other.

How does this affect the argument? 'Living' and 'dead' are not extremes, lying at either end of a range. Nor can things be 'very living' or 'very dead'. None the less, 'living' and 'dead' are contrary opposites. They may both be truthfully denied of a subject. For their logical asymmetry, compare 'married' and 'divorced'. To argue that what is living must earlier have been dead, and therefore still earlier living, is like arguing that someone who is, at a given time, married, must at some earlier time have been divorced, and therefore still earlier married. Yet just as someone *not yet* married cannot be divorced, so something that is *not yet* living cannot be dead. See also next note.

70e4–71a11. All the adjectives used here are in comparative form. Hackforth (64) thinks that such pairs as larger and smaller 'weaken the argument, since they are not genuine opposites'. Since opposites are never defined, it is not clear what would constitute 'genuine' ones. But the use of comparatives seems actually to strengthen the argument at this point. Socrates could hardly infer from a thing's coming to be *weak* that it must previously have been *strong*, for it might have been neither. But he can plausibly argue that if a thing comes to be *weaker* (than it was before), it must previously have been *stronger* (than it is now). This inference is valid, provided that both comparatives are filled out in the appropriate way. An inference from, e.g., 'Simmias comes to be weaker than Socrates' to 'Simmias was stronger than he now is' would be invalid. Note also that where the comparative after 'comes to be' is filled out by 'than it was before', the difference between '*x comes to be F*-er' and '*x is F*-er' becomes unimportant. For the latter implies that *x* has come to be *F*-er, and therefore that it was *G*-er (than it is now). It is, perhaps, assumed that a thing's coming to be large is equivalent to its coming to be either larger than something else or larger than itself at some previous time. For the question whether the distinction between simple and comparative forms is recognized in the *Phaedo*, see on 100e5–101b8, 102a10–d4.

The next stage of the argument will enable Socrates to dispense with comparatives altogether. But no argument relying entirely upon them could, in fact, support the claim that 'all things come to be in this way, opposite things from opposites' (71a9–10). For some opposites, such as 'odd' and 'even', have no comparative form. And no argument based solely upon comparatives could cater for 'living' and 'dead', since these do not admit of degree.

'That which is weaker' and 'that which is faster' (71a3–4) have been used here for the definite article with a neuter singular adjective in comparative form. Greek uses 'the *F*' to denote either the property *F*-ness, or a thing characterized by that property, or the class of things so characterized. The second use is relevant here. A particular thing that comes to be weaker (or faster) must previously have been stronger (or slower). This point is implicit in the use of 'things' (a10), and will be made explicit later (103a–b). See on 103a4–c9.

Socrates' 'law of opposites' may look like an inductive generalization based on the instances he gives. But it should be recognized that it owes any plausibility it has to the concepts used in its formulation. Bluck (18–19, 57) regards the Cyclical Argument as relying on 'mechanistic' principles, and suggests that Plato offers it only for the benefit of those who find mechanistic arguments impressive. But the present law is not genuinely 'mechanistic', nor is it derived from 'the study of physical phenomena'. It takes no empirical study to discover that what comes to be larger must have been smaller, or that what comes to be worse must have been better. Nor do these truths apply only to physical phenomena.

71a12–b5. A new phase of the argument begins here. Between each of a pair of opposites there is a process of coming-to-be. Every such process requires the postulation of a converse process. For the noun here translated 'process of coming-to-be' see on 70d7–e4 and 95e7–96a5 (p.170).

This passage seems to introduce a further argument to show that the living are born from the dead. After concluding at 71e2 that our souls exist in Hades, Socrates will insist that there must be a process of coming to life again, and will continue (72a4–6): '*In that way too*, then, we're agreed that living people are born from the dead.' This suggests that the appeal to reciprocal processes is meant as a second, independent argument for the conclusion.

In fact, however, the claim that there must be processes in both directions is vital for any effective use of the principle that opposites come from opposites. For the principle that whatever comes to be *F* must previously have been *G* requires that there actually *be* such a process as 'coming to be *F*'. If, for a given opposite *F*, there *is* no such process as 'coming to be *F*', the argument will break down. If, for example, there is no such process as 'coming to be unripe', it cannot be inferred from a thing's coming to be unripe that it was previously ripe. For this reason the appeal to reciprocal processes is not really a separate argument, but is essential for the working of the Cyclical Argument as a whole. It is not, indeed, clear whether Socrates recognizes it as such. But if he does, this might explain why it is introduced here, and interwoven with the reasoning that ends at 71e2.

Is there, in fact, such a process as 'coming to be alive'? In one sense there clearly is. Things come to be alive when they come into being at birth or conception. But from a thing's coming to be alive in this sense, the proper inference is not that it was previously dead, but that it did not exist previously at all. The sense of 'come to be alive' required for the argument is not that in which a living thing comes into being, but that in which a soul 'becomes incarnate' in a living body. Yet it cannot do this unless it already exists before birth or conception. And whether it does so or not is just what is at issue. See on 70c4–8 (p.105).

71b6–d4. The examples of complementary processes have a Heracleitean ring about them. Cf., e.g., DK 22 B 88, 126. That 'there are' such processes as cooling and heating is true enough. It does not follow, of course, that they continually recur in each individual thing subject to them. What has cooled down may never warm up again.

The parallel between dying and going to sleep owes its appeal, in part, to a superficial resemblance between sleep and death. Sleep, however, is a temporary state, whereas the permanence of death could not be denied without begging the question. There is, moreover, a basic difficulty in the analogy between waking up and coming to life again. Someone who wakes up exists before waking, whereas someone who comes to life, in the sense of being born or conceived, has not previously existed. A thing cannot be said to 'come to life *again*' in the sense required by the argument, unless the persistence of an independent subject, 'the soul', is already assumed. Yet this is just what has to be proved. See on 70c4–8 and previous note.

Note also that 'coming to life *again*' implies a previous life, whereas 'waking *up*' does not imply a previous waking state. The argument exploits a purely formal resemblance between the two Greek verbs. The prefix common to both of them has a quite different function in either case, shown in the words italicized. See T. M. Robinson, *Dialogue* 1969, 124–5.

What is meant by 'even if in some cases we don't use the names' (71b7–8)? Is it, as most editors assume, that not all processes have names, as do those just mentioned? Or is it that not everything that is in fact a 'process of coming-to-be' would normally be so called? On the first interpretation, the point will be that the available terminology for processes is defective; on the second, that the ordinary use of 'coming-to-be' is unduly narrow. For the relation between names and realities see on 107c1–d2.

71d5–e3. The noun 'death' is ambiguous in Greek as in English. It may refer either to (1) the process of dying, or (2) the event terminating that process, or (3) the state succeeding that event. The verb translated 'be dead' at 71c5 and 71d6 is ambiguous between (2) and (3)—see 64a6 and note 4. Here, however, (3) is clearly the sense required, both for noun and verb. For the opposite of 'death' in senses (1) and (2) would not be 'life' but 'birth' or 'conception'.

'That which is living' and 'that which is dead' have been used at 71d10—13 for the definite article and neuter singular participle. Note that when Socrates shifts to plural participles at 71d14—15, he uses both masculine and neuter forms, and thus distinguishes between 'living people' and 'living things'. The masculine form is used by itself at 70c9, 70d3—4, 72a1, 72a4—5 and 72d9, and the neuter by itself at 71d10—13, 72c7—d2 and 77c9. The argument was extended to non-human beings at 70d7—9. It is nowhere suggested, however, that human and non-human beings are animated only by the souls of their own respective kinds. On the contrary, see 81e—82b.

71e4—72a10. The word here translated 'obvious' (e5) may mean either 'observable' or 'certain'. Thus the meaning may be either that people can be observed to die, or that it is certain that they die. The process of 'coming to life again' is, as Socrates seems to recognize, neither observable nor certain. It is not, of course, made any more believable by the fact that dying is both observable and certain. There is, moreover, a peculiar difficulty in understanding what 'coming to life again' means. Socrates is thinking, evidently, not of 'resurrection' or 'rising from the dead', in which bodily identity is maintained, but rather of 'reincarnation', in which the soul is conceived as entering a fresh body. Yet the whole idea of the soul's 'entering' a body is perplexing. For it seems to require that the body be thought of as already existing, prior to incarnation, just as a gaol exists prior to a man's imprisonment in it. Yet there is, of course, no separate body existing before conception in the way that a corpse exists after death. The genesis of a living thing cannot, therefore, consist in the animation of an already existing, but previously inanimate, body. Nor is it easy to suppose that the soul, if it is a 'life-principle', enters the body at any point after conception has occurred. For it is natural to associate the start of life with conception itself.

72a11—d5. The logical role of this passage is not very clear. It is sometimes treated as merely ancillary to the main argument. Note, however, that it is introduced to justify 'admissions' made earlier (72a11—12). These have rested partly upon the postulate that there is such a thing as coming to life again (see on 71a12—b5). Socrates has so far gained assent to this postulate by simply rejecting the possibility of nature's being 'lame' as an obviously unpalatable alternative (71e9). As if the point were not yet firmly established, he has said (71e14—72a2) that *if* there is such a thing as coming to life again, it will consist in a process of coming-to-be from dead to living people. The present passage may be meant, therefore, to secure the postulate: a process of coming to life again must be assumed, to prevent everything from ending up dead. Taken in this way, the passage supplies a fundamental principle for the whole argument. But several uncertainties remain.

(1) At 72b5 the translation 'they would cease from coming to be' differs from Hackforth's 'the coming into being of things would be at an end', and from Bluck's 'everything . . . would cease from being born'. The supposed consequences of a linear universe may be not merely that things would cease from 'being born' or 'coming into being', but that they would cease from 'coming to be *anything*', i.e. from acquiring any new character at all. For they would remain permanently frozen in one of a pair of opposite states.

(2) The idea that in a linear universe all things would end up having 'the same form' (72b4) is illustrated with the examples of all things being asleep, and Anaxagoras' 'all things together' (72b7–c5). It is not clear, however, whether these suppositions are meant merely to lead up to the crucial case of life and death (72c5–d3), or whether they are thought of as absurd in themselves. Is it being suggested that a perpetually dormant universe is inconceivable? If it is, Socrates does not say why he finds it so.

(3) The argument at 72d1–3 is too cryptic to be reconstructed with confidence. The translation 'if the living things came to be from the other things' follows Burnet's text. But what are 'the other things'? They cannot be 'the dead' (Bluck: 'the other world'). For the hypothesis that living things come from them seems to be counterfactual, whereas Socrates holds that living things actually *do* come from the dead. Burnet takes 'the other things' to mean 'things other than the dead', and Hackforth (62, n.5) emends the text to obtain this sense. Alternatively, the hypothesis may be that living things come from 'things other than the living', i.e. from non-living sources. In that case, if living things were to die, without subsequently being reborn (cf.72c7–8), then when the 'other', non-living sources were exhausted, all possible sources would be used up. Everything would then be 'spent in being dead' (72d3). Note, however, that if 'the other things' are conceived as 'sources', from which new living things are generated, there has been a shift from the sense in which opposite things were originally said to 'come to be' from each other. See on 70c4–8 (p.104).

(4) It is apparently assumed without argument that the possible sources of life are finite and constant. Support for this assumption is sometimes found in *Republic* 611a, where it is argued that the number of souls must be 'always the same'. There, however, constancy in the number of souls does not support, but rests upon, acceptance of their immortality. For it is adduced as a rider to the conclusion

that the soul is immortal. The proof of this rider assumes, without further explanation, that everything's 'ending up immortal' is inconceivable.

(5) The present argument makes the complementary assumption that everything could not conceivably end up dead. This also is left unexplained; and it is natural for a modern reader to ask why the implication that all life would eventually be exhausted should discredit a view that gives rise to it. For it seems to us conceivable, and even likely, that this will happen. It has to be recognized that Plato's view of the physical world as a whole is organic. The universe is itself a living thing. The present assumption may be connected with the principle that 'nothing can come from nothing or disappear into nothing'. See on 105e10–107a1 (p.220).

72d6–e2. The three main propositions which the Cyclical Argument purports to have established are resumed here in order of logical priority. The translation follows Burnet and most editors in omitting the final words (72e1–2), 'and it is better for the good souls, and worse for the bad ones', as an edifying 'enrichment' of the text. In substance they recall 63c6–7, but they are logically and grammatically out of place here.

3.2 The Recollection Argument (72e3–78b3)

It is now argued that what we call 'learning' consists in 'recollection', the recovery of knowledge possessed in a former existence. The soul must, therefore, have existed before birth.

72e3–7. The doctrine of Recollection (*anamnēsis*) is one of the best-known of all Platonic themes. It is prominent in the *Meno* (80d–86c), and is briefly mentioned in the *Phaedrus* (249e–250c). It is introduced here as a familiar tenet (e4–5), and its significance goes well beyond the present context. Both here and in the *Meno* the immortality of the soul is inferred from it, but its philosophical interest is largely independent of that conclusion.

Although the doctrine states broadly that so-called 'learning' is recollection (73b5, 75e5, 76a6–7), it does not cover everything to which the term 'learning' would ordinarily be applied. It does not, for example, include the learning of factual information, learning by rote, or the learning of skills. It should be borne in mind that the word translated 'learn' can also mean 'understand'. For it is with coming to understand certain concepts, in particular those that give rise to the Theory of Forms, that the doctrine of Recollection is concerned.

'Recollection' has been used throughout the translation, and in these notes, for the noun *anamnēsis*, and 'be reminded' has been used for the cognate Greek verb. Note, however, that 'recollection', as ordinarily used, is too broad a term for the context and is used here only for want of a suitable English noun cognate with 'remind'. The key element in the process that Socrates describes at 73c–74a is that on perceiving one thing, a person should think of another. But 'recollection' need not be occasioned by any such experience. 'Be reminded' is closer to the Greek verb both in grammar and sense. In Greek as in English, one is 'reminded of Y by X', where Y and X are the thing remembered and the reminding item.

The translation and the notes on this section of the dialogue owe numerous points to the valuable article by J. L. Ackrill in *Exegesis and Argument*, 177–195.

72e7–73a3. The Recollection doctrine is here taken to imply that the soul existed before being born into human form. The reasoning has some force. If 'we', who are now reminded of certain things, are to be identified with 'we' who formerly learned them, and if, as the coming argument will try to show, 'we' learned them before entering human form, then 'we' who learned them cannot be identified with the whole human being, the present composite of body and soul, since before our entry into human form our present bodies did not exist. Hence prenatal learning requires a pre-existing subject—'the soul'. See also on 76c11–13.

The Recollection Argument partly resembles the Cyclical Argument. Both turn upon the idea that if, at any given time, we are *re-X*ed ('*re*-born', '*re*-minded'), we must already have existed before that time. For if we had not thus existed, we could never have been *X*ed, and therefore could not possibly be *re-X*ed. But the Recollection Argument escapes an objection raised earlier against the previous argument. 'Being reminded' is a familiar predicate, intelligible without special assumptions. But 'being reborn' is not intelligible unless a previously existing soul is presupposed (see on 70c8–d6). The Recollection Argument cannot be convicted in this way of assuming what has to be proved.

At 73a2 the word translated 'immortal' occurs for the first time in the dialogue. For the difficulty of interpreting it consistently with the earlier definition of 'death', see on 64c2–9 (p.87). It may surprise a modern reader that the soul's prenatal existence should be taken as evidence for its immortality. 'How', it has been asked, 'can pre-existence be evidence for post-existence?' (E. J. Furlong, *Hermathena* 1940, 65). But 'immortality' must cover more than 'post-existence'. Cebes will say later (77c1–2) that only half what is needed has been shown. The Recollection Argument proves only the prenatal 'half' of the total immortality thesis. Cf. *Meno* 81b3—6, 81c5—7, where 'immortality' is understood not merely as 'post-existence', but as persistence through a series of incarnations. See also on 95b5—e6, 105d13—e9.

73a4—b10. For the translation at 73a7—b2 see note 19. These lines, although not necessarily an allusion to the *Meno*, clearly refer to the method there followed. Socrates questions a slave boy, previously unversed in geometry, and elicits from him the right solution to a geometrical problem. The present argument for Recollection is offered as an alternative to a proof of that sort (b3—4), and differs from the 'reminding' of the slave boy in several respects. (i) It makes no reference to any mathematical problem, but mentions only judgements about the deficiency of sensible things. (ii) It is concerned with the understanding of concepts, rather than with the proof of propositions. (iii) It does not introduce the Recollection doctrine in the context of a 'what is *F*?' inquiry, or to overcome an apparent obstacle to such an inquiry. (iv) In the *Meno* no stress is placed upon the use of the senses, whereas Recollection will here be said to be occasioned by their use (74b4—5, 75a11—b2, e3—4). (v) No mention is made in the *Meno* of Forms, whereas in the *Phaedo* they are of central importance.

Nevertheless, both passages are concerned with the mathematical and value notions that give rise to the Theory of Forms (see on 65d4—e5, p.95). Both may be viewed as concerned with '*a priori* knowledge'. See R. E. Allen, *R.M.* 1959—60, 165—74, N. Gulley, *C.Q.* 1954, 194—213, G. Vlastos, *Dialogue* 1965, 143—67.

'Knowledge' and 'correct account' (a9—10) are interrelated, the former involving the ability to provide the latter—see on 76b4—c10. At 73b1 the word translated 'diagrams' could mean 'proofs'. Cf. *Cratylus* 436d2, and see Gulley, op.cit. 197. 'Diagrams' would fit the context well enough, however, and the words 'or anything else of that sort' can then be easily explained as referring to solid models (cf. Hackforth, 67, n.1). The words 'that this is so' (b2) are consistent with either the 'diagram' or the 'proof' interpretation. They may refer to the fact that people can answer well-framed questions correctly, or to the inference that 'knowledge and a correct account' are present within them. Either of these things could be made clear by introducing them to proofs or to diagrams.

73c1—3. Socrates here begins to formulate conditions for 'being reminded'. Are these conditions intended as necessary or sufficient, or as both? This point is critical for the structure of the Recollection Argument. Necessary conditions would enable inferences to be drawn

from the Recollection doctrine. Sufficient conditions would enable
the doctrine itself to be inferred. Unfortunately, the conditions
seem to vary in this respect. The one given here, that what one is
reminded of one must previously have known, is represented, like the
one given at 74a5–8, as necessary. But the requirements that on
perceiving one thing one think of another (73c4–d1), and that one
should have forgotten the latter (73e1–4), seem meant as sufficient
('whenever' 73c4, 73d5, 73e2). The application of these conditions
to the case in which we think of the Form Equal on perceiving its
sensible instances is therefore problematic.

J. Gosling (*Phronesis* 1965, 155) has suggested that all of the
conditions are meant as both necessary and sufficient. But there is
nothing in the text to suggest this, nor could it reasonably be maintained. Thinking of one thing upon perceiving another is obviously
not a necessary condition for being reminded of the former. At 73e1
it is said to constitute 'a kind of' Recollection, i.e. only a single form
of it. And Simmias' joking use of the word at 73b7 shows that it is
possible to be reminded of things in a very different way, namely by
verbal prompting from another person. Cf. also 60c9, 105a5.

73c4–d11. Two further conditions for 'being reminded' are now
given: (1) on seeing, hearing, or getting some other sense-perception
of a thing, one 'not only recognizes that thing, but also thinks of
something else' (c6–8); and (2) what is thought of must be the
object 'not of the same knowledge but of another' (c8).

(1) The meaning of the first condition depends on the sense of
the verb translated 'recognize' at 73c7 and 73d7. This is an ordinary
word for 'know', but is distinct from the verb that will mainly be
used for 'knowing' the Forms. It can, like the English 'know', mean
'recognize'; and it is plausible to hold that if one is to be reminded
of Y on perceiving X, one must, indeed, not merely perceive X, but
must also notice features of X by reference to which the association
of Y with it in thought can be explained. Cf. J. L. Ackrill,
E.A. 182–3.

At 73d5–8 lovers are said to 'recognize' their favourite's lyre,
and get in their minds the form of its owner. Does 'recognizing' here
consist merely in recognizing the instrument as *a lyre*? Or do they
recognize it as *its owner's* lyre? If the latter, it may be asked if their
thinking of the boy is a separate mental act, distinct from recognizing
the lyre. Are they not already thinking of the boy, in recognizing
the lyre as his? A similar question arises in the crucial example of
Simmias and his picture (73e9–10). In recognizing the picture as
one *of him*, it seems that we should *eo ipso* necessarily be thinking
of Simmias himself. If so, the question would arise whether the

thing thought of and the thing perceived are, in this case, objects of 'another knowledge', i.e. whether the *second* condition here laid down for 'being reminded' has been met. This bears on the later suggestion that sensible equals 'remind' us of the Form Equal (74c7–d3). For it might be objected that in recognizing sensible equals as such, we are *eo ipso* thinking of Equality. The Form and its instances would not then be objects of 'another knowledge', and the conditions for our being reminded of the former by the latter would not be met.

(2) Hackforth (67, n.4) rightly rejects Burnet's view that the point of the second condition is merely to exclude cases where one member of a pair of opposites, such as odd and even, or darkness and light, reminds us of the other. Although the idea that opposites are objects of the same knowledge will appear later (97d5), it has no relevance here. But Hackforth's own explanation is also dubious. He suggests that Socrates means to exclude cases in which perceived features of a man might remind us of things we know about him but do not perceive. For the latter features would form part of 'our total knowledge of the man', and would therefore be objects of 'the same knowledge'. But, in that case, how should 'our total knowledge of the man' be defined? Why should it not include his lyre or his cloak, so that these too, contrary to the suggestion of 73d3–4, would be objects of 'the same knowledge'? Moreover, why should the cases Hackforth refers to be excluded as irrelevant for Socrates' purpose? The point of the exclusion remains obscure.

At 73d3–4 it is agreed that 'knowledge of a man is other than that of a lyre'. This might be taken to mean merely that the concept of a man is different from that of a lyre. But such an interpretation would not suit all the examples of 'being reminded' that follow. One may be reminded of Cebes on seeing Simmias (d9). Yet these two, since both are men, would presumably instantiate the same concept, and thus, if concepts were meant, would be objects of 'the same knowledge'. If the knowledge of Cebes is different from that of Simmias, what makes it so? Not the mere fact that they are numerically distinct, for it would then be otiose to add the condition at all. It would be met automatically in any case where the thing thought of was numerically distinct from the thing perceived.

Ackrill has suggested (op.cit. 184–5) that knowledge of Y is 'other' than knowledge of X if the thought of the former is not already given in the recognition of the latter. Thus, one may see and recognize Simmias, or a picture of Simmias (73e6–7), without *eo ipso* thinking of Cebes. If this is the meaning, then, as Ackrill says, the condition will be infringed by the case of Simmias and his picture, since one cannot recognize a picture of Simmias without *eo ipso* thinking of Simmias himself. It is unclear whether the condition, as thus interpreted, would be satisfied in the case of the Form Equality and its sensible instances. See (1) above. In any case, no use appears to be made of it in what follows. Socrates will make no effort to show that the Form Equality is, in fact, the object of a different knowledge from its sensible instances. He will show only that it is non-identical with them (74b7–c6).

73e1–74a4. The further examples of Recollection given here are so arranged as to lead up to the case of Simmias and his picture (a9–10), which best illustrates the relation between Forms and sensible particulars. But it is hard to see why so many examples are given, and in particular why 'being reminded by dissimilars' is illustrated at such length, since cases of this sort will play no part in the coming argument about Forms and particulars. Why does Socrates insist that there is Recollection from dissimilar things (74a2–3, cf.74c11–d2, 76a3–4), as well as from similar? Hackforth (68, n.1) suggests that he does so because 'a particular is obviously "like" a Form, and yet may be said to be unlike it because they belong to different orders of existence'. But the case of Simmias and his picture would seem well suited, and sufficient, to make a point of this sort, whereas the case of a lyre and its owner seems quite unsuited to it. For those objects, although unlike each other, both belong to the *same* order of existence.

As J. L. Ackrill has pointed out (*E.A.* 188–9), recollection from similars is, in one important respect, not parallel with recollection from dissimilars. One may think of Simmias on seeing his picture *because* it is like him. But one does not think of a boy on seeing his lyre *because* it is unlike him. Similarity may be part of the associative mechanism, whereas dissimilarity is not. See on 74c7–d3 and 75d7–76b3.

74a5–8. It is here agreed that whenever one is reminded of a thing by something like it, one must consider whether the reminding object 'is lacking at all, in its similarity, in relation to what one is reminded of'. This assertion could hardly be defended as a necessary condition for all cases of being reminded from similars. Only in the special cases in which the reminding item is not merely *like*, but also *a likeness of*, what one is reminded of, does it have any plausibility.

But the claim is dubious even in these cases. J. Gosling (*Phronesis* 1965, 151–61) has argued that it would be implausible to hold as a necessary, or even as a common, condition of 'being reminded' of a person by his picture, that one must assess it as a likeness of him. He therefore suggests that a picture is judged as 'lacking' simply in virtue of its being an image, and thus, precisely because it is an image, failing to possess some features of its original (cf. *Cratylus* 432b–c). Thus, one who is reminded of Simmias by his picture must judge that it 'falls short', e.g. in virtue of its being two-dimensional.

The point is crucial for the interpretation of the later assertion (74d4–8) that sensible equals appear to us to 'fall short' of the Form. On Gosling's view they do so, not because they are not as equal as the Form, or because they fail to be exactly equal, but because they are mere sensible instances of Equality, and must, as such, differ from the Form itself.

This interpretation is attractive. It frees Socrates from making the unsupported claim that sensible equals, unlike the Form, are never exactly equal. However, (i) is it, in fact, necessary that, in being reminded of someone by his picture, one should consider whether it falls short of him, and always hold that it does so? Must one, if one is to be reminded of somebody by a pencil sketch of him, attend to the fact that it is black-and-white and only a few inches long? Are not such things simply taken for granted and disregarded, rather than consciously noticed? (ii) At 74e2–5 it is asserted that whenever one judges that this X falls short of that Y, one must have known Y previously. But this could hardly be held necessary for judging that a picture 'falls short' of its original in Gosling's sense. One may readily judge that a picture falls short of its original in this way, whether one has previously known the original or not. Only if the picture has to be compared with its original, as Socrates says we 'compare' sensible particulars with Forms (76e2), is prior knowledge of the original required.

74a9–b1. The Form Equal is introduced here, and will be used as a specimen Form in the coming argument. For the Theory of Forms generally see on 65d4–e5.

The words translated 'we say, surely, that there is something *equal*' (74a9–10) might be rendered 'we say, don't we, that equal *is* something', in conformity with the Greek idiom 'X is something' for 'there is such a thing as X' (see on 64c2–9). However, the continuation 'I don't mean a log to a log, or a stone to a stone' follows more naturally if 'equal' is taken predicatively. The translation follows the explanation of these lines given by G. E. L. Owen, *A.D.* 114–5. See also note 5, and on 100b1–c8.

74b2–3. More literally, 'we know it, what it is'. The pronoun 'it' refers to the Form Equal, and functions both as direct object of 'know' and as subject of the 'what' clause. Cf., e.g., *Republic* 354c, and see note 21. Verbs of knowing, in Greek as in English, can govern a direct object or an indirect question. Note that 'he knows the man who is on duty' could mean either 'he is acquainted with the man who is on duty' or 'he knows which man is on duty'. These are logically independent statements (neither entails the other), but their meanings converge in the common Greek construction in which a noun is taken both as direct object of 'know' and as subject of the interrogative clause. This construction helps to assimilate 'knowing what F is' to 'knowing the Form F'. The assimilation is natural, given Plato's use of 'what F is' as a standard designation for the Form F (see on 75c7–d6), and given also his tendency to treat the quest for definitions as a search for Forms (see on 65c2–4).

The assertion that 'we know what the Form Equal is', assuming its equivalence to 'we know the Form Equal', appears to be contradicted at 76b4–c3. It is there denied that all men know the Forms, on the ground that they cannot give an account of them, and that the ability to do so is necessary for knowledge (see on 76b4–c10). This contradiction could be avoided in one of two ways. (i) The sense of 'know' might be less strict here than at 76b–c. Here it might be meant merely that we have the concept of equality, 'know what it is' for normal human purposes; whereas the 'knowledge' referred to at 76b–c would require the ability to give a philosophical analysis of it. This, however, would involve (a) an unacknowledged shift in the meaning of 'know', and (b) a shift in the reference of 'we' from 74b1, where it means 'we philosophers', to 74b2, where it would mean 'people in general'. Alternatively, (ii) 'we' might be taken to mean here not 'people in general', but 'we philosophers' (cf.74a9–b1, 75d2, 76d8, and 78d1). This would limit the scope of the Recollection Argument to the souls of philosophers. But no such limitation is indicated in the Recollection Argument itself. Indeed, 76c4 says that even those who cannot 'give an account' of the Forms are reminded of them. This suggests that Recollection is not a philosopher's privilege, but, as in the *Meno*, is possible for human beings generally. See also next note.

74b4–6. The claim that we thought of the Form Equal, or got the knowledge of it, from sensible things recurs several times (74c7–10, 75a5–7, 75a11–b3, and cf.75e3–5), and is evidently vital to the argument. Yet its meaning depends upon that of the question at 74b4 'where did we get the knowledge of it?', and this is far from obvious. Is Socrates asking (i) from what source we (people in general) acquired the concept equality, i.e. how we learnt, for ordinary purposes, to recognize things as equal, and to describe them as such? Or is he asking (ii) from what sources we (philosophers) became acquainted with the Form Equal, i.e. how we came to acknowledge its existence and to discover its nature? Is he concerned with ordinary concept formation, or with philosophical clarification? Uncertainty on this point pervades the whole argument.

There is difficulty on either view. (i) The assertion that we acquired the concept of equality 'from' sensible equals, or 'from' sensing them, although perhaps congenial to common sense, would be a jejune answer to a complex empirical question. Clearly, much more would need to be said about how we learnt to compare and measure sensible things in order to judge them equal. The role of counting would have to be considered. And it would need to be shown that we could have acquired the concept in no other way (75a6) than through sensing.

Alternatively, (ii) if Socrates is talking about the clarification of concepts, his insistence that we could acquire knowledge of the Form Equal only from sensing particular equals must seem surprising, in view of his continual disparagement of the senses elsewhere (65a9− 66a10, 79a, 83a−b). They are denounced as nothing but a hindrance in the quest for Forms (see on 65b1−7). Socrates will later tell how he gave up using them in his own inquiries (99d4−e6). How then could we, in using the senses (75e3), regain the very knowledge to which they have been said to deny us access?

74b7−c6. This passage is of the utmost importance for understanding the Theory of Forms, since it argues that the Form Equal, and by implication many other Forms (cf.75c10−d5), must be nonidentical with their sensible instances. It should therefore throw light upon the motives from which the Forms are 'separated' from sensible things in the fully-fledged version of the Theory adopted in this dialogue (see on 65d4−e5, p.94). Unfortunately, the argument itself is much vexed, and has become a notorious philosophical crux. See especially J. L. Ackrill, *P.R.* 1958, 106−8, and K. W. Mills, *Phronesis* 1957, 128−47, 1958, 40−58.

The non-identity of the Form Equal with its sensible instances is inferred from the fact that the latter do, but the former does not, possess a certain property. Thus, the argument is of the following form: sensible equals have the property P; but the Form Equal does not have that property; therefore sensible equals and the Form Equal are not the same thing. However, (1) what exactly is P? And (2) why does Socrates use the expression 'the equals themselves' (plural) at 74c1, unparalleled elsewhere in the dialogue, instead of 'the equal itself', his usual expression for the Form, which reappears in the conclusion at 74c4−5?

(1) The property ascribed to equal stones and logs at 74b8−9 has

been interpreted in four different ways. Socrates may be suggesting (a) that equal stones and logs, while remaining the same, seem equal to one observer but not to another; or (b) that they seem equal to one thing but not to another; or (c) that they seem equal in one respect (e.g. length) but not in another (e.g. weight); or (d) that sometimes, while remaining the same, they seem equal at one time, but not at another. (a), (b), and (c) are all based upon Burnet's text. (d) is based upon a variant reading with good MS. authority (see note 22).

Each interpretation has its supporters, and none can be conclusively disproved. It is, however, doubtful whether the Greek will bear sense (c), and it will not be further considered here. (d) is defended by Verdenius, who glosses the lines thus: 'under certain conditions, e.g. when you are walking around two equal stones, they in turn seem equal and unequal, whereas under other conditions, e.g. when you are sitting in front of them, they do not show such a variation in their mutual relation.' Verdenius argues that the temporal reference at 74c1 ('did the equals themselves *ever* seem . . .') requires a temporal contrast at 74b8–9. But just such a contrast is provided by the word 'sometimes', so the variant reading is not needed to obtain it. Nor does the fact that Socrates refers at 74c1 to only a single observer ('to you') tell in favour of the variant reading, as Verdenius supposes. For if Burnet's text is not interpreted in sense (a), as referring to different observers, the fact that only a single observer is mentioned at 74c1 would not tell against it at all. (d) is therefore a possible interpretation, but by no means necessary.

The present translation, 'sometimes seem equal to one, but not to another', is deliberately ambiguous between (a) and (b). With (a) the point will be that two different observers could disagree as to whether logs or stones were equal, whereas no such disagreement would be possible with respect to the Form Equal. With (b) the point will be that logs and stones can have contrasted predicates in different relations, whereas the Form Equal cannot.

Both interpretations are grammatically acceptable, but neither is without logical difficulty. For (a) see Mills, op.cit. 129–31. For (b) see N. R. Murphy, *I.P.R.* 111, n.1, answered by Hackforth, *C.R.* 1952, 159. It is, indeed, a common enough Platonic reproach to sensible *F*s, that they are only relatively *F*, and may, when viewed in a different relation, appear not to be *F*, or to be the opposite of it, *G*. Cf., e.g., *Republic* 479–80, 523c–524c. However, (i) since any given sensible equal is always unequal to something, it is somewhat odd to say that this seems to be the case only 'sometimes'. (ii) It is very hard to suppose that the Form Equal is itself free from this defect, if this means attributing equality to it (see on 74d4–8, p.128).

And (iii) the names of the Forms mentioned at 75c11–d1, to which the argument in general is supposed to apply, could not, on interpretation (b), be directly substituted for 'equal' at 74b8 without any further changes of wording, whereas on interpretation (a) they easily could. None of these objections to (b) is decisive, however, and the argument, if taken in this sense, can readily be adapted to the other relevant Forms–see G. E. L. Owen, *S.P.M.* 306. Either (a) or (b) therefore remains a defensible reading of Burnet's text.

Note that *all* the defects of sensible equals that feature in the above interpretations are implicitly ascribed to instances of the Form Beauty at *Symposium* 211a1–5. The doubt as to which particular defect is here in question should not be allowed to obscure the basic case for 'separating' Forms from sensibles to which they all contribute. The essential point, on any interpretation, is that no sensible F can be the true nominatum of 'F', can be 'that which F is', because all sensible Fs admit also of being called 'G'. Yet 'F' and 'G' are names for two different and opposite things, so anything that admits of both names cannot be 'what F is'. The Form F must therefore be something 'other than', distinct from, its sensible instances. See Mills, op.cit. 145–7, and R. E. Allen, *R.M.* 1961, 328–9.

(2) Plato's use of the unusual plural, 'the equals themselves', has been variously interpreted. Burnet, Hackforth (69, n.2), Bluck (67, n.3), and W. D. Ross (*Plato's Theory of Ideas*, 23–5, 60) take it to refer to non-sensible mathematical objects, such as the angles at the base of an isosceles triangle. But equals of that sort would be irrelevant to the conclusion that sensible equals differ from the *Form* Equal, which is what the argument purports to prove. Moreover, as Ackrill has pointed out (op.cit. 108), the premiss would on this interpretation be false, since one might, if unfamiliar with the relevant Euclidean theorem, suppose that the angles at the base of an isosceles triangle were not equal, or not suppose that they were.

R. S. Bluck (*Phronesis* 1959, 5–11) proposes to read back into the present passage the distinction drawn later (102d6–103b5) between the Forms Large or Small and the Large or Small 'in us'. The Forms 'in us', which he calls 'Form-copies', may also, he thinks, be exemplified by 'the equals themselves' of 74c1. But it seems unlikely that a distinction not drawn till much later, having no obvious relevance to the present context, should suddenly be introduced here without explanation. See J. M. Rist, *Phronesis* 1964, 28–9.

If the premiss at 74c1–3 is to be both relevant to the argument and true, 'the equals themselves' is best understood as an alternative designation for the Form Equal, used, like 'equality' later in the same line, as a variant for 'the equal itself'. Cf. *Parmenides* 128e–

129b, and see Rist, op.cit. 29–30. The plural designation is sometimes attributed to the fact that 'equal' implies at least two terms.
It has been further suggested that this Form was conceived by
Plato as a set of two (or more) Equals, a bipartite (or multipartite)
entity, that could appropriately serve as a standard to which sensible
equals approximate. See P. T. Geach, *P.R.* 1956, 76, Mills, op.cit.
49–50, and G. Vlastos, *S.P.M.* 287–91. But this explanation of the
plural is neither free from difficulty nor necessary. 'Equal' has just
been used (74b8) in the plural of logs and stones. As Owen has
suggested (*A.D.* 114–15), the word is quite naturally picked up in
its plural form when Socrates switches attention to the Form. In any
case, whatever the explanation of the plural may be, there need be
no shift of subject in the two halves of Socrates' question at 74c1–2.
When he adds the second half, 'or (did) equality (ever seem to you
to be) inequality?', he is asking a question about the same entity as
in the first half, namely the Form of Equality.

It may still be asked, however, how the predicate terms 'unequal'
and 'inequality' in the two halves of the question are to be understood. Do they both alike stand for the Form of Inequality? If so,
the second half of the question will simply be a doublet of the first,
the 'or' between them having the force of 'i.e.' or 'that is to say'.
In both halves, Socrates will be scouting the possibility of identifying
Equality with Inequality. But this view appears to render the whole
question inappropriate to the argument. For the predicate which will
then be denied of the Form Equality in the second premiss will
differ from that which was affirmed of the logs and stones in the
first. They, it was said, can seem to be 'unequal', whereas the
Form of Equality, it is now said, cannot seem to be 'inequality'. Yet
the predicate in question needs to be the same in both premisses if
the argument is to go through.

It might therefore be supposed that the first half of the question
is scouting the possibility of the Form of Equality's being unequal,
whereas only the second is denying that it could be identified with
Inequality. This would make the first half of the question relevant
to the argument. But the second half would still need to be explained.
For the alleged impossibility of identifying Equality with Inequality
would then be left without a clear role in the reasoning.

Robin translates the lines as follows: 'Mais quoi? L'Égal en soi
s'est-il en quelque cas montré à toi inégal, c'est-à-dire l'Egalité, une
inégalité?'. Such a translation would enable 'inequality' to be understood as meaning '*an* inequality', i.e. an instance of inequality. This
would bring the second half of the question into line with the first.
In effect, Socrates would be asking, once again, whether the Form
of Equality has ever seemed unequal. But 'inequality' is not easily

taken in this way. For given that 'equality' has just been used as the name of a Form, 'inequality' is naturally read likewise as standing for a Form, rather than for an instance of one. What is needed for the argument is a premiss to the effect that the Form of Equality can never (seem to) be unequal. The required premiss is of the form 'the Form F can never (seem to) be G'. Now, as noted earlier (see on 64d4–e5, p.93), Forms are designated with apparent indifference by adjectives and abstract nouns alike. We may therefore suppose that assertions of the form 'the Form F can never (seem to) be G' were not felt to be as distinct from those of the form 'the Form F can never (seem to) be G-ness' as they appear to us to be. Failure to distinguish between (A) 'Equality can never (seem to) be unequal' and (B) 'Equality can never (seem to) be Inequality' would be understandable if the Form Equality was taken to be the true bearer of the names 'unequal' and 'inequality' alike. It would be all the more intelligible if the predicative function of the verb 'to be' was not yet clearly distinguished from its role as an identity sign (see on 65c2–4). For it might then be thought that (A) and (B) were simply equivalent ways of denying that equality could ever (seem to) be unequal. On this view the second half of the question at 74c1–2 would appear as a perfectly natural variant for the first. For an explanation along these lines see Mills, op.cit. 48–9.

Note, however, that Inequality, if it is to be construed as a Form, cannot be understood in a manner altogether parallel to Equality, as the latter Form figures in the ensuing argument. For sensible unequals could hardly be held to 'fall short' of Inequality in the way that sensible equals may be held to fall short of Equality. On a common interpretation of 74d4–e8, it will be suggested that equal logs and stones exemplify Equality imperfectly. But *un*equal logs and stones would seem to exemplify *In*equality as well as could be desired. If so, it would be strange to postulate a paradigm of Perfect Inequality. This illustrates a general difficulty about the scope of the Theory of Forms, which arises if their roles as 'universals' and 'paradigms' are confused. For certain pairs of opposites, notably for value concepts such as 'good' and 'bad', 'just' and 'unjust', it is only one member of the pair that is naturally thought of as an ideal, of which particular things fall short. It may therefore be doubted whether 'paradigmatic' Forms are admissible for certain concepts whose title to 'universal' Forms is as good as any. See on 65d4–e5 (p.97).

74c7–d3. For the interpretation of 74c7–10 see on 74b4–6. Here, as above, Socrates speaks simply of our getting knowledge of the Form from particular sensible equals. He draws no distinction between acts of sensing and objects sensed. But he later uses a variety of expressions (75a7, 75a11, 75b1, 75b6, 75e3, 76d9) which suggest that it is, strictly, our sensing of things, rather than the things themselves, that occasions our thought of the Form. It is, however, unclear in several of these passages whether the translation 'senses' or 'sense-perceptions' more nearly expresses the meaning. See on 65b1—7.

At 74c11—13 it is noted that the Form may be either similar or dissimilar to its sensible instances, but that this 'makes no difference': provided that from seeing X we think of Y, recollection has occurred, whether X and Y are similar or dissimilar. The point of insisting on this here is not clear, but there seems no reason to follow Archer-Hind in excising the lines. It has not yet become apparent that being reminded of a Form by its sensible instances is a case of being reminded by similars. And the claim that one may be reminded either by similars or dissimilars will be reiterated at 76a3—4.

Bluck translates 74c11: 'Presumably either because it is like them, or else because it is unlike?' But it is incorrect to take 'being' in this line as a causal participle. It would be inappropriate to suggest that we might be reminded by sensible equals of the Form *because* it is unlike them (see on 73e1—74a4). Bluck glosses the line: 'because they resemble it, or because they are associated with it only in thought' (67, n.4). But 'being associated with it only in thought' is not equivalent to 'being unlike it', nor does it correctly express the relation between unlike objects, one of which reminds us of the other. The boy at 73d5—8 is not associated with his lyre or cloak 'only in thought', but because he has been observed to use them. Any causal explanation of someone's being reminded of him on seeing them would have to mention this fact.

74c13—d3, like 73c4—d1, represents 'thinking of Y from seeing X' as a sufficient condition for 'being reminded of Y'. But one might, surely, think of Y from seeing X, without being reminded of the former, e.g. when one imagined Y or made it up. The condition mentioned is not, in fact, sufficient for 'being reminded', unless it be stipulated that Y is something previously known. But, with respect to the Form Equal, this is precisely what has to be proved. See J. L. Ackrill, *E.A.* 186—7.

74d4—8. Socrates now makes the point, to be repeated several times, that we think of sensible equals as 'falling short' of the Form Equal. The Form is here referred to as 'what it is itself'. For this phrase see on 75c7—d6 (p.131) and note 24. The phrase translated 'the instances in the logs' contains no word as specific as 'instances'.

More literally: 'the things in the logs'.

Why, and in what sense, are we said to think that sensible equals 'fall short' of the Form, or that they 'strive', unsuccessfully, to be like it (75a2–3, b1–2, b7–8)? The usual interpretation of these remarks is that the Form is never perfectly realized in its sensible instances. Cf. Burnet's notes on 65d4, 74a9, 74e9, 75c11, and see on 65d4–e5 (p.96). The Form F serves as a paradigm, a perfect exemplar or standard F, to which sensible Fs can only approximate, and against which they may be judged: no sensible equal is ever exactly equal; only the Form Equal is so. On this view, 'F' not only names the Form F, but can be predicated of it. Indeed, strictly, it is only of the Form F that it is predicated correctly.

The Theory of Forms, as thus interpreted, gives rise to a number of acute difficulties. (i) It is hard to imagine how the Form Equal could function in the way proposed, or to believe that in practice it ever really does so. To suppose that we might determine whether one log is equal to another by comparing either or both of them with a non-sensible Form, to see if they share its character, seems a travesty of what we actually do. To find out if they are equal, or how nearly equal they are, we measure them not against Equality but against each other, or against some other sensible object, such as a ruler.

(ii) The judgement that two logs are not exactly equal is no doubt of a kind that we do sometimes make. We know that our senses or instruments are inaccurate, and we may therefore suppose that closer measurement would always reveal inequalities that had previously escaped us. But in judging that two logs are not exactly equal, we do not take ourselves to be comparing them with a non-sensible Form, and finding that they lack a property which it alone possesses. Indeed, we may make such judgements without supposing that any such entity exists.

(iii) It is debatable whether, in order to be able to make such judgements as 'these logs are not exactly equal', we must previously have been acquainted with something which *is* exactly equal. More generally, it is not clear that judgements to the effect that 'X is not exactly F' require prior acquaintance with an x that *is* exactly F. Must we have encountered perfection in order to recognize imperfection?

(iv) As noted at 65d4–e5, the Form F functions, in some contexts at least, as a 'universal': it is the character F-ness common to all particular F things. But if the Form is construed as a universal, it seems, for many values of F, nonsensical to say that it, and it alone, is perfectly F. Equality cannot itself be equal; no more can smallness be small, or largeness large. Forms, as universals, cannot, in general, *have* the characters that they *are*. The paradoxes incurred by attributing the character *F* to the Form *F* were recognized by Plato and explored in the later *Parmenides* (132a–b, 132c–133b). They can easily be generated if the paradigmatic and universal roles of the Forms are confused. Whether Plato himself confused them in the *Phaedo* and other dialogues of his 'middle period' has been a major crux of recent scholarship. See *S.P.M.*, Chs. 4, 12–14.

(v) If 'equal' is predicated of the Form Equal, even in its purely paradigmatic role, it may be asked whether it is equal *to* anything, and if so, to what. It could hardly be equal to everything. If it is equal to some things but not to others, it will suffer from the very defect from which Forms are supposedly immune, and which, on one plausible interpretation of 74b8–9 above, was said to distinguish sensible equals from it. If it is equal only to itself, it will fail to be a genuine paradigm for items that are said to 'strive to be like it'. Should we conclude, then, that the Form Equal is not equal to anything, either to itself or to anything else, but is just equal *simpliciter*? On this view, it would fail, once again, to be a genuine paradigm for the things supposed to approximate to it. And to treat 'equal' as a non-relational attribute seems a patent misconstruction, deserving to be characterized, as a case of 'Greek mistreatment of "relative" terms in the attempt to assimilate them to simple adjectives' (G. E. L. Owen, *S.P.M.* 310).

Does the present passage, in fact, improperly predicate 'equal' of the Form? Undeniably, it implies that the word 'equal' is grammatically predicated of it. For it must be taken to mean that sensible equals seem to us to fall short of being equal in the same way as the Form Equal *is equal*. The italicized words, though not in Burnet's text at 74d6, clearly have to be understood. See note 24 and cf.100c4–5, 102e5. But in what way 'is' the Form Equal equal? Is it possible to interpret 'the Form Equal is equal' without raising the difficulties mentioned above? A possible solution is to understand it not as attributing equality to the Form, but simply as an identity statement: the Form Equal *is* (identical with) Equal. Sensible equals are therefore not equal in the way that it is. For they are not identical with the Form, but only (to use the terminology introduced later) 'participate' in it. They 'fall short' of it, not in failing to be exactly equal, a claim for which the present passage has provided no argument whatever, but rather in that they are nonidentical with it, as argued at 74b7–c6. They 'strive to be like it', but they fall short. For they suffer from the defects that characterize sensible particulars as such.

On this view, the judgement that sensible equals 'fall short' of the Form Equal will not be that of a plain man confronted with logs that he regards as not quite equal. It will be the judgement of a philosopher, who has recognized that the Form is distinct from its sensible instances, and who, on sensing the latter, reflects upon how different they are from the former. This interpretation avoids some difficulties in the traditional view. See H. F. Cherniss, *S.P.M.* 368–74, R. E. Allen, *P.R.* 1960, 147–64. It is not clear, however, that it will fit all contexts. In particular, it runs into difficulty in the later discussion of Largeness and Smallness. See on 102a10–d4 (p.194).

74d9–75c6. It is now argued that on perceiving sensible particulars, we 'refer' them to the relevant Form (75b7, cf.76d9–e2), and judge that they 'fall short' of it (74d9–e2, 75a1–3, 75a11–b3). Such judgements are held to require prior knowledge of the Form (74e2–75a4), and consequently (75a5–b9) knowledge of it before we began to use the senses, which was at birth (75b10–11). For the expression *'what equal is'* see notes 25, 26, and on 75c7–d6 (p.131).

Is it legitimate to infer, as Socrates does at 75c1–6, that we possessed knowledge of the Forms before birth? At 75b4–9 he argues that we must have gained knowledge of the Form before we began to use our senses. Yet it has so far been shown only that we gained knowledge of the Form before the *first occasion* on which we referred sensible equals to it (74e9–75a4). Might this occasion not have been some time after we began to use the senses? Cf. J. L. Ackrill (*P.R.* 1958, 108): 'One could admit that we saw and heard from birth, and that referring what one sees and hears to standards implies prior knowledge of the standards, and one could still deny that we had prenatal knowledge of standards. For we may have done a good deal of infantile seeing and hearing before we began to refer what we saw and heard to any standards (in fact we certainly did).'

Socrates would no doubt ask when and how prior knowledge of the standards was acquired. If referring sensible things to standards requires 'direct acquaintance' with those standards, then it would follow, given his assumptions, that the referring of sensible things to standards implies prenatal acquaintance with the latter. For we can have had no direct acquaintance with them since birth, given (a) that there is no direct acquaintance with them through sense experience (65d9–e5, cf.79a1–5), and (b) that it is only through sense experience that we have thought or could think of them at all (75a5–7). But this line of thought is not made explicit. The argument is therefore defective as it stands.

The inference at 75c1–6, that we must have gained knowledge of the Equal before we were born, would suffice to prove the soul's prenatal existence directly. Yet it takes a further page of argument, proving the Recollection doctrine, before prenatal existence is inferred at 76c11—13. What is the role of this further argument? If, as seems to be the case, the Recollection doctrine is premissed upon the conclusion drawn in the present lines, and prenatal existence is then derived from it, the reasoning from 75c7 to 76c13 will be circular. See on 76c14—d6.

75c7—d6. Hackforth (71, n.1) rightly notes that the clause 'if, having got it before birth, we were born in possession of it' (c7—8), like that at 75d7 below, expresses a hypothesis that Socrates does *not* accept: it will shortly be argued that we do not possess knowledge of the Forms at birth (cf.76d2—3). But although the protasis of the present sentence will prove false, the apodosis is clearly held to be true. It extends the conclusion that we knew the Form Equal before birth to the whole range of Forms posited in dialectical question and answer. The correctness of this extension cannot be meant to depend upon the truth of the 'if' clause.

Note that the claim that a Form's instances 'fall short' of it, as often interpreted in connection with Equality, would be untenable with respect to some of the Forms mentioned here. The interpretation considered at 74d4—8 was that sensible equals are judged only approximately, never exactly, equal. But it could make no sense to suggest that on seeing two logs, one larger than the other, we judge the former to be only approximately, never exactly, larger than the other. It may be answered that there is no question of postulating a Form of Larger, as distinct from that of Large. The language is, as Hackforth says (71, n.2), loose, and the Forms of Large and Small are meant. But even so, do we judge sensible objects to be only approximately large in the way that such objects may be judged only approximately equal? In what sense could anything be, or fail to be, 'exactly large'? The interpretation clearly breaks down in this case. Yet a satisfactory interpretation of 'falling short' of the Form should preferably fit as many of the Forms mentioned here as possible.

The phrase at 75d2 translated '*what it is*' is a standard Platonic expression for the Forms. It occurs, with variations, at 65d13—e1, 74b2, 74d6, 75b1—2, 78d4—5, 92d9, and often in other dialogues. The phrase is here recognized as semi-technical—'we set this seal' on the Forms. Often the name of the relevant Form is included, but sometimes, as here and at 92d9, no name is specified. The phrase then consists simply of the neuter singular relative pronoun followed by 'is'. The word 'itself', though sometimes added, seems not (despite Burnet's note on 75d2) to have been an integral part of the phrase. For the departure from Burnet's text at 75d2, see note 28. Cf. also notes 25 and 31.

Where the name of a Form '*F*' is included, the phrase may be taken in three different ways:-

(a) that *F* which *is*:
(b) that thing which *F* is:
(c) that thing which is *F*.

In (a) 'is' will be the 'complete' or 'absolute' use of the verb 'to be'. In (b) and (c) it will be 'incomplete' (see on 65c2–4). In (b) it must function as an identity sign. In (c) it could be taken either (i) as an identity sign, or (ii) as attributing to the relevant Form the character *F*. If the 'is' is an identity sign, the choice between (b) and (c) (i) will be unimportant. On interpretation (c) (ii), however, the Form will be 'self-predicated' in the manner that gives rise to the difficulties discussed above (see on 74d4–8).

Interpretation (a) can be ruled out in some passages on grammatical grounds. See notes 7 and 25. Other passages are less clear, however, and it cannot, perhaps, be assumed that occurrences must be construed uniformly, even within a single dialogue, or with respect to a single Form. K. W. Mills (*Phronesis* 1957, 146) takes the phrase in sense (b), as correlative to the question 'What is *F*?', where this is understood to mean 'What is the thing of which "*F*" is the name?' Similarly, G. F. Else, *H.S.C.P.* 1936, 43–4. This fits the reference in the present passage, and at 78d1–5, to dialectical questions and answers, which may indicate the provenance of the phrase. It could well have arisen from asking and answering the question 'What is *F*?'–the Form being designated, in answer to that question, as 'the thing that *F* is'. Mills's view of the phrase has been adopted throughout the present translation. Occurrences of the phrase without '*F*' have been rendered '*what it is*'. Alternative renderings for these occurrences, corresponding to (a) and (c) above, would be 'that ... which *is*' and 'that which is ...' respectively.

See, further, H. Cherniss, *S.P.M.* 372, A. R. Lacey, *C.Q.* 1959, 51, G. Vlastos, *R.M.* 1972, 452–8, and R. Loriaux, *E.F.P.*, reviewed by K. W. Mills, *Gnomon* 1957, 325–9.

75d7–76b3. Simmias is now presented with two hypothetical statements, the first (if *P*, *Q*) at 75d7–e1, and the second (if *R*, *S*) at 75e2–8. He is then offered a choice (76a4–7) between their respective consequents, *Q* and *S*. *Q* will be rejected, for reasons to be given in 76b4–c3. *S* will then be inferred at 76c4–5. The argument down to 76c5 is therefore of the following form:

(1) If *P*, *Q* (d7–e1).
(2) If *R*, *S* (e2–8).

So (3) Either *Q* or *S* (a4–7).

But (4) Not-Q (c1–3).
So (5) S (c4–5).
In this argument, step (3) follows if, but only if, it is assumed that:
    (2*) Either P or R.
In terms of the actual argument, this is the contention that at birth, *either* (P) we did not forget our prenatally gained knowledge of the Forms, *or* (R) we lost it. In view of the equivalence between 'losing it' and 'forgetting' (d10–11), P = Not-R, so that (2*) is an application of the Law of Excluded Middle. Its presupposition, that we did gain knowledge of the Forms before birth, is built into (1) and (2) by the wording at 75d7 and 75e2. Both antecedents, P and R, begin with the words 'having got them'—i.e. having acquired the knowledge prenatally. *If* we gained knowledge before birth, it is supposed that we must either have retained it at birth or lost it. But Simmias' suggestion at 76c14–15 will cast doubt upon whether we *did* get it before birth. His point does not seem to be satisfactorily answered. See below, and on 76c14–d6.

At 75d7 'on each occasion' must refer to each occasion on which the soul becomes incarnate. At 75e3 the meaning of the phrase translated 'using the senses about the things in question' is far from clear. See on 65b1–7 and 74c7–d3.

At 76a1–4 Socrates recalls points agreed earlier (73c6–d1, 74c13–d2): one may, on perceiving X, think of Y, which one had forgotten, whether X and Y are similar or dissimilar. Note, especially, the condition that one should have 'forgotten' Y, repeated from 73e1–3. The claim that we 'forgot' the Forms at birth is an important element in the argument summarized in the first paragraph of this note. However, since prenatal knowledge of the Forms is presupposed in this claim, such knowledge cannot be inferred from it without begging the question.

Hackforth translates at 76a3–4: 'something with which the first object was connected, whether by resemblance or contrast'. The suggestion that dissimilarity is itself the source of the association is no more implied in the Greek here than at 74c11. See on 74c7–d3. The nature of the association is not clearly specified in the verb translated 'was related', but the idea is, perhaps, that dissimilar items have frequently been found together.

76b4–c10. The ability to 'give an account (*logos*)' is said at 76b5–7 to be a necessary condition for knowledge. 'Correct account' was also linked with knowledge at 73a9–10.

What is it to 'give an account'? The phrase can mean 'give a definition', and this would be a natural way of taking it here, where the things about which an 'account' has to be given are Forms. On this interpretation, no one has knowledge of the Form *F* unless he can give a definition of *F*, say what *F* is. See also 78d1–5, and cf. *Republic* 534b. However, 'give an account' can also mean 'give proof' (cf.95d7), and it may be the having of grounds for a proposition, or the ability to prove it, that Socrates has in mind as requisite for knowledge. Reasoning of this sort is said to distinguish knowledge from correct belief at *Meno* 98a. On this interpretation, 'giving an account' about the Forms will mean defending propositions about them by rational argument. 'Giving an account' in this sense, and giving one in the definitional sense, are, of course, related, the former being required for the latter.

Inability to give an account is agreed at 76b8–c3 to preclude most men from knowing the Forms. For the conflict with 74b2 see on 74b2–3. Hackforth (76) would reconcile the present lines with 74b by saying that it is moral Forms, as distinct from mathematical ones, that Socrates here has in mind. But there is no hint in the text of any such restriction. On the contrary, 'moral' and 'mathematical' Forms are expressly said to be on a par (75c10–d2).

76c11–13. The inference is drawn here that our souls existed before entering human form 'apart from bodies'. The most natural interpretation of this last phrase is 'apart from bodies altogether'—i.e. in a discarnate state, cf.114c3. It might be objected that on this interpretation the inference does not, strictly, follow. For our present incarnation might have ensued immediately after a previous death, without any discarnate intermission. The most that could then be claimed would be that our souls existed apart from our present bodies, incarnate in some previous one. This seems a less likely interpretation of 'apart from bodies'. But even if it were correct, the required point could still be made. 'We' are not to be identified with our present bodies, since we already existed before they did. Nor can 'we' be identified with our previous bodies, since we still exist when they no longer do. Hence, 'we' who once knew the Forms, and are now reminded of them, must be identified with a persisting non-bodily subject. See on 72e7–73a3.

There can be no doubt, however, that the argument does envisage us as having known the Forms in a discarnate state. As W. D. Ross pointed out (*P.T.I.* 25), the Recollection doctrine would not explain how we can now come to know Forms on the suggestion of sensible things, merely by referring back to a previous knowing of them in the same way. For this previous knowledge would require explanation no less than does our knowing them on the suggestion of sensible things now. The Recollection doctrine therefore points to a direct and immediate knowledge of the Forms. But since we have no such knowledge of them while the soul is incarnate (66d7–67b2), the Recollection doctrine, if it is to explain what it is introduced to explain, requires that the soul must at some time have existed in a discarnate state.

76c14–d6. Simmias tries to resist the conclusion that our souls existed before birth, by suggesting that we might acquire the relevant bits of knowledge at the time of birth. He is silenced by being asked at what other time we could lose them.

But he gives in too easily. For why should it be inferred from our lacking knowledge when we are born, that we must 'lose' it at that time? An analogy may be useful here. We should not think of a child born blind as losing his sight at birth, since he never had it. No one would argue from his lack of sight at birth that he must have lost it at that time, and therefore possessed it prenatally. Someone born without sight has never possessed it, and therefore could not be said to have 'lost' it at all. Nor, if he should later acquire sight, could he be said to 'regain' what he had never had.

If, then, we are born lacking knowledge, the inference that we 'lose' it at birth, and subsequently 'regain' it, is justified only if it is already assumed that we once possessed it. Why should this be assumed here? Only, it would seem, because, the idea that we acquired it before birth is contained in the disjunctive hypotheticals at 75d7–11 and 75e2–7. Both disjuncts assume prenatally acquired knowledge. See on 75d7–76b3. But this assumption is precisely what Simmias is here questioning.

It is true that Socrates has already, at 75c4–5, obtained the admission that we gained knowledge of the Form Equal before birth. But once this is granted, he already has all he needs to prove pre-existence, and the ensuing argument for the Recollection doctrine will be otiose. Alternatively, if the Recollection doctrine is meant to be a ground for holding the thesis of prenatal knowledge, the reasoning seems circular. For, as argued above, the thesis of prenatal knowledge is used at 75d7–76c5 in establishing the doctrine. Simmias is here challenging the thesis. But he is rebutted only by appealing to the very assumption his objection calls in question, that we did in fact gain knowledge before birth. It should therefore be asked whether prenatal knowledge and existence are logical consequences of the Recollection doctrine, or whether it is a consequence of them. It cannot function both as premiss and conclusion of the same argument.

76d7–77a5. Socrates refers to the Forms as 'what was formerly ours' (e1–2), meaning that they were objects of our knowledge before birth. Cf.92d8–9 and note 50.

At 76e2–7 the existence of the Forms and the pre-existence of the soul are said to be equally necessary. Socrates then adds: 'and if the former don't exist, then neither did the latter'. Simmias' reply shows that he too thinks of the Forms' and the soul's existence as logically interdependent. But the nature of the relation is not entirely clear. The passage might be taken to authorize a bi-conditional: 'If the Forms exist, our souls existed before birth; and if they don't exist, our souls didn't exist before birth.' But Socrates can hardly mean that the pre-existence of the soul and the existence of the Forms are materially equivalent, so that either can, without further premises, be inferred from the other. He means, more likely, that the existence of Forms necessitates the pre-existence of the soul in virtue of the Recollection Argument; and that their existence is also necessary for the success of that argument. 'If they don't exist, this argument will have gone for nothing' (76e4–5). The words 'if the former don't exist, then neither did the latter' are perhaps only a somewhat inaccurate restatement of the latter point. The existence of the Forms is, indeed, essential to the Recollection Argument, and is the ruling hypothesis of the dialogue. Cf.92d, and see on 65d4–e5 (p.97).

At 77a3–5 Simmias says that the Forms *are* 'in the fullest possible way'. Degrees of 'being' may sound paradoxical to a modern reader; but the use of 'are' is 'complete' here, and seems undeniably existential, in view of the connection with the pre-existence of the soul. See on 65c2–4 and 83b2–3.

77a6–d5. Simmias and Cebes object (b1–c5) that only half what is needed has so far been shown—the soul's pre-existence. Socrates replies (c6–d5) that its post-existence has been proved as well, if the Recollection and Cyclical Arguments are 'combined'. But how exactly is this to be done?

Archer-Hind (45, n.3) takes the arguments as two halves of a single proof, one showing the pre-existence and the other the post-existence of the soul. But what Socrates here claims to have been proved by conjoining the two arguments is simply 'post-existence'. For 'that's been proved' (c6) must refer back to the claim that our soul 'will exist after we've died' (c3–4). It is not, therefore, the whole of Socrates' thesis for which the two arguments are to be combined, but only the post-mortem half of it. But if so, how? As E. J. Furlong has argued (*Hermathena* 1940, 62–72), the Cyclical Argument, whatever its defects, seems equally relevant to pre-existence and to post-existence. It would 'prove' either without combination with the Recollection Argument. On the other hand, the Recollection Argument has no bearing upon post-existence at all.

It is usually supposed that whereas the Cyclical Argument is meant to prove the bare existence of the discarnate soul, the Recollection Argument meets Cebes' further demand to be shown that it possesses 'some power and wisdom' (70b3—4). This latter inference has indeed been drawn, with respect to pre-existence, at 76c12—13. But its bearing upon the present problem is doubtful. It is not mentioned here, nor would it be to the point. The objection Socrates faces is not that our souls have not been proved to exist after death possessed of power and wisdom, but simply that they have not yet been proved to exist after death at all. He would merely evade this objection by replying that they possessed power and wisdom before birth.

At 77c9—d5 Socrates explains the combination of the arguments as follows: the soul 'must also exist after it has died, given that it has to be born again' (d3—4). This is inferred from a conjunction of (1) 'the soul does have previous existence' (c9—d1), and (2) 'when it enters upon living and being born, it must come from no other source than death and from being dead' (d1—3). (1) and (2) appear to invoke the Recollection and Cyclical Arguments respectively. Yet, as noted above, (1) is derivable from the Cyclical Argument alone. So if Socrates thinks that the Recollection Argument is needed at this point, he is in error.

Hackforth (80, cf. *C.R.* 1925, 12) interprets Socrates as wanting to show that 'the soul *as conceived in the Recollection Argument*, the soul which apprehends the Forms, exists after death as well as before birth'. Hackforth claims that the principle 'all that is living comes from that which is dead' (c9), derived from the Cyclical Argument, justifies us in regarding the conclusion of the Recollection Argument—'the soul does have previous existence' (c9—d1)—as involving the corollary that the soul must also exist after it has died. For, he suggests, 'the time before birth *is* the time after death'.

If this is the reasoning, it supports the required conclusion by a mere sophism. For to say that 'the time before birth *is* the time after death' would be true only in the sense that the time before the birth of one living thing is the time after the death of an earlier one. The argument would show that a soul animating any given living thing must have survived the death of some previous one. It would not show that it *will* survive the death of the living thing in which it is now incarnate. So the argument gives the speakers no assurance that their own souls will survive death. Essentially the same objection will be raised by Cebes later (88a—b, cf.95c4—e1).

Note that at 77d4 Socrates speaks of the soul as 'dying'. This, although formally inconsistent with its 'immortality', must mean merely that it becomes separated from the body. See on 64c2–9 (p.86) and 84a2–b8.

3.3 The Affinity Argument (78b4–84b8)

Socrates next argues that the soul must be immortal in virtue of its affinity to the unchanging and eternal Forms. He then speculates upon the after-life of purified and unpurified souls, and renews his advocacy of the philosophic life.

78b4–10. 'What kind of thing is not liable to it?' (78b7): the translation follows Burnet in supplying 'not', which is omitted in the MSS. at this point. The passage sets out concisely the programme that will be followed in the coming argument. Socrates asks (1) which class of thing is liable to destruction and which is not, and (2) to which of these classes soul belongs. (1) will be considered at 78c1–79a11, and (2) at 79b1–80a9. The conclusions will be drawn at 80a10–81a3.

78c1–9. Socrates here links (1) incompositeness with indestructibility (c1–4), and (2) constancy with incompositeness (c6–8).

(1) The supposition that incomposite things are indestructible has a strong intuitive appeal. For the destruction of a material thing seems to require the separation of its component parts. How an incomposite material thing could be destroyed it is not easy to conceive. So it seems that if the soul were material and incomposite, it could not be dispersed 'like smoke'. But according to the present argument, the soul is essentially *im*material. And it is doubtful whether the principle that incompositeness entails indestructibility applies to immaterial things. Simmias will later (85e–86a) give an example of something immaterial—the attunement of a lyre—that is clearly destructible, but (although composite) is not destroyed through the separation of its own components. Perhaps, then, immaterial things, even if incomposite, might nevertheless be destroyed. In that case, the soul's incompositeness would not show its indestructibility.

At 78c3–4 it is suggested that 'if there be anything incomposite, it alone is liable, if anything is, to escape this (sc. destruction)'. The first 'if' clause need not be taken to imply doubt as to the existence of something incomposite. Nor need the second 'if' clause be taken to cast doubt upon there being anything indestructible. Cf.106d2–4.

(2) There seems no difference in meaning between the phrases translated 'constant' and 'unvarying', or their respective opposites. At 78e5 Cebes uses one of these phrases to answer a question framed in terms of the other. Both mean 'being in the same state',

'admitting of no kind of alteration' (cf.78d6—7). For the kinds of alteration envisaged, see on 78d10—e5.

At 78c6—7 it is not clear which of the phrases 'the things that are constant and unvarying' and 'the incomposite' is to be taken as subject and which as complement. Is it being said that unvarying things are likely to be incomposite, or that incomposite things are likely to be unvarying? Or are the classes of unvarying and incomposite things thought of as coextensive? On the translation adopted, Socrates is saying that unvarying things are likely to be incomposite. Logically, this makes better sense, since he is arguing that the Forms, being unvarying, are likely to be incomposite, and he therefore needs the premiss that unvarying things are likely to be incomposite rather than the converse. Hackforth's translation makes him say that incomposite things are likely to be unvarying. But this, since its converse would not hold, unless the classes were assumed to be coextensive, would not further the argument.

Socrates claims only that unvarying things are 'likely' to be the incomposite. It therefore could not be certain that members of any sub-class of unvarying things, such as Forms or souls, are incomposite. Nor is the basis for the alleged 'likelihood' explained. Perhaps change is thought of as depending upon rearrangement of parts within a complex whole. The characterization of the Forms as incomposite is, indeed, often taken to imply that they are without parts, and therefore incapable of such change. 'Incomposite' may, however, mean merely 'not having been put together', and might thus be ascribed to something that has possessed parts from all eternity. See K. W. Mills, *Phronesis* 1958, 45—7, answered by R. S. Bluck, *Phronesis* 1959, 5, and J. M. Rist, *Phronesis* 1964, 32—3. See also on 80a10—c1.

The question whether Forms can have parts, and if so in what sense, raises the question whether the soul, in virtue of its kinship with the incomposite Forms, is supposed to be without parts, and if so, whether this account of it can be reconciled with the teaching of the *Republic* and the *Phaedrus*. See R. W. Hall, *Phronesis* 1963, 63—82.

For many different ways of understanding 'composite' see Wittgenstein, *Philosophical Investigations*, I,47.

78d1—5. The grammar and sense of the words translated 'the Being itself, whose being we give an account of' (d1—2) are uncertain. 'The Being itself' clearly refers to the domain of Forms (see note 7). But 'giving an account' could mean either 'giving a definition' or 'giving a proof'; and the use of 'being' may be either 'incomplete' or 'complete' (see on 65c2—4). 'Giving an account' of a Form's 'being' may therefore mean either 'defining its essential nature' or 'proving that it exists'. Loriaux (152–3, 164–5) defends the existential interpretation. See also *E.F.P.* 26–34. Similarly Hackforth. For the view adopted here see Bluck and Burnet. The non-existential reading has been preferred, in view of the reference to 'asking and answering questions'–cf.75d2–3. It seems far more natural to associate this with the Socratic quest for definitions than with proofs of the Forms' existence. To 'give an account of the being of *F*' is to answer the question 'what is *F*?'. Questioning and answering of this sort are familiar in Plato's writings, and typical of dialectical inquiry (cf., e.g., *Republic* 538d6–e3), whereas questioning and answering to prove that the Forms exist can hardly be said to occur in the dialogues at all.

The phrase 'what . . . is' has been translated accordingly at 78d4 and 78d5. See note 31.

78d10–e5. For the text at 78d10–e1 see note 33. At 78e2 Socrates speaks of 'all things that bear the same name as those objects'. 'Those objects' are, of course, the Forms, here treated as the prime bearers of their names. Particulars are 'named after' them. Cf.102b2, 102c10, 103b7, and see on 65d4–e5 (p.96), 102a10–d4.

In contrasting sensible particulars with Forms, two kinds of variation are mentioned (e3): particulars may vary in relation either 'to themselves' or 'to one another'. Hackforth (82, n.1) rightly rejects Burnet's view that the latter phrase refers to things presenting different appearances to different people. But there seems no need to suppose, with Hackforth, that the words 'or to one another' may be added because equality requires two terms. The point is simply that particulars may become more or less *F* at t_2 than they were at t_1 (they vary 'in relation to themselves'), or they may become more or less *F* than some other particular thing (they vary 'in relation to one another').

The stress here is upon the mutability of sensible particulars, their liability to be characterized by different attributes at different times, rather than (as at 102b–d) their being characterized by opposite attributes at the same time in relation to different things. They are also, of course, mutable in that they are ephemeral: particular *F*s come into being and pass away, whereas the Form *F* is conceived as eternal, 'that which is always existent' (79d2).

79a1–b17. 'Two kinds of beings' (a6): more literally, 'two kinds of the things that are'. See on 65c2–4 and note 34. For the inaccessibility of the Forms to the senses (a1–4) cf.65d9–e4.

At 79a9–10 the 'invisible' is said to be always constant, and the

139

'seen' never constant. This is best taken as referring to the Forms and the sensible world as such, rather than as asserting, quite generally, that whatever is unseen is constant, and whatever is seen is inconstant. In effect, it recapitulates the premises of 78d1−8 and 78d10−e5, enabling the Form world to be designated in what follows either as 'the invisible' (79b16) or 'the unvarying' (79e4).

The assumption that we are 'part body and part soul' (b1−2), upon which the argument of the whole dialogue rests, is simply posited and accepted without demur. For the concept of 'soul' see on 64e4−65a3. The inference that it is 'more similar' to the invisible than body (b16−17) rests simply on the claim that it is invisible (a14). The 'seen' is defined (b9−10) with reference to human nature, perhaps to forestall the objection that the soul is not invisible to the gods.

'Similarity' is not defined. But if 'being more similar' means 'having more features in common', the fact that the soul shares with the Forms a given feature that the body lacks would not show that it is 'more similar' to them than is the body. Even if this were shown, it would not follow that the soul has *all* features in common with the Forms that the body lacks. Taken as an analogy, the argument is weak. It would be stronger if the feature common to the soul and the Forms were to entail the other relevant features, i.e. if invisibility were to entail invariability, invariability incompositeness, and incompositeness indestructibility. A chain connecting these concepts can, indeed, be derived from 78c1−9 and 79a9−10, but its links are weak. See on 78c1−9.

79c2−e7. A tacit assumption underlying the argument here is the Empedoclean doctrine that 'like knows like' (see DK 31 A 86, B 109). The soul's knowledge of the unvarying Forms shows its likeness to them; its confusion when it is in contact with varying sensibles shows that it is unlike them. Hence soul is 'more similar to what is unvarying than to what is not' (e3−5). Note that this conclusion is of a different form from the earlier 'soul is more similar than body to the invisible' (79b16). That conclusion was of the form '*A* is more similar than *B* to *C*'. This one is of the form '*A* is more similar to *C* than to *D*'.

Socrates claims only that the soul is 'more similar to the unvarying', not that it *is* unvarying. He could hardly say this after just saying that in using the senses it is 'dizzy, as if drunk' (c7−8). This recalls his earlier criticism of the senses (65a−b). But he does not explain their defects any more clearly here than before—see on 65b1−7. Why should use of the senses make the soul 'dizzy'? In dizziness objects are experienced as changing when they are really at rest. Yet if the sensible world is, in fact, changing, the senses would not be deceiving us by representing it as doing so. Cf. *Cratylus* 411b–c. There is, perhaps, a further reason for Socrates' reluctance to say that the soul *is* unvarying. That the soul is, in fact, subject to change seems an inescapable consequence of (1) its liability to incarnation, and of (2) its role as a 'life-principle'. For (1) apparently requires that such properties as 'being in Socrates' body' should be truly predicable of the soul at one time but not at another. And (2) if, as a life-bearing agent, the soul is itself characterized by the property it imparts, and if life entails change, then soul must be subject to change. For the resulting tension with the present view of it as akin to the changeless Forms, see T. M. Robinson, *P.P.* 30.

For 'wisdom' (79d6–7) see on 69a6–c3.

79e8–80a9. The soul's kinship with the divine is derived from its being 'naturally adapted' (a4–5) to rule the body, i.e. to discipline it and resist its desires (cf.94b–e). This may seem odd, in face of Socrates' continual stress upon the soul's bondage to the body (e.g. 66b–d, 83c–e). If 'rulership' indicates divinity, and 'being ruled' mortality, why should the soul's servitude to the body not suggest that *it* is mortal and the body divine? No doubt the conception of 'nature', here as elsewhere in Plato, is normative. What 'nature ordains' (80a1) is what ought to happen, not what usually does. The soul's 'natural' fitness to rule the body does not mean that it always does so, just as in the *Republic* (430e–431a) the 'natural' superiority of reason does not mean that it is actually in control. Even so, the notion of the soul's 'rulership' sits awkwardly with the theme of its imprisonment within the body. See on 64e4–65a3 (p.90).

'Rule' is more naturally attributed to gods than to Forms. But the Form world is virtually identified with the gods—see on 81a4–11. For human service to the gods, cf.62b–63a and see on 58a6–c5.

80a10–c1. The contrasts that have been drawn between Forms and the sensible world are summarized at 80b1–5. Forms are called 'intelligible' (b1) versus 'non-intelligible' (b4). The word translated 'non-intelligible' can also mean 'unintelligent', and there may be a hint of this sense here: body is 'stupid'. For 'body' without the article see next note.

At 80b2 the Forms are said to be 'uniform', by contrast with the material realm, which is called 'multiform' (b4)—cf.78d5, 83e2. Hackforth (81, n.2) understands 'uniformity' to mean 'the denial of internal difference or distinction of unlike parts'. If the Forms' incompositeness is taken to imply that they have no parts (see on 78c1–9), then no distinction of parts of any kind, whether like or unlike, could be allowed them. However, the notion of parts may be irrelevant here. For 'uniform' may be explained as meaning 'of just one character'. See K. W. Mills, *Phronesis* 1958, 45–6 and W. F. Hicken, *S.P.M.* 191.

At 80b3–5 soul and body are said to be 'most similar' (superlative) to their respective domains, and not merely, as at 79a16 and 79e4, 'more similar'. 'Most similar' could be intensive–'very similar', or could mean 'more similar than anything else'. These interpretations of the superlative are logically distinct. Neither entails the other, and they call for different kinds of support. On neither interpretation would it follow that the soul shares all the features of the Forms, or that it shares any particular feature with them, or that it shares every feature that the body lacks. These inferences would be stronger on the intensive interpretation. But the claim that the soul is 'very similar' to the Forms is hardly warranted by the foregoing argument, which has shown merely that it has a few properties in common with them.

At 80b9–10 Socrates concludes that soul must be completely indissoluble 'or something close to it'. It is not clear whether this last phrase is meant to qualify the soul's indissolubility, or to signal reservations about the argument. Does Socrates mean that the soul may be nearly (but not quite) indissoluble, or that the argument nearly (but not quite) proves the soul indissoluble? Or are these two things confused? No suggestion that the soul might be 'nearly indissoluble' appears elsewhere, nor would it be consistent with the final conclusion that soul is 'immortal and imperishable' (106e9–107a1). On the other hand, 'nearly indissoluble' seems the more natural way of reading the present text.

80c2–d7. The meaning and text at 80c2–9 have been much disputed–see note 35. But the main argument is clear: even the body lasts for a considerable time after death, so the soul, being of superior nature to the body, may be expected to last longer still. The best comment on this argument is supplied by Simmias' and Cebes' parodies of it at 86a6–b5 and 87b6–c5.

It is somewhat odd that 'the body' should here be said to last for 'a fairly long time' (c5–6) after death, when only a few lines above (80b8) 'body' was said to be 'quickly dissolved' (cf.87e5). 'Body', which occurs at 80b8 without the article, as often (79b16, 80a1, 80b5, 81e2, 91d3, 91d7, 105c9), might be used generically ('matter'), or might perhaps mean 'a body' (i.e. 'a material thing'). However, 'the body' normally means 'the human body' (cf.79c2–6), and is explicitly equated with the corpse at 80c2–4. If its meaning varied in the course of the argument, there would be serious equivocation. For what is true of 'body' in the generic sense need not be true of individual 'bodies'. The same goes for 'soul'—see on 64e4–65a3 (p.89–90). At 80d5–7 (cf.81a4, 81c11) there is a play on the words 'Hades' (*haides*) and 'invisible' (*aides*). The Form world is 'Hades in the true sense', i.e. 'unseen' but an object of thought. For Hades as the place of departed souls, cf.58e5, 68b1, 70c4, 71e2, 83d9, 107a1. The place is named after the god whose realm it is. This suits the identification of Forms and gods as the soul's destination—see next note. The derivation of 'Hades' from 'unseen' is rejected at *Cratylus* 404b, but may be sound—see L.S.J. s.v. ἄδης and Bluck, 197.

80d8–81a3. 'Blown apart' (80d10) is a reference to the materialist view of the soul under attack. Cf.70a2–6, 77d7–e2, 84b4–8. The cumbersome sentence beginning 'Far from it' (80e1) has been broken up in the translation, which assumes a comma after 'shunned it' (e4). The sentence breaks at 80e5, and the sense is not completed until Socrates' next speech, the 'suppose' clause beginning at 80e2 being picked up by 'if it is in that state' at 81a4.

81a4–11. 'The divine and immortal and wise': Hackforth (88, n.4) says that these epithets belong properly to the gods or God (cf.80d7) rather than to the place of the departed soul. But in this section of the dialogue, God (or gods) and the Forms are spoken of interchangeably as the soul's destination. They are, in effect, identified, and divine attributes are applied to both alike. See 79d2, 83e2, 84a8, and on 80c2–d7.

81c4–d5. Unpurified souls are here portrayed not as immaterial substances, but as phantoms or insubstantial wraiths. They are described in terms that could not literally apply to the soul in its essential, incorporeal nature. How could an incorporeal thing be 'interspersed with a corporeal element' (c4–5), be 'weighed down' (c10), or 'fall back into another body, and grow in it' (83d10–e1)? Such language, taken literally, describes interaction between one material substance and another. Even the purified soul of the philosopher is said to 'gather itself together' (83a7–8, cf.67c8, 80e5), which suggests, as Hackforth says (52, n.3), the spatial diffusion of a vital fluid throughout the body. The fact is that, despite the tenor of his argument for the soul's nature, Socrates does not consistently speak of it as immaterial. Note also that at 83d7 he speaks of the soul as 'sharing opinions and pleasures with the body', implying, strictly, that the body as well as the soul can have pleasures and opinions. He may be speaking 'loosely' here, as Hackforth says (93,

143

n.1), but his language at least is not that of a Cartesian dualist, for whom soul and body could have no attributes in common.

81d6–82d8. The notion of reincarnation in animals is Pythagorean (cf. DK 21 B 7), and is developed here with savage irony. Cf. *Phaedrus* 248e–249b (ed. Hackforth, 88–91), *Republic* 619e–620c, and *Timaeus* 41e–42d, 91d–92c. See also 113a5 below.

How can the soul be essentially rational in virtue of its kinship with the Forms, and yet be reborn in animal bodies? This is a further point of conflict (see previous note) between the view of the soul's nature espoused by the Affinity Argument and what is actually said about it. E. R. Dodds remarks: 'The notion of reincarnation in animals was in fact transferred from the occult self of Pythagoreanism to the rational *psychē* which it did not fit' (*G.I.* 229, n.43, cf.215).

At 82a7–8 the meaning may be 'And it is clear that the way every other class also would go depends upon the nature of their previous practices' (Bluck). With this translation, what is clear is the general principle that souls will be reborn into appropriate forms of life, rather than the form of life that each soul will actually enter.

At 82c1–8 the philosopher is said to practise restraint not for ordinary prudential reasons (cf.83b8–c2), but to become purified, and thus escape from reincarnation. This should not be taken to mean, or to imply, that virtue should be practised *only* for the sake of reward in the after-life. See on 69a6–c3 and 107c1–d2.

83b2–3. 'And not to regard as real what it observes by other means and what varies in various things': what the soul observes 'by other means' is, of course, the sensible world, observed by means 'other' than the soul itself, i.e. the senses (cf.83a3–5). The soul's mediated observation of sensible things is contrasted with its unmediated observation of the Forms. Note the stress (83b1–2) upon the soul's being 'alone by itself', which is correlative to the state of the Forms (cf.66e–67a).

The sensible world is characterized, literally, as 'what is other in other things'. Bluck (82, n.1) argues for the meaning 'appearing variously in various other things', on the ground that the emphasis is not so much upon the invariability of the soul's object as upon its purity, corresponding to that of the soul itself, when it is 'alone by itself'. However, the variability of sensible things is itself one among several features that render them 'impure', and the phrase 'other in other things' is too vague to be tied closely to any single feature.

The word translated 'real' can also mean 'true' (see on 66b1–c5), but 'real' is clearly required here, as at 81b4, where the unpurified soul was said to regard nothing but sensible things as 'real'. Cf.83c7 below, where pleasure and pain are said to dispose the soul to regard their objects as 'most clear and most real' (see also 83d6). The superlatives there may be merely intensive ('transparently clear and utterly real', Hackforth). But Plato elsewhere speaks of Forms as 'more real' than sensible things, notably in the *Republic* 514a–516a, 585b–e.

What sort of 'reality' is at issue when sensible things are said not to be real, or not to be the only, or the most, real things there are? G. Vlastos (*N.E.P.A.* 1–19, *A.P.A.* 1965–6, 5–19) has argued that in questioning the reality of sensible things, Plato does not mean to deny their 'existence'. Nor, in denying that they are 'most real', does he ascribe to them a lesser degree of 'existence' than to Forms. Rather, the Form F is 'more real' than sensible Fs in that 'it yields a better disclosure of what an F is' (*N.E.P.A.* 5). Would such an interpretation fit the present passage? Philosophy tells the soul not to regard what it observes through the senses as 'real'. Could this mean 'not to regard, e.g., sensible equals as really equal'? Or does it mean 'not to regard sensible things as real beings'? The latter surely suits the context better. The error to which sense-bound souls were said to be prone at 81b4 is not that of taking objects of sensual enjoyment to be the only real Fs, but that of taking them to be the only 'real beings'. In the wider context, the point required is that sensible bodies are not the only real beings, and the survival of the soul therefore need not depend upon the continued existence of the body. It would be irrelevant to this point to insist that sensible things are unreliable exemplars of attributes such as equality or beauty. The essential point would be to maintain that they are not the only 'realities' or 'things that *are*'. It is the Forms that 'are' in the fullest possible way. Cf.77a2–5, where their 'being' seems undeniably existential, and see on 76d7–77a5.

If this is correct, the point of denying that sensible things are (fully) real, or of asserting that Forms are more real than sensible things, is that the latter are more properly said to be 'real' or to 'be'. The so-called 'realities' and 'beings' of the sensible world are, strictly, miscalled. High standards for the proper use of 'being' are thus imposed, to which Plato does not always adhere himself. See, e.g., 79a6 and note 34.

83b5–e3. Bodily pleasure and pain are reproached here for compelling belief in the reality of their objects. There is no suggestion that they are themselves unreal or not fully real. But see on 60b1–c7. For the alleged 'greatest and most extreme of all evils' (83c2–3) see on 89d1–4.

84a2–b8. The phrase 'not the object of opinion' applied to the Form world at 84a8 glances at the important Platonic contrast between 'opinion' and 'knowledge'. These are differentiated in the *Republic* (476d–480) according to their 'objects', Forms being the only objects of true knowledge, and sensible things being the objects of opinion. The distinction is not drawn in these terms in the *Phaedo*. But its essence is everywhere present in the contrast between philosophers and other men—e.g. 82a11–b3.

At 84b2 the soul is said to 'die'. Strictly, this is inconsistent with the thesis that it is 'deathless'. The meaning, however, is clearly that it ends its association with the body. Cf.77d4 and see on 64c2–9 (p.86).

Socrates ends (b5–8) by scouting all fears that the soul could be 'blown away by winds'. This reminds us that the Affinity Argument has been concerned to correct the popular misconception of the soul's nature. See on 80d8–81a3.

3.4 Simmias' and Cebes' Objections (84c1–88b8)

Counter-arguments are now advanced by Simmias and Cebes. Simmias likens the soul to the attunement of an instrument, and Cebes compares it with the weaver of a series of cloaks. These images suggest that it perishes at death.

84d4–85d10. Socrates' comparison of himself with his fellow servants, the swans, illustrates the theme of mortal obedience to divine rule (80a). See on 58a6–c5. For 'eleven Athenian gentlemen' (85b9) see on 59e6–60a1.

Simmias' remarks about philosophical inquiry (85c1–d10) are notable on several counts. In recognizing that certainty is either difficult or impossible to attain in this life (85c3–4, cf.107a8–b3), he echoes what was said at 66e–67a and 68a–b. The reference to a 'divine doctrine' (85d3–4) may be to Orphic teaching, but Simmias seems to entertain little hope of a revelation. He conveys a clear sense of the difference between philosophic inquiry and religious dogma. His characterization of fallible human reason as a 'raft', and his 'voyage' metaphor, are expressive of the open-minded tone of the discussion. Indeed, Simmias is committed to the very method that Socrates will later describe as his own (99c–100a). The parallel may escape notice in translation, because uniform rendering of *logos*, a key word in both passages, is impossible. Among its commoner meanings are 'discussion', 'account', 'definition', 'reason', 'argument', and 'statement', none of which will suit the present contrast between the human and the divine (85c9, d3). 'Doctrine' has therefore been used here. Later, where Socrates speaks of his own recourse to *logoi* (99e5, 100a1), it has been translated 'theories'. But the close similarity between the passages should be observed. Cf. especially, 85c7–d2 with 99c8–d1. See also on 90b4–91c5, 92c11–e3, and 100a3–9 (p.181).

85e3–86a3. *Harmonia* has been translated 'attunement' rather than 'harmony', except in the joking allusion to Harmonia, wife of Cadmus, who personifies Simmias' argument at 95a4. In a musical context 'attunement' is less misleading than 'harmony', whose modern musical sense the word never bears. 'Attunement' is also conveniently related to 'tune', which is needed for the verb at 93a–94a. The noun is formed on this verb, whose primary meaning is 'fit together' or 'join'. It has a basic sense of 'fitting together', 'adjustment', or 'arrangement', in which Simmias applies it to 'all the products of craftsmen' (86c6–7). It can thus mean the 'adjustment' of the parts of an instrument, and specifically the tuning of its strings. Hence it comes to mean a musical scale or mode, or, more broadly, music. See L.S.J. s.v. ἁρμονία. For various Platonic uses, cf. *Symposium* 187a–188a, *Republic* 398e–400a, 430e3–4, 431e8, 443d5–e2, 531a–b. The interpretation to be placed upon it in connection with Simmias' theory of the soul is far from clear. See on 86b5–d4.

86a3–b5. Simmias here parodies the argument of 80c2–d10. The properties ascribed earlier to the soul—'unseen', 'incorporeal', 'divine'—belong also to an attunement. But just as an attunement does not outlast lyre and strings, so the soul's possession of these properties need not entail that it outlasts the body. This is a powerful objection, and, as Bluck notes (22, 86), the force of the attunement analogy as a criticism of the Affinity Argument is never denied. However, the parallel between attunement and soul, as the latter was represented in the Affinity Argument, is not exact: (1) The case for the soul's indestructibility rested upon its supposed incompositeness. But an 'attunement', however interpreted (see next note), is evidently not incomposite. Socrates later calls it 'a composite thing' (92a8, cf.93a1). (ii) The soul was said to resemble the divine by virtue of its ruling the body (80a). But, as will be argued later (94b4–e7), an attunement is incapable of ruling its constituent elements. So 'divine' must apply differently to soul and attunement (cf.94e5–6). (iii) An attunement, although 'unseen' (85e5), is—on at least one interpretation—capable of being heard, whereas the soul is not accessible to the senses at all.

86b5–d4. The attunement analogy is now developed further.

147

Simmias says that something of this sort is 'what we actually take the soul to be' (b6–7): the soul is a blending or attunement of the bodily elements. Here he goes beyond criticism of the Affinity Argument. The attunement theory of the soul is not merely consistent with its destruction at death, but actually entails it. Two problems arise here: (1) Who are 'we' who are said to hold the theory? (2) What exactly does it maintain?

(1) Does Simmias mean, as might seem natural for a disciple of Philolaus (see on 61d3–e9), 'we Pythagoreans'? It is true that the theory has some appeal for the Pythagorean Echecrates (88d3–6). But it is flatly inconsistent with the Pythagorean orthodoxy that seems implicit in Philolaus' teaching on suicide, if this is correctly represented by 61e–62b (cf. DK 44 A 23, B 14). Simmias must be associating himself either, as Burnet suggests (note on 86b6), with a heterodox Pythagorean group, or with 'people in general'. The latter seems preferable for the reasons given by Hackforth (102–3). Cf.92d1–2 and see note 49. The attunement theory is acutely criticized, from very different perspectives, by Aristotle (*De Anima* 407b27–408a30) and Lucretius (*De Rerum Natura* iii. 94–135), but neither refers to the *Phaedo* or identifies the theory with any particular school. Aristotle simply calls it 'persuasive to many' (407b27–8), and ascribes a wholly different theory of the soul to the Pythagoreans (404a16–20). For the view that the attunement theory is of Pythagorean origin, see F. M. Cornford, *C.Q.* 1922, 145–50. For a full discussion of the relation between the present passage and later versions of the attunement theory, see H. B. Gottschalk, *Phronesis* 1971, 179–98.

(2) Is Simmias identifying the soul with (a) a ratio according to which bodily elements are combined; or (b) the condition of the body when they are thus combined; or (c) some complex product, analogous to the 'music' of a lyre, yielded by the bodily parts? A. E. Taylor (*P.M.W.* 194) takes the theory in sense (c): '"mind" is the tune given out by the body, the music made by the body.' He compares it with the epiphenomenalism of T. H. Huxley. *Harmonia* could, perhaps, bear this meaning (see on 85e3–86a3), and occasional phrases give the interpretation some support: 'very lovely and divine' (85e5–86a1) seems well suited to music; at 86c6–7 Simmias refers to attunements 'in musical notes', which might be regarded as elements in a musical scale or melody (cf. 'notes' at 92c1); and at 94c5 an attunement is assumed to depend not only upon the tension of the strings, but upon their being struck (cf.93a9).

Nevertheless, this interpretation, which is unmentioned by Aristotle, is probably mistaken: (i) The soul is expressly said (86b9,

d2—3) to be a 'blending and attunement' of the bodily elements, the
hot and cold, wet and dry, which are more closely analogous to the
physical components of a lyre than to musical notes. (ii) Simmias
refers to attunements 'in all the products of craftsmen' (86c7).
These presumably include such things as painting, weaving, building,
and furniture (cf. *Republic* 400d11—401a8), which exhibit 'structure', but produce nothing analogous to the music of an instrument.
(iii) 'Attunement' will be contrasted several times with 'non-attunement' (93c5, 93e4, 93e8, 94a3), which means 'being out of tune'
rather than 'lack of music'. Above all, (iv) Simmias is comparing the
soul with something that is destroyed as soon as the tension of the
strings is altered: 'when our body is unduly relaxed or tautened by
illnesses and other troubles, then the soul must perish at once'
(86c3—5). Clearly, it is the tuned state of the strings that 'perishes'
in this way rather than the music. For music could hardly be said to
'perish', even though it can no longer be produced, as a result of
relaxing or tightening the strings. It is true that the tuned state,
once lost, may be restored by restringing, and retuning the instrument, whereas the soul cannot be restored to a dead body. But
equally, a musical scale or melody can be replayed many times on
the same instrument. The analogy breaks down at this point on any
interpretation.

There remain the alternatives (a) and (b), that are distinguished
and separately refuted by Aristotle. The distinction between these
is rather a fine one, and may not even have been recognized by Plato
himself. But if a choice has to be made, (b) is perhaps preferable. The
notion of the soul as a mathematical ratio is rather abstruse, and
would be less likely to have appealed to 'most people' (92d2). It is
true that if 'attunement' means the tuned state of an instrument, it
will be hard to understand the suggestion at 93a11—12 that an
attunement itself could be tuned. But this is a difficulty on any view.

However interpreted, the attunement theory is a notable ancestor
of the many accounts of the soul, from that of Aristotle onwards,
which have denied its independent existence either as causally impossible or as logically absurd. It makes the essential point, central
to all such accounts, that the soul is not an entity separate or
separable from the body. The theory thus challenges a basic assumption of Socrates' arguments, that we are 'part body and part soul'
(79b1—2). In confronting him with it, Plato recognizes it as a
plausible and popular rival to his own view (cf.92d).

86e6—87a7. Cebes here accepts the conclusion of the Recollection Argument that our souls existed before birth (a1—4). His own
account of the soul will be consistent with that view, whereas that of

Simmias is not (cf.91e—92a). Unlike Simmias, therefore, he can preface his objection by harking back to the state of the argument at 77b5—c5.

At 87a5—7 he dissociates himself from Simmias' objection 'that soul isn't stronger and longer-lived than body'. Here he speaks as if Socrates had asserted and Simmias had denied that soul is 'stronger' and 'longer-lived' than body. Neither of them had used those words. But Socrates' argument at 80c—d was based on the supposition that soul is more durable than body, and Simmias had countered by comparing the soul with an attunement. Cebes here rejects the implications of that comparison. He goes on (87a7—b2, c1—5) to parody the argument of 80c—d in his own way.

87b4—8. It is essential to Cebes' analogy, as Hackforth rightly argues against Burnet, that the weaver should both weave and wear his own cloaks (b7—8). This introduces a new and striking picture of the relation between soul and body: the latter is causally dependent upon, 'made by', the former. In this respect Cebes' theory is antithetical to Simmias', exactly reversing the order of causal dependency between body and soul. If the soul, in some sense, 'makes' the body, it must exist before it. Makers exist before their products. But they need not survive them. Indeed, many kinds of product, such as statues and buildings, last longer than men. Cloaks are not among these, however, and the special implications of weaving are developed further below. See on 87d3—e5.

Since cloaks are relatively short-lived, it is of some importance that the weaver should die in old age (b5). An old weaver would quite likely die before his last cloak wore out, whereas a younger one might be expected to outlive the cloaks he was currently making. Accordingly, the soul would have less chance of surviving its last 'cloak', if the weaver were old. His age would not matter, of course, if it were stipulated that he goes on weaving and wearing cloaks till he dies. For he would then have to predecease his last cloak in any event.

87c1—3. 'Which class of thing is longer-lived, a man, or a cloak in constant use and wear': the terms of Cebes' parody suggest a distinction between classes and their members. From the premiss that *X*s as a class are more durable than *Y*s as a class, it cannot be inferred that *this X* will last longer than *this Y*. Even if souls as a class are stronger than bodies as a class, the fact that the body is preserved for some time after death does not show that the soul survives also. Men as a class last longer than cloaks in constant use. But some cloaks last longer than some men, and even the longest-lived of men will perish before a cloak finished on his dying day. It should be noted that men and cloaks alike have a finite life-span, and that a member of the longer-lived class may thus predecease a member of the shorter-lived one. This is why Socrates must show not merely that soul is 'stronger' or 'longer-lived' than body, but that it is 'completely immortal and imperishable' (88b5–6).

87d3–e5. Cebes now deploys his analogy in a more damaging way. If it is correct, the soul's immortality is not only not proven, but is actually disproved. The soul does not survive the last of the 'many bodies' that it weaves and wears out (d7–8). These 'bodies' are, it should be observed, the series of tissues that are successively wasted and rebuilt in the course of a single life-time. At 87d9 and 87e5 'the body' reverts to its usual meaning. For Cebes, it is, of course, only a series of 'bodies' in the special sense of 87d8. On his theory, our ordinary concept of 'the body' as a single, persistent entity is, strictly, a fiction. Cf. *Symposium* 207d–e. The body is in constant flux, and must be continually 'rewoven' by the soul (87e1, cf.91d7). Death occurs when, and because, the soul itself perishes (e3–5). The soul is conceived here as a source of vital energy, an agent of continuous organic renewal, finally exhausted at death. Thus, it is later suggested that death might be 'just this, the perishing of soul'. See on 91d2–9.

Note that Cebes does not, as yet, raise the possibility that the soul might occupy a succession of 'bodies' in the ordinary sense, i.e. become incarnate in one living body after another (95d5). The words 'especially in a life of many years . . . while the man is still alive' (87d8–9) show that his 'weaving' image cannot be taken in that way. The idea of a series of incarnations is not broached until 88a (see next note).

Cebes' statement of his theory should be compared with Socrates' restatements of it at 91d and 95b–d. Significantly, it is never refuted in the sequel. Unlike the attunement theory, it is not recanted or denounced as an impostor (92d1–4). Socrates will, indeed, argue that the soul, unlike the weaver, is imperishable. But otherwise he never disputes the theory as a model for understanding the relation between body and soul. Perhaps, therefore, it expresses his own view of the soul's animating function (cf.105c9–d5), though it is incompatible with the notion of soul as a 'prisoner' in the body.

88a1–b8. For the text and grammar of this passage see note 43. It might be granted, Cebes suggests (a4–7), that some souls could have undergone many previous incarnations. But unless the soul can be proved 'completely immortal and imperishable', no one can feel assured that his own soul is not incarnate for the last time, and will not perish at his death (b3—8).

To admit that reincarnation is possible would, of course, preclude inferring from the mere fact of death that the soul had perished, as was suggested above (87e4—5). But even so the soul, conceived as a source of vital energy, might eventually wear out. Successive incarnations might have weakened it (a8—9), or incarnation might be the start of a 'terminal illness' for it (cf.95d1—4). Socrates will try to meet this objection by arguing that soul is not the kind of thing that can 'wear out' at all. The effect of Cebes' remarks here is to show that previous incarnations, even if admitted, would give no 'inductive' grounds for a belief in survival. For we can never tell how many previous incarnations a soul has undergone, or what its present condition is.

'No one can know this death or detachment from the body which brings perishing to the soul—since none of us can possibly perceive it' (a10—b3). Hackforth (100, n.2) translates and interprets these words as if they supported the viewpoint of someone who grants, improbably, that the soul 'does not suffer in its many births', i.e. one who holds that the soul could survive many deaths and rebirths without ill effect. But they are much more likely to support the sceptical position for which Cebes himself is arguing, the view that, for all we can tell, our soul's present incarnation may be its last. It is not, indeed, very clear exactly what it is that we cannot 'perceive', since the object of that verb is not expressed. But perhaps Cebes means that, since we cannot perceive *the soul*, we cannot tell how badly 'worn' it is, and therefore cannot gauge its chances of survival. Hence, no one can know whether his own death, or—more generally—whether *any* particular death, will bring perishing to the soul.

At 88b1 the words translated 'detachment from the body' are taken by most translators to mean 'dissolution of the body'. The present version takes 'from the body' as genitive of separation, and makes the phrase explanatory of 'this death' which precedes it. It will then be parallel with 'its present disjunction from the body' at 88b7—8. It shows that 'death' is here used in the sense established at 64c2—9, and suggests that the soul's repeated 'deaths', like its 'births' (a6—9), may be traumata, one of which proves fatal to it. The usual interpretation would imply that the soul might be destroyed by 'dissolution of the body', i.e. decomposition. But this would be inapposite. For decomposition does not ensue immediately at death (80c4—5), and there is no reason, on Cebes' theory, to suppose that it affects the soul at all.

The words 'completely immortal and imperishable' (b5—6) are

significant. Socrates' answer to Cebes will consist in trying to show that soul has just these properties (cf.95c1, 106e9–107a1).Hackforth (100, n.3, cf.122, n.1, 164, n.1) thinks that 'immortal' and 'imperishable' are 'as yet' used synonymously. But Socrates will first argue that soul is 'immortal' (102b–105e), and then that it is 'imperishable' (106a–e). D. O'Brien (*C.Q.* 1968, 97) rightly argues that the distinction is anticipated here. See on 91d2–9, 95b5–e6, 105e10–107a1 (p.217).

3.5 Reply to Simmias (88c1–95a3)

Socrates prefaces his reply with a warning against 'misology', the hatred of arguments. He then counters the objection of Simmias by refuting the attunement theory.

88c1–89c10. Echecrates' dismayed reactions to Simmias' and Cebes' objections introduce the parallel between arguments and people that occupies this section. Note that the argument for immortality is itself personified at 89b9–c1. Socrates is determined that it shall not 'die', that it shall be 'revived'. The fate of the argument thus parallels his. He is the human counterpart of his own thesis.

At 88d8 Echecrates wants to be convinced that when a man dies, his soul does not 'die with him'. Comparison of this passage with 88a4–6 reveals a shift in the usage of 'die'. In the earlier passage Cebes grants that when we have died, nothing prevents our souls from being born and 'dying over and over again'. 'Dying over and over again' must mean 'being repeatedly separated from the body'. This is consistent with the definition of death at 64c2–9, and with the soul's being said to 'die' at 77d3–4 and 84b2. But in the present passage, the compound verb translated 'die with him' cannot mean merely 'be separated from the body'. It must mean something like 'cease to exist (along with the man himself)'.

At 89c5–6 Phaedo says: 'even Heracles is said to have been no match for two'. Heracles, while fighting the hydra, was attacked by a large crab, and called his nephew Iolaus to his aid (cf. *Euthydemus* 297c). The 'two' opponents meant here must be (1) Simmias and (2) Cebes, and not, as K. Dorter suggests (*Dialogue* 1970, 570), (1) their joint case against immortality, and (2) the consequent threat of misology. Since Socrates does not mention misology till 89d1, Phaedo could not be alluding to it at 89c5. 'While there's still light' (89c7–8), however, glances forward to Socrates' execution, which was due at sunset (cf.61e4, 116e1–2).

89d1–4. Socrates here says that one could suffer no greater evil than 'misology', whereas at 83c2–9 the greatest of all evils was said to be taking the sensible world to be fully real. These alleged evils, although surely not the same, may, in Plato's view, be related. One who has lost all faith in rational argument will not recognize Forms as the true 'realities'. He will assume that the sensible world alone is real, and will thus be 'deprived both of the truth and of knowledge of things that are' (90d6–7).

'Misologist' and 'misology' have been used to parallel 'misanthropist' and 'misanthropy'. The Greek words are rare, but cf. *Laches* 188c6, *Republic* 411d7. 'Arguments' suits the emphasis in this context upon rational discussion, but is not altogether satisfactory (see next note). At 90b6–8 and 90c9, arguments are said to be 'true' and 'false'. These words do not go naturally with 'arguments', but have been kept to preserve the required parallel between arguments and people. 'Skill in arguments' (90b7) perhaps includes not only 'knowing how to assess arguments' (Hackforth), but the capacity to handle arguments in live discussion. This is not only parallel with 'skill in human relations' (89e5–90a2) but actually requires it. Socrates is shown as a master at handling people and arguments alike (88e4–89a7, 95a8–b4). See also on 84d4–85d10.

90b4–91c5. The misologist's distrust of arguments is extended at 90c3 to the 'things' that they concern. Cf.88c6–7. Finding arguments neither true nor secure, the misologist supposes that 'things' lack these properties as well. Thus, since arguments seem to him 'now true and now false' (d2–3), there can be for him no fixed truths: 'the things that are' share the arguments' instability, like things fluctuating in the rapid currents of the Euripus (c5–6).

The assumption that 'arguments' and 'things' have properties in common underlies Socrates' own resort to 'arguments' (*logoi*) at 99e–100a, where it has been translated 'theories'. In studying in them 'the truth of the things that are' (99e5–6, cf.90d6–7), he supposes that they reflect that truth. Indeed, the Theory of Forms, in one aspect, is precisely the assumption that truth is discoverable through philosophical arguments. The Forms are the 'truth' that 'true arguments' express. Here the inadequacy of the translations 'true' and 'argument' becomes apparent. 'Truth' not only belongs to 'arguments', but also characterizes or designates 'the things that are'. It is a property not only of arguments, but of what they express. And 'arguments' are not merely pieces of reasoning, to be assessed for their internal logic, but are characterizations of a 'reality' external to themselves. These nuances defy translation, and are a constant source of difficulty. For 'truth' and 'reality' see on 66b1–c5 and 83b2–3. For 'arguments' see on 84d4–85d10, 100a3–9 (p.178), and previous note.

At 90c1 the translation 'antinomies' preserves the sense of 'arguments for and against' a given proposition. For the prevalence of such argumentation, see G. Ryle, *Plato's Progress*, Ch.4, and Hackforth, 108−11. Good specimens are to be found in the treatise *Dissoi Logoi*, 'Arguments Both Ways', trans. R. K. Sprague, *Mind* 1968, 155−67. The style of argument is parodied by Plato in the *Euthydemus*. 'Contradiction-mongers' has been used to translate the same notion at 101e2, where it is applied to those who trade in arguments of this kind, caring nothing for truth but only for victory. Plato denounces them elsewhere for inducing intellectual or moral scepticism (cf., e.g., *Republic* 538d−539e). The motive to which they appeal, the desire to be proved right and to prove others wrong, is endemic in philosophy. Socrates may even be semi-serious in confessing to it himself (91a−b). But his primary concern to convince himself (91a7−b1) is genuine. It is a mark of the true philosopher, and shows continually in what he says (96b1, 96e7, 97b4, 100d9).

91d2−9. In restating Cebes' position, Socrates asks 'whether death might not be just this, the perishing of soul' (d6−7). D. O'Brien (*C.Q.* 1968, 98−100) interprets this as a new definition of 'death': instead of meaning, as at 64c2−9, 'separation of soul from body', it now means 'perishing of soul'. Consequently, soul must now be proved not only 'immortal' but 'imperishable'. For it might survive separation from the body once or many times, as Cebes had allowed (88a4−7), and yet be unable to survive all such separations. To be shown capable of this, it must be proved immune from 'death' in the new sense, i.e. imperishable.

O'Brien (op.cit. 98, n.2) links the present passage with 88a10−b2 and 95d2. But neither of those passages points to a redefinition of 'death', and both use the term in its familiar sense. The former (see on 88a1−b8) expressly recalls the sense established at 64c. The latter suggests that incarnation might be the start of the soul's perishing, and that it might finally perish 'in what is called death' (95d4), i.e. in 'death' as that term is commonly used. Could Socrates here be operating with the new sense of 'death' that O'Brien suggests? If so, he would be speculating that 'death', in this new sense, might begin with the soul's entry into the body, and be completed at the time of 'death' in the familiar sense. This would be a confusing way of redefining the term.

It seems preferable to take the present lines either (i) as restating the idea of 87d8−e5 that the death of *the man* might be due to the perishing of his soul, or (ii) as recalling the idea of 88a9−b3 that one of *the soul's* deaths might 'bring perishing' to it. With (i), 'death is the perishing of soul' will be an explanation rather than a redefinition of death. Death is due to the perishing of soul, somewhat as a black-out is due to a power-failure. The cessation of vital functions is due to a breakdown of their source. On this view, the words simply resume Cebes' original idea of soul as an agent of bodily change. With (ii), 'death is the perishing of soul' will mean that the trauma of separation from the body will sooner or later prove fatal to the soul. This would link the words closely with 88a10–b2, and 'death' would be used in precisely the sense there specified. It is possible that both these ideas are in Socrates' mind, but the emphasis on constant bodily flux (cf.91d7 with 87d9) strongly suggests that he is thinking at least of (i). If he is thinking only of (i), there is no reference here to Cebes' concession at 88a4–7 regarding reincarn-ation. That will be glanced at only in the second restatement of his position (95d4–6).

On any interpretation of these lines 'death' must, here as at 88a10–b4 and 95d4, mean the 'event' of dying rather than the 'state' of being dead. See note 4, and on 71d5–e3. For the concept of 'death', see also on 57a1–b3, 64c2–9, 88a1–b8, 88c1–89c10, 105c9–d12, 105d13–e9, 105e10–107a1 (p.221).

92a6–c3. Socrates here points out that the attunement theory of the soul conflicts with the belief in its prenatal existence, which Simmias had accepted. This point is *ad hominem*, and would, of course, be ineffective against someone who rejected the Recollection Argument. But how effective is it against someone who accepts it? As noted above (see on 86b5–d4), the attunement theory may be variously interpreted. An attunement may be (a) a ratio, (b) a tuned state, or (c) music. On any of these interpretations, Simmias might reply that an attunement could, in fact, have existed before the particular body in which it inhered. Thus, (a) the ratio governing the lengths of lyre strings could be said to exist before any given lyre; (b) the tuned state of lyres in general could be said to exist before some particular lyre came into existence; and (c) music, e.g. a scale or melody, could exist before any given instrument on which it might be played. In short, neither tunings nor tunes depend for their existence upon that of particular instruments.

Simmias makes no such response, however. To do so would require 'attunement' to be understood in such a way that different lyres could share the same attunement. On such a view, Simmias' theory would entail that different bodies could share the same soul. To avoid this consequence, it must be supposed that the attunement of each instrument is unique to it, and numerically distinct from the attunements in all others. It could not then exist before its own lyre, or survive that instrument's destruction. Understood thus, the attunement theory would make Simmias' original point, and would also be defeated by Socrates' present objection.

At 92b7–8 Socrates says: 'attunement isn't, in fact, the same kind of thing as that to which you liken it' (sc. the soul). This interpretation follows Burnet's text, and assumes a slight looseness in the use of 'likening', since it is, strictly, the soul that has been likened to an attunement, and not vice versa. For this reason Verdenius prefers a variant reading, and would replace 'as that to which you liken it' with 'as you represent it' or 'as you guess it to be'. But if Simmias can be said to have 'represented' an attunement as being of any particular nature, it is only as being liable to perish before its component elements, and Socrates is not disputing that.

This note, and subsequent notes on Socrates' refutation of the attunement theory, owe much to an unpublished paper by Mr. C. C. W. Taylor.

92c11–e3. Simmias now renounces the attunement theory as incompatible with the theory of Recollection, which was in turn derived 'from a hypothesis worthy of acceptance' (d6–7, cf.e1–2), i.e. the Theory of Forms. It is plausible to see his withdrawal as an application of the 'hypothetical method' that Socrates will describe at 100a3–7, the positing of the theory he judges to be strongest, and the taking of things not in accord with it to be untrue. Admittedly, Simmias has not yet been told of the hypothetical method. But it is because he believes in adopting 'the best and least refutable of human doctrines' (cf.85c8–d1 with 100a3–4) that he now has to retract the attunement theory. He is committed, unawares, to Socrates' own method. See on 84d4–85d10.

The sense of the words translated 'just as surely as its object exists—the Being, bearing the name of *"what it is"* ' (d8–9) is uncertain. Loriaux (155, cf. *E.F.P.* 31) argues that the phrase 'bearing the name' must have a causal nuance, and embodies a proof of the Forms' existence. This, he thinks, dictates the interpretation 'in virtue of its bearing the name of that which *is*'—i.e. 'that which exists'. The present version follows Loriaux in taking the main verb of the 'just as' clause (the first 'is' at d9) existentially. But the sense of 'is' in the 'what' clause cannot be fixed as he argues. To derive the Forms' 'being' from the nomenclature used to refer to them would be a singularly weak 'proof' of their existence. See also note 50.

92e4–93a10. Socrates here begins a new assault on the attunement theory. The section that follows, 93a11–94b3, is extremely difficult, and its analysis remains highly problematic. Reference should be made to Archer-Hind, Burnet, Hackforth, Verdenius, Bluck, and W. F. Hicken, *C.Q.* 1954, 16–22. Olympiodorus' commentary (ed. W. Norvin, 169) and Philoponus on Aristotle *De Anima* I,4. (ed. M. Hayduck, 141–5) are also relevant.

The argument of 93a11–94b3 will be referred to here as 'Argument B'. It is followed at 94b4–95a3 by a further argument against the attunement theory, which will be called 'Argument A'. Steps in each argument will be numbered accordingly (A1 etc., B1 etc.). The attunement hypothesis itself will be referred to as H.

The admissions of 92e4–93a10 serve as premisses for Argument A. At 93a11 Socrates appears to start afresh, eliciting a new set of admissions (93a11–c10), to be used as premisses for Argument B. The structure of the whole passage 92e4–95a3 is therefore as follows:

    (1) Premisses for Argument A (92e4–93a10);
    (2) Premisses for Argument B (93a11–c10);
    (3) Argument B (93d1–94b3);
    (4) Argument A (94b4–95a3).

Here the pattern A-B-B-A is well marked (cf. Hicken, op.cit. 17). Yet it is hard to see why Plato has cast the arguments in this form. If the A premisses are left unused until Argument A, the train of thought begun by them is interrupted for more than a page. Archer-Hind (78) provides continuity by linking the A with the B premisses: the admission at 93a6–10 that an attunement is governed by its constituent elements is supposed to support the claim at 93a11–b3 that the extent of every attunement depends upon the extent to which it is tuned. But this seems unlikely. The words 'Again now', which preface the B premisses at 93a11 (cf.92e4, 94b4), serve to divide them from the A premisses rather than to link them. Nor, in fact, are these sets of premisses logically connected. The dependence of an attunement upon its constituent elements does not imply its dependence upon the extent to which it is tuned. The former dependence concerns the state of an attunement (a1), how 'it acts and is acted upon' (a4), whereas the latter concerns the extent to which it is an attunement (93b1–2). Moreover, the constituent elements are not mentioned in the B premisses at all. The extent to which an attunement is an attunement is said to depend not upon how its elements are tuned, but upon how it is tuned itself (93a12, a14).

The A and B arguments, and their respective premisses, are therefore better taken as logically unrelated. Further discussion of the A premisses will be deferred until Argument A is considered. See on 94b4–95a3.

93a11–b3. The B premisses begin here. Socrates asks (i) 'Isn't it natural for every attunement to be an attunement just as it's been tuned?' (a11–12). Simmias fails to understand, and is next asked (ii) 'Isn't it the case that if it's been tuned more and to a greater extent, assuming that to be possible, it will be more an attunement and a greater one, whereas if less and to a smaller extent, it will be a lesser and smaller one?' (a14–b2).

(1) What difference, if any, is intended between 'more' and 'to a greater extent', and between 'less' and 'to a smaller extent'? (2) Does this passage imply that degrees of attunement are possible, or that they are not, or does it imply neither of these things?

For (1), which is of minor importance, see note 51. Whatever difference may be intended between the two pairs of terms, no use is made of it in the argument. For simplicity, therefore, only the antithesis between 'more' and 'less' will be used in these notes.

(2), however, is critical for the argument. Burnet takes the passage as an admission that no attunement admits of degree. Socrates first asks (i) whether the nature of every attunement depends upon how it has been tuned, i.e. whether it varies according as it has been tuned to the interval of a fourth, a fifth, or an octave. He then suggests (ii) that if, *per impossibile*, an attunement were more or less tuned, it would not be more or less an attunement. On this view, (ii) would have to be understood as asking: 'And it isn't the case, is it, that (even) if it has been tuned more, it will be more of an attunement, whereas if it has been tuned less, it will be less of one?' However, if framed in this way, Socrates' question would expect the answer 'No', and Simmias' 'Certainly' at 93b3 would be inappropriate. Moreover, on Burnet's interpretation, (ii) would be an inept reply to Simmias' 'I don't understand.' For it would not explain what Socrates has asked in (i), but would make a completely fresh point. Yet (ii) must be meant to clarify for Simmias what he had been asked in (i) (cf. W. F. Hicken, *C.Q.* 1954, 19). It must, therefore, be suggesting that if an attunement has been more or less tuned, assuming that to be possible, it must be more or less an attunement. The characterization of the attunement will depend upon that of the tuning process. The first premiss of the argument may therefore be interpreted thus:

B1. If an attunement has been more or less tuned, assuming that to be possible, it will be more or less an attunement.

What is meant, however, by the proviso 'assuming that to be possible'? Burnet says that this plainly indicates that it is not possible for an attunement to be more or less tuned, hence that it could not be more or less an attunement than another. However, the 'assuming' clause need not, in itself, imply '*per impossibile*'. Socrates does not say 'if, in fact, that *were* possible', but 'if, in fact, that *is* possible'. Cf.93e8 and 94a9, where 'assuming' introduces supposedly true premisses of the argument.

If Socrates were talking about the attunement of an *instrument*, Burnet's view would be clearly mistaken, for different degrees of tuning in a lyre obviously are possible. However, the subject of the sentence is 'attunement', and it is not easy to attach sense to an attunement's being tuned in different degrees, or even at all. Moreover, there would seem no point in adding the proviso 'assuming that to be possible', if the possibility were obviously beyond dispute. It therefore seems preferable to suppose, with Hicken, op.cit. 20, and Bluck, 100, n.1, 198, that the question whether an attunement can be tuned more or less is here simply left open. The argument will then turn neither upon its possibility (Philoponus, Archer-Hind, Hackforth), nor upon its impossibility (Burnet). A quite different account of the proviso given by Verdenius (see note 52) leaves the argument equally unaffected.

93b4–7. The next premiss is:
B2. One soul is not, even in the least degree, more or less a soul than another.
Burnet takes this as derived from the previous admission together with the hypothesis that soul is attunement. The present sentence certainly could be translated as an inference, but has not been so taken here. That one soul is not more or less a soul than another seems hard to deny, and would be ill supported by the far more questionable proposition that attunement admits of no degrees (cf. W. F. Hicken, *C.Q.* 1954, 19). But in any case, there are serious objections to taking the latter proposition as a premiss (see previous note).

Philoponus, partially followed by Hackforth (118), takes 93a11– b7 as a self-contained argument. Thus:
(1) An attunement can be more or less an attunement;
(2) A soul cannot be more or less a soul;
Hence,
(3) A soul cannot be an attunement.
However, (i) (1) has not been asserted (see the account of B1 in the previous note). (ii) Such an argument would be defective. Attunement as such might admit of degrees, while specific kinds of attunement, such as souls, did not. As Philoponus says, the argument would have to run '*every* attunement admits of degrees' (cf. Hicken, op.cit. 18, n.1). Moreover, (iii) if Simmias' theory were already refuted at 93b7, Socrates might be expected to say so, before passing on to a fresh point. 'Well, but' at 93b8 is therefore better taken as

continuing with a further phase of the same argument (cf. the same phrase at 79b1), than as introducing a new one.

93b8–c10. Two further premises are now added:
B3. Some souls are good, and others bad (b8–c2).
B4. Good souls contain attunement, and bad souls contain non-attunement (c3–8).

Both premises are accepted as self-evident, and must be assumed to be stronger than the attunement theory itself, if the argument is to succeed as a *reductio ad absurdum* of it. The denial of B3 will constitute the absurdity to which the theory will be reduced (94a8–10).

B4 suggests an account of goodness and badness like that of the *Republic* (430e, 443d–e), where temperance and justice are defined in terms of attunement within soul and state. Socrates will argue here that such an account would be incompatible with Simmias' attunement theory. But would it be any more compatible with his own earlier suggestion that the soul is 'incomposite'? The account of goodness in the *Republic* is based upon a doctrine of 'parts' of the soul. If attunement or non-attunement can be contained only by that which is composite, they would require a different account of the soul from that which the *Phaedo* suggests. Plato recognizes and tries to resolve the conflict between the doctrine of a composite soul and that of immortality at *Republic* 611a10–612a7. See also on 78c1–9.

Philoponus finds in 93c3–8 a further self-contained argument against the attunement theory: taken together with B3 and B4, it implies that an attunement (a) may have a further attunement, or (b) may have a non-attunement, within itself, either of which would be absurd. It is true that to a modern reader (a) sounds ill-formed, while (b) appears to breach the principle maintained later (102d5–103c8) that opposites cannot admit each other. Some such objection to (b) might be read into the argument at 94a2–4, but there is no indication that Socrates is appealing to it here. As for (a), the idea of an attunement's having a further attunement within itself seems no more objectionable than that of its being tuned, which figures twice in the argument (93a11–b1, 93d6–9), yet is never dismissed as improper. Nor is the conclusion required by Philoponus' interpretation, that soul is not attunement, actually drawn at 93c9–10. The argument therefore remains, as yet, incomplete (cf. W. F. Hicken, *C.Q.* 1954, 17, n.3).

93d1–5. Socrates now reaffirms B2, and then says: 'and this is the admission that no one attunement is either more or to a greater extent, or less or to a smaller extent, an attunement than another'.

Thus:

> B5. One attunement is not more or less an attunement than another (d3–4).

Burnet takes B5 as reiterating 93a11–b3, which he interprets as claiming that attunement admits of no degrees. Thus he translates: 'this is just our admission, (namely B5)'. But his interpretation seems untenable for the reasons given above. See on 93a11–b3. The natural sense of the present lines is 'this (sc. B2) amounts to the admission that B5'. See note 53. On this view, B2 yields B5 by substitution of 'attunement' for 'soul', based on Simmias' hypothesis (H). This raises two questions: (1) Is B5 consistent with B1? (2) Is it validly derived from B2?

(1) B5 will be inconsistent with B1, if, but only if, the latter is construed as asserting categorically that an attunement *can* be more or less an attunement. There need be no inconsistency, if B1 is taken as non-committal regarding this possibility, as urged above (see on 93a11–b3). Some, however, find the present lines irreconcilable with 93a11–b3, and would therefore emend the text at 93d4. For the effect of the emendation upon the argument, and some objections to it, see note 53.

(2) Those who would retain the MS. reading (e.g. Archer-Hind, Hicken) sometimes construe B5 as restricted to the attunements specifically under discussion, namely soul-attunements. Nowhere in the text is any such restriction stated. But if B5 extends to attunements in general, or refers to 'attunement' as such, its derivation from B2 is fallacious. From the premiss that no soul is more or less a soul than any other, conjoined with the hypothesis that soul is an attunement, it would not follow that no attunement whatever is more or less an attunement than any other, but only that no soul-attunement is more or less a soul-attunement than any other.

It should be noted that Greek lacks the indefinite article, and the sense of 'is' in 'soul is attunement' (H) is therefore unclear. In English we may distinguish more easily between (H1) 'soul is (identical with) attunement' and (H2) 'soul is an (or a kind of) attunement'. Socrates' refutation of H depends upon interpreting it as H1, and treating 'soul' and 'attunement' as interchangeable *salva veritate*. Substitutions of 'soul' and 'attunement' are made, accordingly, at 93d1–4, 93d12–e2, and 94a2–6. The attunement theory is, indeed, often expressed simply as 'soul is attunement' (92c9–10, 92e3, 93c3, 94a2, 94b1–2, 94c4, 94e2–3). But Simmias clearly need not be committed to the view that 'soul' and 'attunement' are equivalent terms. It is clear from several passages (86c2–3, 88d4–5, 91d1–2, 92a8, 94e8–95a1) that his meaning would be better expressed by H2. If so, Socrates' refutation of him is open to the above criticism.

93d6–e6. The argument continues:
B6. That which is not more or less an attunement has not been more or less tuned (d6–8).
B7. That which has not been more or less tuned participates in attunement to an equal degree (d9–11).
Hence,
B8. Soul has not been more or less tuned (d12–e3).
Hence,
B9. Soul does not participate more in non-attunement or in attunement (e4–6).

With Burnet's text at 93d4, the subject 'that which' (d6, d9) in B6 and B7 must be 'the attunement' rather than 'the soul', as would be required if the text were emended—see note 53. B6 then follows from B1 by contraposition. B7 introduces the new terminology 'participating in attunement', which seems to mean 'being in a state of attunement' as distinct from 'being an attunement'. If so, it is best taken as an independent premiss, rather than (with W. F. Hicken, *C.Q.* 1954, 21) as derived by conversion from B6: an equal degree of tuning entails an equal state of attunement. For the distinction between 'being in a state of attunement' and 'being an attunement' see next note.

B8 is prefaced by a repetition of B2, but is presumably derived by substituting 'soul' for 'attunement' in B6. B9 is derived from B8, together with a similar substitution in B7. The point of repeating B2 in obtaining B8 is not clear, but it may be meant to recall its role at B5, and consequently to suggest resubstitution of 'soul' for 'attunement' in B6 and B7. Strictly, however, what is needed to obtain B8 and B9 is the reintroduction of H. For the validity of substitutions based upon H, see previous note.

93e7–94b3. The attunement theory is now reduced to absurdity as follows:
B10. One soul does not participate more in goodness or badness than another (e7–10).
B11. A soul could never participate in badness (94a1–7).
B12. All souls of all living things are equally good (a8–11).
B13. B12 conflicts with B3 (supplied).
Hence,
B14. H is not correct (a12–b3).

Here B10 is derived from B9 by substituting 'goodness' for 'attunement' and 'badness' for 'non-attunement', on the strength of B4. B11 is given as a still more paradoxical conclusion than B10. B12 is based upon B10 and B11, with further reference to B2.

B10 and B12 are straightforward steps. The derivation of B11, however, is much more problematical. It is obtained from H (94a2) together with:

B5*. An attunement is completely itself, namely an attunement (a2–3).

This yields:

B5**. An attunement could never participate in non-attunement (a3–4).

B11 then follows by substitution of 'soul' for 'attunement' and 'badness' for 'non-attunement', based on H and B4 respectively, in B5**.

How is B5** supposed to follow from B5*? No doubt B5* should be taken as an abbreviated form of B5, 'One attunement is not more or less of an attunement than another'. The reasoning will then be from this assertion to B5**. But this transition is highly dubious. For it is arguable that, although every attunement is, indeed, as much an attunement as any other, nevertheless some attunements lack attunement, and some may, to use the terminology introduced at B7, 'participate' in attunement more or less than others. The shift to this terminology was represented in the previous note as a change from 'being an attunement' to 'being in a state of attunement'. This distinction must now be clarified.

'Attunement' may be taken to mean either a tuning (attunement[1]) or a correctly tuned state (attunement[2]). It might be agreed that every attunement[1] is an attunement[1] equally, no one attunement[1] more or less so than any other. But it may also be held that some attunements[1] participate in attunement[2] more or less than others, and that there is no contradiction in holding that an attunement[1] participates in non-attunement[2], i.e. lacks attunement[2]. Thus it could be admitted that every attunement[1] is equally an attunement[1], yet denied that every attunement[1] is equally in a state of attunement[2].

For example, the normal tuning of a guitar is E-A-D-G-B-E. This might be held to be no more an attunement[1] than the variant tuning D-A-D-G-B-E, which involves lowering a single string by one tone. It might also be held to be no more an attunement[1] than, say, F-A-D#-G-A#-C, a random combination of notes to which the strings could be, but are not in practice, tuned. Either of these latter tunings might be said to be no less an attunement[1] than the usual one. But if the usual tuning is assumed to be the only 'correct' one, then the second and third tunings mentioned could be regarded as participating less in attunement[2] than the usual one. There would be no contradiction in holding that they participated in non-attunement[2], or lacked attunement[2]. The third tuning might intelligibly be said to participate in attunement^2 less than the second, because it is, in an obvious way, further from the normal tuning than is the second. Note that these points are quite independent of a distinction that might be drawn between any of these tunings and particular instances of them. They could be expressed equally well in terms of the tunings themselves or in terms of their particular instances.

It seems, then, that B5 is defensible if it is interpreted solely in terms of attunement^1. But 'being an attunement^{1}' does not entail 'being in a state of attunement^2'. B5** therefore does not follow from B5, and seems, moreover, actually false. Applying this result to the soul, it may be argued that its being an attunement in the sense required by Simmias' theory need not preclude it from lacking attunement in some sense that would enable good and bad souls to be distinguished in the way proposed at B4. And if the derivation of B11 is fallacious, the further conclusion at B12, that all souls are equally good, will be open to similar objections.

It is hard to be sure that the argument equivocates upon 'attunement' in the way just suggested. But if it does, the root ambiguity is one that pervades the use of many abstract nouns, in both Greek and English, such as 'height', 'length', 'depth', 'size', 'weight', 'thickness', or 'speed'. In sense 1 we may speak of David's height as well as Goliath's, of the tortoise's speed as well as the hare's. But in sense 2 it is only Goliath who has height, and only the hare who has speed. Thus, David's height^1 can lack height^2; the tortoise's speed^1 can lack speed^2; and a lyre's attunement^1 can lack attunement^2.

Possibly, in denying that attunement can participate in non-attunement, Socrates would rely on the principle of 102d5–103c8, that 'opposites will not admit each other'. But it will be evident that that principle would not really be infringed by the supposition that an attunement^1 can admit non-attunement^2. For attunement^1 and non-attunement^2 are not opposites of each other.

A stronger reply for Socrates to make would be to deny that the attunement theory is correctly represented in terms of attunement^1. Soul, according to the theory, was not just *any* tuning of the bodily elements, but their correctly tuned state, i.e. attunement^2. Cf.86c1–2, 'when they're blended with each other in due proportion'. It therefore remains debatable whether good and bad souls (attunements^2) could, in fact, be distinguished in terms of a further attunement^2 in the way proposed at B4.

Hackforth (119–20) takes 94a2–5 as withdrawing the assumption, provisionally made at 93a14–b1, that one *can* tune a lyre more or less exactly. But that assumption was neither made nor denied in the earlier passage (see on 93a11–b3). Nor is it here denied that varying degrees of tuning in a lyre are possible. Bluck (100, n.1) cites *Republic* 349e10–16 as denying this, although, in fact, it suggests just the opposite. But controversy over whether a lyre can be tuned more or less exactly is largely irrelevant. For the soul is not being compared with a lyre, but with an attunement; and it is with the implications of an attunement's (not a lyre's) being tuned that the whole argument is concerned.

The *reductio ad absurdum* is finally sprung at 94a12–b3. B13 has been supplied in the summary above, to enable the attunement theory (H) to be represented as generating a contradiction: since B12 conflicts with the common-sense intuition B3 accepted earlier, H has to be withdrawn.

Note that at 94b1 the attunement theory is called a 'hypothesis' (cf.93c10). The argument is evidently an application of the 'hypothetical method' described at 100a and 101c–d. The hypothesis that soul is attunement has been shown to lead to 'contradiction', i.e. to a consequence (B12) which conflicts with an earlier admission (B3). It is rejected because its 'consequences' are in discord with each other (cf.101d4–5). See R. Robinson, *P.E.D.* 142. Of course, B3 is not itself a logical consequence of H but an independent assumption. But cf. Robinson (op.cit. 133): '[A hypothesis] may have conflicting consequences on our standing assumptions, that is, when combined with some of our permanent beliefs.' This is the kind of 'contradiction' involved both here and in the refutation of the attunement theory (Argument A) that follows. See also on 92c11–e3.

94b4–95a3. Argument A runs thus:

A1. The soul can control and oppose the bodily feelings (94b4–c2, 94c9–e1).

Furthermore, as was agreed earlier (92e4–93a10):

A2. An attunement can never be in a state other than that of its components (92e4–93a3).

A3. An attunement can neither act nor be acted upon in any way different from its components (93a4–5, 94c3–8).

Hence,

A4. An attunement cannot control or oppose its own components (93a6–9).

Hence,

A5. The soul cannot be an attunement (94e8–95a1).

A1 develops and applies the principle used earlier (80a), that soul 'rules' body. It often opposes bodily inclinations and prevents their gratification. These include anger and fear, hunger and thirst (94b8–

10, d5). All such states are here lumped together as 'bodily', and are viewed as sources of conflict between soul and body. In the *Republic* Plato will treat similar conflicts as evidence of different 'parts' within the soul itself. The first of the two lines quoted from the *Odyssey* (xx.17) at 94d8–e1 is used at *Republic* 441b6 to support a distinction between 'rational' and 'spirited' elements in the soul. See on 64e4–65a3 (p.89).

A2 and A3, if taken strictly, are overstatements. The attunement of a lyre is clearly capable of 'being acted upon' in a way in which its components are not. For it may be destroyed, while the strings and wood remain intact. Moreover, the strings may be 'acted upon' in such ways as being stretched or severed. These operations, although they affect the attunement, could hardly be regarded as affections of the attunement itself: *it* is not stretched or severed. Its affections need not, therefore, coincide with those of its components. But this does not alter the essential point. A lyre's attunement depends wholly upon the state and relationship of its material components, whereas they in no way depend upon it. The causal relation is in one direction only. By contrast, the soul is not only acted upon by the bodily elements, but acts upon them. This is the point at which the attunement theory is being held to break down.

All that would follow from this argument, however, is that the soul is not an attunement of bodily feelings. It would not follow that it is not an attunement at all. To this it might be replied that bodily feelings *are*, according to the attunement theory, the components of the soul. But this is not quite in line with Simmias' original account. The components there specified were 'hot and cold, dry and wet, and the like' (86b8–9). Bodily feelings, such as hunger and thirst, or anger and fear, were not mentioned. Yet they are now referred to as 'alleged sources' of the soul's existence (94c10–d1). No doubt they are to be thought of as due to the presence of the basic physical elements in various proportions, thirst, for example, being associated with heat (94b8–9). But they are clearly not on a par with those elements, and it therefore remains uncertain whether, according to the theory, the 'components' of a soul-attunement are the basic physical elements (as at 86b), or their psychic products (as here), or both.

More generally, the strength of the argument will depend upon whether the phenomena of conflict and self-control demand explanation in Socrates' terms. A defender of the attunement theory might deny that they evidence the activity of an autonomous soul. The soul's so-called 'opposition' to the body, he might object, is itself simply the effect of a bodily state.

3.6 Socrates' Story (95a4–102a9)

Cebes' objection leads Socrates into an account of his own intellectual history. He tells of his early interest in natural science, and his abandonment of it in favour of a quest of his own. His method is described and illustrated with reference to the Theory of Forms.

95b5–e6. Cebes' position is here restated once again. As before (88b5–6), it is required that soul be proved 'imperishable and immortal' (c1). Hackforth's view (122, n.1) that these terms are still being used synonymously is rightly rejected by D. O'Brien (*C.Q.* 1968, 97). But the addition of 'imperishable' does not seem to be dictated, as O'Brien suggests, by Cebes' concession regarding reincarnation. This concession would, he thinks, allow the soul a limited or 'partial' immortality, i.e. survival of one or more deaths, but would not guarantee it 'full' immortality, i.e. survival of any and every death. 'Imperishability' is therefore added, O'Brien suggests, to fill this potential deficiency in the notion of 'immortality'. See on 91d2–9.

If this were so, we should expect Cebes to allow that, were reincarnation granted, the soul would have been proved 'immortal' in the limited sense, and only its 'imperishability' would remain to be shown. But this is not how Socrates presents Cebes' position here. He argues that the soul's strength, divinity, and prior existence need not prove its *immortality* (c7, d1); and that it would make no difference whether the soul was incarnate once or many times (d4–5): one would still be foolish not to fear death, unless one could prove the soul *immortal* (d6–e1). A proof of 'immortality' would still be needed, then, even if the soul were reincarnate many times. It follows that 'immortality' cannot be used here in any sense less stringent than the ability to survive every death. And since Cebes agrees that the present résumé expresses his position exactly (e4–6), he can hardly have had anything else in mind at 88a–b.

It is doubtful whether the concept of 'partial' immortality finds any place in the dialogue. At 73a2–3 (see on 72e7–73a3) Cebes had referred to the doctrine of Recollection as showing that the soul is immortal, in virtue of its prenatal existence. But he later complains (77c1–5) that the Recollection Argument has shown only 'half' what is needed. It must also be shown that our souls will exist when we have died, 'if the proof is going to be complete'. That objection, essentially, is repeated here (c6–d2), and it is added that it would not be met, even if many incarnations were admitted. All this strongly suggests that for Cebes 'immortality' never connotes anything less than 'full' immortality in O'Brien's sense, the capacity to survive any number of deaths without perishing. Nevertheless, there is an important point in the addition of 'imperishable', which will become clear later. See on 105e10−107a1 (p.217).

95e7−96a5. Socrates' account of his intellectual history is, as G. Vlastos has said (*P.R.* 1969, 297), 'one of the great turning points in European natural philosophy'. It is, in fact, a striking counterpart in ancient philosophy of Descartes's *Discourse on Method*, despite its rejection of 'mechanistic' explanations that Descartes was to revive. Cf. A. E. Taylor, *P.M.W.* 200, n.1. Like Descartes, Socrates professes to be confused by the senses and to abandon their use. Both are pioneers of a new philosophical method. Both seek metaphysical foundations for mathematics and natural science. And both formulate basic certainties that fortify their religious convictions. Moreover, the autobiographical form of Socrates' story, as of Descartes's, disguises the true rigour of its author's thought.

For philosophical purposes it hardly matters whether Socrates' story is authentic, and if so, whether it is true of the historical Socrates or of Plato himself, or whether part is true of each. For a balanced review of these alternatives see Hackforth, 127−31. It is more important to ask how it bears upon Cebes' position. Why is his objection here said to require an inquiry into the reason concerning coming-to-be and destruction? This demands an elucidation of two key concepts: (1) 'reason', and (2) 'coming-to-be and destruction'.

(1) The primary sense of the noun translated 'reason' (*aitia*) is 'charge' or 'accusation'. The related adjective, applied to human agents, means 'responsible' or 'at fault' (cf.116c8), and the cognate verb means 'accuse' or 'blame'. The concept is thus rooted in the notion of human responsibility (cf.98e2−99a4). In a secondary and frequent use, the noun, and the adjective in its neuter form, are applied to a wide range of non-human things, to which events or states of affairs may be attributed. Similarly, the verb can mean 'impute' or 'ascribe' (98b9, c2, e1).

In its secondary use the noun has traditionally been rendered 'cause'. This hallowed mistranslation is particularly unfortunate here, since it covers, at most, only part of the field with which Socrates is concerned. Many of the things he will mention are not amenable to what we should call 'causal' explanation. They are not, and could not be, subsumed under causal laws, or related to sets of antecedent conditions sufficient for them to come about. See on 96c1−e5.

Socrates' interest in natural science prompts a number of questions of the form 'why is x F?', which are generally answered by a noun in the dative case ('by y') or by a prepositional phrase ('on account of', or 'owing to', or 'because of', y). It becomes clear from the discussion that these questions mean, initially at least, 'in what does x's F-ness consist?' or 'what constitutes x's F-ness?'. To ask 'why' x is F need not be to ask what 'causes' it to be F, but may rather be to ask for the feature in virtue of which it *is F*. The range of possible interests covered by Socrates' questions is well reflected in the English question 'what makes x F?', which may embody a request either for causal explanation or for conceptual clarification. Socrates' disenchantment with the natural sciences stems from their failure to pursue the latter. It is not, however, clear that the conceptual sense of the question is the *only* one relevant to the discussion. It is arguable that Socrates will later formulate an *aitia* that is not constitutive of a thing's being F, but causally imparts F-ness to it, and thus explains how it comes to be F. If such an *aitia* is provided, then a concern with something like 'causes' in the modern sense is not, after all, to be ruled out. See on 100c9–e4, 105b5–c8 (p.211).

The Protean nature of the concept, and the restrictions that will be placed upon it, make it impossible to find a translation of *aitia* that fits all of Socrates' multifarious examples, but 'reason' is perhaps the least unsuitable. It has been used for the noun, and for relevant occurrences of the adjective, throughout. See also G. Vlastos, op.cit. 292–6, and E. L. Burge, *Phronesis* 1971, 1–13.

(2) As noted earlier (see on 70c4–8), the verb translated 'come to be' has both complete and incomplete uses. Similarly, the noun translated 'coming-to-be' (*genesis*) can mean either a thing's coming-into-being (its 'genesis' in the English sense) or its acquisition of an attribute (see on 71a12–b5). Accordingly, an inquiry into the reason concerning 'coming-to-be' might be either (i) an inquiry into the reason for the coming-into-being of things, or (ii) an inquiry into the reason for their acquisition of attributes. In the ensuing discussion Socrates will confine himself to (ii) (cf. Hackforth, 144–6). Yet some contribution to (i) is surely demanded from the perspective of Cebes' objection. His conception of the soul as a source of vital energy calls for an improved account of things' 'coming-into-being', and not merely of their coming to be, e.g., large or beautiful. Moreover, it is just such an account that Socrates' language leads us to expect. When he asks repeatedly (96a9–10, cf.97b5–6, 97c6–7) 'why each thing comes to be, why it perishes, and why it exists', it is natural to take 'comes to be' as the counterpart of 'perishes', i.e. as meaning 'comes into being'. Hackforth (145, n.1) rightly remarks, of the verb cognate with the noun translated 'destruction' at 95e9, that it cannot mean 'lose an attribute'. We should expect, then, that Socrates will explain not merely the acquisition and loss of attributes by already existing things, but the coming-into-being of things that do not exist, and the perishing of things that do.

We find, however, no explicit discussion of these issues. Why are the major questions raised by Cebes' objection apparently disregarded? Perhaps because, as Socrates' very first example will suggest (96b2—3), he is concerned primarily with the genesis of *living* things. And in their case 'to be' is 'to be alive'. 'Coming-into-being' can thus be equated with 'coming to be alive'. Where the value of F is 'alive', 'coming to be F' and 'coming to be *simpliciter*' will coincide. So too will 'ceasing to be F' and 'ceasing to be *simpliciter*', i.e. 'perishing'. A living thing's birth (or conception) is its 'coming-into-being', and its death is its 'perishing' or 'destruction'. If these equivalences are assumed, it follows that Cebes' objection demands an inquiry into 'coming to be (alive)', i.e. being born (or conceived), and into 'ceasing to be (alive)', i.e. dying. A conceptual examination is needed of being and coming-to-be, birth and life, death and destruction. This huge task is, as Socrates aptly remarks, 'no trivial matter' (95e8), and his own narrative and discussion are mere prolegomena for it. Apart from a few hints (see on 105e10—107a1, p.220), he does not pursue it himself. He merely offers his 'own experiences' (96a2—3) to Cebes (and the reader) for further reflection.

96b1—8. The question at 96b2—3 seems concerned with the origin and nourishment of the earliest animals, not with the development of individuals. The theory mentioned, perhaps that of Archelaus (see Burnet's note), conspicuously makes no reference to 'soul'. Similarly, in the next example (b4—5), 'what do we think with?', the answer 'soul' or 'intelligence' is avoided. The verb translated 'think' occurs at 66c5 with different overtones (see on 66b1—c5). Here it seems to be used in a general way to cover various conscious states from sensation upwards (b5—8). It is perhaps implied that the stock scientific account of perception and thought is inadequate, as providing for no subject of consciousness (cf. *Theaetetus* 184b—186a and see on 64e4—65a3, p.89).

96c1—e5. G. Vlastos (*P.R.* 1969, 309, n.50) treats Socrates' 'unlearning' of his former beliefs about nutrition as quite distinct from the 'puzzles' introduced at 96d8—97b3. It marks, he thinks, a preference for 'windy theorising' over homespun explanation, born of Socrates' passion for natural science. But this interpretation destroys what looks like a continuous sequence of thought running from 96c2 to 96e7. At 96c3 Socrates begins to specify what he formerly 'supposed' he knew (c6, cf.d6). He then gives four more examples of what he 'supposed was an adequate view' (d8—e4). When Cebes asks (e5) what he thinks about these things now, he answers

171

(96e6–7) that he is 'far from supposing' that he knows 'the reason' about them. All this suggests a simple contrast between a state of confidence preceding his 'scientific' phase and one of confusion following it, which still, in a manner, persists.

For reasons that will emerge shortly (see next note) Socrates is confused by standard explanations of growth in terms of aggregation. All such explanations, whether couched in simple or sophisticated terms, lead to problems. His claim to have been 'blinded' by science (c5) is ironical (see also on 99d4–100a3). He pretends that his inability to accept even the simplest common-sense explanation, which rendered him 'unfit' for scientific study, was actually produced by it. In reality, his problems are conceptual. They arise from philosophical reflection, not from empirical study. His profession of 'puzzlement' may seem disingenuous, considering that he has the Theory of Forms up his sleeve (cf. Hackforth, 124, n.2). But the Theory offers only a provisional solution, which is itself in need of further exploration (107b4–10). And Socrates' puzzlement is no doubt meant to be infectious. A reader who first has to puzzle over the nature of his puzzles will come to feel them as his own. See also on 100e5–101b8.

The general nature of these puzzles may be brought out by the following expansion of the text at 96d8–e4, linking the difficulties posed in that passage with the questions of growth at 96c2–7: 'A thing grows, anyone would think, in virtue of its "coming to be large" (d4–5) (i.e. larger than it was. But what does "larger" mean?). Is one man or one horse "larger" than another in virtue of (the measure of the difference between them, namely) "a head"? (If "larger" means "containing a greater number of units of measurement", then what does "a greater number" mean?) What makes (a given number of units, such as) ten "greater" than (another number, such as) eight? Is it "greater" in virtue of the accruing to it of two? And is (a given length, such as) two cubits "larger" than (another, such as) one cubit in virtue of exceeding it by half (of itself)?'

Note that Socrates is not seeking a 'causal' explanation of one thing's being larger or more numerous than another, but an account of the concepts 'larger' and 'more numerous'. If this concern is not understood, some of his problems will appear unreal or meaningless. Thus, Hackforth (131) complains that 'there is no more a cause of 10 being greater than 8 than there is of Thursday coming after Wednesday'. Certainly, ten's being greater than eight neither needs nor admits of causal explanation. But this is to miss Socrates' point. In considering 'why' ten is greater than eight, he is interested in what constitutes it as 'greater', what its being 'greater' consists in.

'By a head' (e1) is a use of the dative case to express the measure 'by' which one thing exceeds another. It need not be supposed that Plato confuses this dative with a 'causal' one. He is using a trivial example to make a serious point: the difference in size between x and y is not what *constitutes* x's being larger than y. For a further implication of this key example, see on 100e5−101b8.

96e6−97b7. Some words added to the MS. reading by Wyttenbach and Burnet have not been translated. If they are supplied, an extra 'or the one that's been added' must be inserted after 'that's come to be two' at 96e9. The words are not essential, but they would enable all possible answers to the question '*what* has come to be two?' to be taken into account.

What exactly are Socrates' puzzles? He says that he does not accept the view that when one is added to one, *either* the latter unit (*or*, on Burnet's reading, the former), *or* both units have 'come to be two because of the addition of one to the other'. For the meaning of 'I wonder if' at 97a2 see on 62a2−7 (p.79), and cf. H. Reynen, *Hermes* 1968, 44, n.3. Socrates is asking himself in astonishment (i) whether it is the process of addition that makes them two, and thus (ii) whether *any* of the things mentioned can properly be said to 'come to be two', i.e. what the subject of the predicate 'come to be two' could be.

These two difficulties are connected. First, Socrates is evidently recognizing that the physical propinquity of two items is not what constitutes their being two. For they were two already, before they were juxtaposed. Cf. Frege: 'Must we literally hold a rally of all the blind in Germany before we can attach any sense to the expression "the number of blind in Germany"?' (*The Foundations of Arithmetic*, §23). This gives rise to the second problem. 'Two' can be predicated of a pair of items taken together, but of neither taken singly. 'One' can be predicated of either taken singly, but not of both taken together. Cf. *Hippias* I, 300−303, where number predicates are contrasted with others in this very respect. In the light of this, the predicate 'come to be two' is, indeed, puzzling. For two items taken singly can *never* be two, and taken together they must *always* be two. A set cannot, it seems, change its cardinal number, whereas the verb 'come to be . . .' suggests that it can. More generally, how can things 'come to be F', where F is a character that they either always or never possess? Number predicates appear to be such that things cannot 'come to' acquire them. Comparable difficulties can be seen to arise over the predicates 'come into being' and 'cease to be', if negative existential statements are disallowed. This problem too, inherited by Plato from the Eleatics, lies close to the surface of Socrates' inquiry into 'coming-to-be and destruction'.

A further source of puzzlement is the idea that two opposite processes, addition and division, should be 'reasons' for the same thing, i.e. for one's 'coming to be two' (97a5–b3). The clear implication of this is that two opposites cannot function as 'reasons' for a thing's coming to have one and the same property, i.e. cannot be constitutive of that property. Vlastos (*P.R.* 1969, 312, n.57) questions both the assumption that opposite processes cannot be 'reasons' for the same state of affairs, and its application to the present case. For, he says, the items that have 'come to be two', by addition and division respectively, are different in either case. But Socrates might reasonably wonder how two different items could acquire a common character in virtue of two opposite processes being performed upon them. If what is sought is a 'reason' that is *constitutive* of the character in question, then two quite different and opposite answers would be unsatisfactory. The 'safe' answer that Socrates will give (101a–c) will be immune from this criticism. See on 101b9–c9.

97b8–98b6. The translation 'Intelligence' has been used here as best suited to the idea that things are arranged for the best, which Socrates thought implicit in Anaxagoras' theory (97c4–d1, 98a6–b1), but which 'mind' and 'intellect' fail, in different ways, to convey. 'Intelligence' (*nous*) should be understood here as a substance term. It is the faculty of thought, or that which thinks, rather than a mental quality, such as 'sagacity' or 'good sense'. It is cognate with the verb translated 'think' (83b1), used for thinking of Forms, and also with the adjective 'intelligible', used to describe their status as objects of thought (80b1, 81b7, 83b4). For the original Anaxagorean theory, see DK 59 B 11, 12, 13, 14.

Note that Socrates' first reaction to the theory (97c3) was that it seemed to him 'to be a good thing' that it should be so. What 'seemed a good thing', i.e. what appealed to his own intelligence, was the hope of understanding all things as the work of another intelligence. Accordingly, at 97d7 he says that he was pleased to think that he had found in Anaxagoras an instructor 'to suit my own intelligence'. The translation tries to capture a pun, which is obscured by 'after my own heart' (Hackforth). Burnet says that such a joke would be 'very frigid'. Not only is it entirely in keeping with Socrates' ironical treatment of Anaxagoras, but a repetition of it may be suspected at 98b8–9: 'I beheld a man making no use of his Intelligence at all'. In explaining things, Anaxagoras failed not only to invoke his theory of a cosmic intelligence, but also to use his own.

The programme of explaining natural phenomena in terms of

'what is best' is carried out in detail in the *Timaeus*, both for the universe as a whole, and for its contents. Cf., e.g., *Timaeus* 29–34, 44d–46a, 68e–71a, and see G. R. Morrow, *P.R.* 1950, 147–63. The present passage marks the transition from a mechanistic to a teleological conception of the natural order that was to dominate European science for the next two thousand years.

At 97d4 (cf.98b6) the better and the worse are said to be objects of 'the same knowledge'. Socrates may mean that an understanding of one member of a pair of opposites (*F*) requires an understanding of the other (*G*). This is clearly the case, where, as with 'better' and 'worse', *F* and *G* are overtly relational, so that (x, y) $(xFy \equiv yGx)$. He may also be hinting that evil is a necessary complement to good, and that a complete explanation of the universe would encompass both.

98b7–99b6. In view of the connection between an *aitia* and the notion of responsibility (see on 95e7–96a5, p.169), it is natural that Socrates should give, as a paradigm instance of a 'reason', his own judgement that it was better to abide the decision of the Athenian court. In his parody of Anaxagoras he charges him with confusing a reason of that sort with the physical conditions necessary for that reason to take effect. The distinction is related to, though not the same as, the modern distinction between necessary and sufficient conditions. The physical conditions specified are necessary not merely for Socrates' sitting in gaol, but for enabling the true reason to function as a reason (99b2–4). This does not mean that Socrates will regard the judgements of rational agents as the only reasons ever admissible, but only that they are indicated by any appeal to 'intelligence' in explaining something. Nor does Socrates mean that he will countenance only the purposive use of the word 'reason'. He himself will use it later (112b1) in the sense disparaged here.

Note also: (i) Socrates' account of his reason for staying in gaol (98e2–99a4) contains a wry contrast between morality and expediency. By implication, the Athenian court's decision was based purely upon the latter.

(ii) Socrates' judgement is in turn attributed to the judgement of the court (e3). Thus, one human decision is explainable by reference to another.

(iii) Explanations of action such as Socrates gives may be loosely labelled 'teleological', and linked with Aristotle's 'final causes'. But the reason here mentioned cannot, strictly, be identified with Socrates' 'end'. It is not an object for the sake of which he acts, but consists simply in its seeming to him that the relevant action would be for the best. This judgement needs to be distinguished from the moral or prudential grounds on which it was based.

(iv) The physical conditions in Socrates' example have their counterparts in the material elements and forces used by the divine craftsman who fashions the universe in the *Timaeus*. They are 'accessories' or 'co-reasons', necessary for realizing his designs. Cf. *Timaeus* 46c7–e6, and see G. R. Morrow, *P.R.* 1950, 151.

99b6–d3. Socrates scolds his predecessors for not acknowledging any supernatural power sustaining the universe, but for thinking to find 'an Atlas stronger and more immortal than this', i.e. a permanent material support to hold up the physical world. Their disregard of 'the good or binding' as the real sustaining force points to the theistic account of the cosmos that Socrates himself envisages. Similarly Leibniz, citing the present passage: 'the general principles of physics and mechanics themselves depend upon the action of a sovereign intelligence and cannot be explained without taking it into consideration' (Letter on 'Explaining the Laws of Nature', *P.P.L.* i.542. Cf. *Discourse on Metaphysics*, §§ 19–20). The word translated 'binding' (c5) means 'obligatory', and is here connected with 'binding' in the physical sense (cf. *Cratylus* 418e).

The nature of Socrates' 'second voyage' (c9–d1) has been much debated. The phrase may mean 'taking to the oars when the wind has failed' or 'making a second, safer journey'. The former sense is well attested, and suggests a second-best method of reaching one's destination. Cf. *Philebus* 19c2–3. But if so, what is Socrates' destination? And in what sense is the approach that he will now describe 'second-best'? For both questions see W. J. Goodrich, *C.R.* 1903, 381–4, 1904, 5–11, N. R. Murphy, *C.Q.* 1936, 40–7, L. E. Rose, *Monist* 1966, 464–73.

Socrates' destination is the discovery of 'the reason', i.e. the reason for coming-to-be and destruction. Note that he does *not* say that he is making a second attempt to find a reason of the kind that he had vainly expected from Anaxagoras. Hence there is no need to interpret the Form hypothesis introduced at 100b in teleological terms, as Bluck and others have supposed. It *may* simply be taken as an inferior pattern of explanation, containing no reference to the teleological ideal. Relative to that ideal it is, indeed, 'second-best', and the phrase may be read without irony. It would not, of course, be second-best in comparison with the cosmologists whom Socrates has just criticized, and the phrase 'second voyage' would be ironical if related to them. But it need not be so understood. The passage is, rather, in the vein of Simmias' remarks at 85c–d. See on 84d4–85d10.

Some commentators would insist that all reference to the

teleological ideal must be excluded. See, e.g., G. Vlastos, *P.R.* 1969, 297, n.15, 302–3, and E. L. Burge, *Phronesis* 1971, 1, n.2. But this seems to be going too far. Whatever state of mind on this point may be imputed to Socrates, his words do not prove that no allusion is intended by *Plato* in what follows to teleological explanation. As Vlastos says (303, n.37), both here and in the *Timaeus* teleological explanations are exemplified solely in the purposeful agency of a mind. But it seems conceivable that the Form hypothesis, and the 'subtler' reason that succeeds or supplements it (105c–d), should point to the action of a divine mind as the 'reason' for coming-to-be. This idea is, in fact, discernible later. See on 105e10–107a1 (p.221).

N. R. Murphy (*I.P.R.* 146–7) holds that Socrates' destination on his 'second voyage' is different from his original one, and thus that he avoids altogether the problems of efficient causation and temporal change. But this would disappoint the expectations aroused by 95e9–96a1. Those expectations are, indeed, very imperfectly fulfilled (see on 95e7–96a5, p.171). But to deny any reference whatever to a source of coming-to-be and destruction would be to sever Socrates' story from the objection of Cebes which gave rise to it.

99d4–100a3. This passage has suffered from over-interpretation, especially in the light of the sun simile in *Republic* vi–vii. See W. J. Goodrich, *C.R.* 1903, 383–4 for a critique of several misunderstandings. When Socrates says that he had tired of studying 'the things that are' (d4–5), he cannot be referring to Forms, which have not yet entered his narrative, but simply means, noncommittally, 'things', i.e. the scientific and mathematical matters raised at 96a–97b, and the conceptual questions arising therefrom. No subtle symbolism need be read into the reference to the sun (d6): its eclipse is mentioned merely as the occasion when people are most inclined to look at it. The 'objects' (e3) that Socrates thought he should not look at with his eyes (e1–4) cannot be Forms, for Forms cannot be observed by the senses at all (65d–e, 79a). They must, presumably, be the scientific and mathematical matters mentioned above.

Why did Socrates fear that by using his senses to examine them he might altogether 'blind his soul'? Is he harking back to his earlier, ironical suggestion that scientific studies had 'blinded' him (96c5)? Or is he hinting that such studies, if continued, would have unfitted him for conceptual inquiry? The soul's 'vision', its capacity for 'seeing' Forms, might be thought of as damaged by sensory observation (cf.79c2–9). But there is no allusion to the Forms, at least until Socrates speaks of his resort to 'theories' and of his studying in them 'the truth of the things that are' (e6). For this phrase, which does seem to contain a presentiment of the Form hypothesis, cf.90d6–7. For 'theories' (*logoi*) at 99e5 and 100a1, see on 90b4–91c5, and next note.

The sentence in which Socrates qualifies his comparison of 'theories' with images (a1–3) is confusing in translation. The point is not to deny that 'theories' or concrete things are images, but to question whether the former are more so than the latter. To look at things 'in concrete' is to study them in images at least as much as is looking at them 'in theories'. It is being suggested that 'theories' are images of a higher grade than objects in the sensible world, and thus closer to the Forms. This idea, in a more developed form, governs the structure of *Republic* ii–ix. See D. Gallop, *A.G.P.* 1965, 113–31.

'Perhaps my comparison is, in a certain way, inept' (99e6–100a1): more literally, 'Perhaps that to which I liken things is not like.' The words for 'liken' and 'be like' are cognate with the word translated 'images' (99e1, 100a2).

100a3–9. These difficult lines, together with the further precepts about method at 101d–e, have been much discussed. See Bluck, 13–14, 111–12, Hackforth, 160–73, 138–42, R. Robinson, *P.E.D.*, Ch.9, K. Sayre, *P.A.M.*, Ch.1, N. R. Murphy, *C.Q.* 1936, 40–7, P. Plass, *Phronesis* 1960, 103–15. The main problems are: (1) What is meant at 100a4 by 'hypothesizing on each occasion the theory (*logos*) I judge strongest'? (2) How can the metaphor of 'accord' (a5) be interpreted in such a way that 'putting down as true whatever things seem to me to accord with it, and as not true whatever do not' will seem a logically defensible procedure? (3) How is this procedure related to its context, especially to the illustrations at 100b–101c?

(1) *logos* has been translated 'theory', so as to leave it open whether it should be taken to mean 'definition' or, more broadly, 'proposition', 'statement'. 'Definition' might seem to fit well with Socrates' account (99e1–100a3) of his resort to theories after giving up using his senses. The quest for definitions could be expected to figure in an account of his development. Adoption of what he judged to be the strongest definition in each case would form a natural part of this quest, and would enable him to set down particular things as *F*, or not *F*, according as they did, or did not, conform to the definition. This reading would link *logos* at 100a4 closely with its occurrences at 99e5 and 100a1, where it could well mean either 'definitions' or 'conceptual discussions' aimed at producing them. Bluck (13–14, 164–6) understands the lines in this way.

But this view is untenable. For the meaning of 'the theory I judge strongest' must be gathered, partly at least, from Socrates' illustrations at 100b1–101c9. Bluck would, indeed, avoid this, by taking the latter passage as marking a deliberate shift from Socratic to Platonic doctrine. Socratic definitions are, he thinks, there being supplanted as 'causes' by Platonic Forms. But this interpretation is itself bizarre. Definitions are nowhere said to be 'causes', and the words 'it's nothing new' (100b1) expressly disclaim the notion that Plato is somehow improving upon what has already been said. Clearly, he is making Socrates elucidate the cryptic utterances of 100a. See R. C. Cross, *P.R.* 1956, 405.

The elucidation consists in (i) 'hypothesizing' that beautiful, good, large, and other Forms exist (b5–7), and (ii) agreeing that particular things are beautiful, large, etc. because they participate in the corresponding Forms. Note that Socrates uses the verb 'hypothesize' at 100b5 as he did for 'the strongest *logos*' at 100a3. The latter therefore almost certainly exemplifies what he will later call a 'hypothesis' (101d2, d7, cf.107b5). For the notions of 'hypothesizing' and 'hypothesis', see R. Robinson, op.cit., Ch.7. 'Hypotheses' need not be hypotheses in the modern sense, i.e. explanatory theories as yet unconfirmed. Nor need they be 'hypothetical' in the sense of being conditional in form, though they may need to be supported by further argument (101d3–e1, 107b5–8). Only (i), and not (ii), is here explicitly said to be 'hypothesized'. But (ii) is evidently inseparable from (i), being integral to the Theory of Forms itself. And if it is taken to form part of 'the strongest *logos*', it will explain why the *logos* is 'strongest'. It is so, in this context, for the same reason that it is 'safe' (100d8–e3): it is proof against certain kinds of counter-argument. It will be convenient to call (i) and (ii) together 'the Form-Reason hypothesis'.

Clearly, neither (i) nor (ii), nor the Form-Reason hypothesis as a whole, amounts to a definition. This precludes *logos* at 100a4 from meaning 'definition'. Whatever it may mean at 99e5 and 100a1, it must here mean 'proposition' or 'statement'. But the notion of definition is not, in fact, far off. For there is an obvious link between the definitional sense of *logos* and its use to characterize the Form-Reason hypothesis. In seeking a definition of *F*, one looks for a feature common to *F* things, in virtue of which they are *F*. The question 'What is *F*?' naturally gives rise to the question 'What makes *F* things *F*?'. The answers to the latter question in terms of Forms at 100b–101c are thus directly relevant to Socrates' interest in the former. If this is borne in mind, no sharp change in the meaning of *logos* between 99e5 and 100a4 need be supposed. The strongest *logos* is an appeal to Forms, when other answers to 'what makes *F* things *F*?', and thus to 'what is *F*?', have proved inadequate.

(2) The main difficulty in the notion of 'accord' has been

succinctly stated by Robinson (op.cit. 126–9). If it means 'be consistent with', Socrates will be putting down as true whatever propositions are consistent with his theory. But it would seem a quite inadequate ground for putting down something as true that it should merely be consistent with a given theory. On the other hand, if 'accord' means 'is deducible from', Socrates will be putting down as not true whatever propositions are not deducible from his theory. And it would seem an equally inadequate ground for holding something to be untrue that it should not be deducible from a given theory. Hence Robinson concludes that Plato 'does not say quite all that he means'. Although 'accord' cannot, strictly, mean deducibility, what Plato here means is that one should take propositions deducible from one's theory to be true, and those whose contradictories follow from the theory to be untrue.

Hackforth initially (139) takes the notion of 'accord' similarly: 'Any proposition arrived at by what the inquirer deems a valid process of deduction is accepted, and the contradictory of any such proposition is rejected.' But his account of 101d–e, which he believes to give the detail of the process described in the present lines, seems inconsistent with this. He introduces a chain of propositions– G - F - E - D - C - B - A —successively deduced, in that order, from an initial hypothesis H. If these propositions survive the test described at 101d3–5, they will be 'in accord' with each other, and may all be put down as true. But if one of them– F, say–is successfully challenged, then it and G will be at variance: 'the one is not a valid inference from the other' (140). However, F's not being a valid inference from G is clearly quite different from its being the contradictory of something that *is* a valid inference from H. And whereas the latter defect would give ground, to one who had adopted H, for putting F down as 'not true', the former surely would not.

As noted in (1) above, a quite different interpretation is favoured by Bluck. He takes 'accord' to mean 'conformity' of things to a definition: 'Having found an "account" or "definition", [Socrates] would accept as genuine instances of the thing concerned whatever seemed to conform to it, and reject what did not' (111, cf.114, n.1). But it seems hardly credible that the Greek at 100a5 should mean 'accept as genuine instances of the thing concerned'. The word that Bluck translates 'genuine' is much more likely to mean here 'true', as used of propositions. Moreover, Bluck's interpretation leaves the words 'both about a reason and about everything else' (a6) inexplicable. For they strongly suggest that the method was used in other spheres besides the inquiry into 'reasons'. Yet the idea of 'putting down as genuine things that conform to a definition' has no wider application. By contrast, a propositional interpretation allows us to see the hypothetical method in operation elsewhere. See on 84d4–85d10, 92c11–e3, 93e7–94b3 (p.166).

(3) The immediate context is, however, all-important. For it is to be expected that Socrates' account of his procedure should be adapted primarily to the matter in hand. If so, the method will be best understood by attending to its role in the quest for 'reasons'. The ensuing passage (100b–101c) may best be regarded as illustrating not only 'the theory judged strongest', but also the putting down as true whatever things seem to accord with it, and as not true whatever do not. Applications of the hypothesis that F things are F because they participate in the Form F are 'in accord' with that theory, whereas alternative 'reasons' yield statements that are not. Thus, 'x is beautiful because it participates in the Form Beautiful' and 'x is large because it participates in the Form Large' may be put down as true, since they are 'in accord' with the relevant Form-Reason hypothesis; whereas 'x is beautiful because of its colour or shape' and 'x is larger by a head' are not 'in accord' with the relevant hypothesis, and may therefore be put down as not true. 'Accord' is not, on this view, used in a sense equivalent to bare logical consistency. Socrates does not mean to accept just *any* proposition that may be logically consistent with the Form-Reason hypothesis. But 'accord' seems a natural enough term to use for the relation between the Form-Reason hypothesis and its applications. If, as suggested in (1) above, the hypothesis includes not only the assertion that the Forms exist, but also the thesis that F things are F 'for no other reason' than that they participate in the Form F (100c5–6, d4–5), then clearly the rejected alternatives will, in the sense just indicated, be 'not in accord' with it. The great mass of propositions, having no relevance to the issue about which any given hypothesis is put forward, will be neither 'in accord' nor 'not in accord' with it. They simply lie outside the scope of Socrates' remarks altogether.

This interpretation has the advantage of making Socrates' remarks directly relevant to their context. It also enables the plurals at 100a4–7 (the 'things' that do or do not accord), and the words 'on each occasion' (a4) to look forward to the plurality of examples that Socrates will give at 100c–101c. Thus, the present lines may be taken as simply enunciating a general schema into which those examples can be fitted.

For a somewhat similar interpretation see P. Plass, op.cit. 104–5. See also on 101c9–102a9.

100b1–c8. Socrates says that he will 'display' (1) the kind of reason with which he has been dealing (b3–4), and (2) 'the reason' (b8). He will thus (1) show what the general requirements for a 'reason' are (see next note and on 100e5–101b8), and also (2) indicate the particular 'reason' that he is seeking, i.e. the reason for coming-to-be and destruction. The word 'display' (cf.99d2) suggests that he will exhibit these things in what he says rather than state them directly.

Once again the Theory of Forms is readily accepted (cf.65d6, 74b1). At 100b5–6 the literal meaning could be 'something is beautiful alone by itself', or 'there is something beautiful alone by itself', or 'beautiful alone by itself is something'. See on 74a9–b1 and note 5. The translation is based on the third interpretation. Cf.102b1.

The next step (c3–8) is to agree that things are beautiful for no reason save that they participate in the Form Beautiful. R. Robinson (*P.E.D.* 127) takes 'what comes next to those things' (c3) to mean 'what logically follows'. But the present step is not so much a logical consequence of the hypothesis that the Form Beautiful exists as an integral element in it. 'Next' may mean only that it belongs next in an orderly statement of the argument—cf. *Gorgias* 454c1–2.

'If anything else is beautiful besides the beautiful itself' (c4–5): note that the words 'besides the beautiful itself' clearly imply that the Form Beautiful is beautiful. This raises the question whether the character of beauty is being attributed to the Form, or whether 'the Form F is F' should be understood in some other way. See on 74d4–8. For Beauty the 'self-predicative' interpretation is defensible (see G. Vlastos, *R.M.* 1972, 456). But what of the Forms Numerousness and Twoness (101b6, 101c5)? Could Twoness be two, or Numerousness numerous, without wrecking the base of the Theory, that there is just *one* Form for each set of things to which we apply a common name (*Republic* 596a, 597c)?

The nature of the relation between beautiful things and the Form Beautiful will be deliberately put aside at 100d5–7 (see next note). The word translated 'participate' (c5, 101c3–6) is the ordinary Greek word for 'share' used semi-technically. 'Partake' is used similarly at 102b2. To say that beautiful things 'share' Beauty is to say that they have that feature in common. The relevant sense of 'share' is that in which x and y may share A, without its being the case that each of them has only a part of A (as two people may share an ancestor or a birthday). This point is exploited in the *Parmenides* (131a–e), where 'share' and 'partake' are wilfully misconstrued.

100c9–e4. The Form 'reason' for things being beautiful is now further elaborated. For the text at 100d5–7 see note 63. Socrates remains non-committal as to the relation between Forms and particulars. This relation is the focal point of criticism of the Theory in the *Parmenides* (131–5). See on 65d4–e5 and previous note. The language of 'presence' was perhaps already a source of sophistical objection. Cf. *Euthydemus* 300e–301b.

It is obvious why such 'wise reasons' as colour and shape are to be rejected. No given colour or shape is either a necessary or a sufficient condition for a thing's being beautiful. The reason why the Form answer would be 'safest' (d8, e1, cf.101d2, 105b7) is that any other answer could be refuted with counter-examples: a certain colour or shape might be present in a thing, and yet that thing might not be beautiful, or might be ugly; and other things might be beautiful, even when that colour or shape was lacking. But the Form reason, and it alone, would be 'safe' from all such objections: participation in the Form F is both a necessary and a sufficient condition for a thing's being F. The 'safety' in question is immunity from rebuttal by the counter-arguments sketched at 97a5–b3 and 101a5–b2.

Forms, interpreted as 'reasons', should not be taken as Aristotelian 'efficient causes'. The Form Beautiful, for example, should not be taken as a beautifying agent, which is somehow supposed to impart beauty to things, or generate beautiful objects. For this interpretation, which naturally thrives on the mistranslation of *aitia* as 'cause', see Aristotle, *De Gen. et Corr.* 335b7–16, and Hackforth, 144–5. If the Forms are causes, Aristotle asks, why do they not generate things continuously instead of intermittently? Hackforth thinks that Aristotle here fastens upon 'the weakest point in the theory', viz. its failure to explain what causes the acquisition of attributes. But since the Forms are not represented as explaining that, the criticism is irrelevant. See G. Vlastos, *P.R.* 1969, 303–7, E. L. Burge, *Phronesis* 1971, 2, n.4.

On the other hand, the text should not be over-interpreted in another direction. Apart from exhibiting the requirement that the 'reason' should be a necessary and sufficient condition for any given concept, and insisting that Forms exist, the Form-Reason hypothesis is wholly uninformative. This, no doubt, is why it is called 'simpleminded' (d4) and 'ignorant' (105c1). It gives no analysis for any of the concepts mentioned. The appeal to Forms side-steps rather than performs this task. Vlastos (op.cit. 314–15) formulates plausible logico-mathematical conditions that such an analysis might yield, in the case of 'numerous' (101b4–6), and represents these conditions as 'what Socrates is telling us, put into more modern language'. However, Socrates refrains from 'telling us' any such things. All we can say is that participation in a Form requires, in each case, that some such conditions be satisfied. We are given no insight, in any particular case, into what they are.

Moreover, it need not be supposed that Socrates' sole concern in the wider argument is with the analysis of concepts, or the formulation of necessary and sufficient conditions. Even when it is recognized that a thing (x) is F in virtue of its participating in the Form F, and even when this latter notion is properly understood, there remains the question how x 'comes to' participate in that Form. Socrates does not answer this question here. But he can plausibly be seen as doing so at 105b−d. So the denial that Forms are 'efficient causes' does not entail that an interest in such causes is altogether extraneous to the argument. See on 105b5−c8 (p.211).

100e5−101b8. The Form-Reason hypothesis is now applied to the cases of 'large' and 'numerous'. Note that at 100e5 the Form Largeness is given as the reason not only for large things being large, but also for larger things being larger. Separate Forms are not posited for comparative adjectives. It is the Form F that accounts for things' being 'more F', just as it does for their being simply 'F'. Cf. also 101b4−7. In general, 'F' and 'more F' are subjects of the same conceptual inquiry. This would explain some looseness earlier (75c9), where Socrates spoke of 'the larger' and 'the smaller'. See on 70e4−71a11, 75c7−d6.

G. Vlastos calls this feature of the account a 'blemish'. It is, he thinks, one of Plato's 'residual confusions and fallacies' that he has failed to bring out that the instances under discussion are 'special cases of the "greater than" relation, and that the absolute numerousness or bigness of the things he is talking about is irrelevant to the reasoning' (*P.R.* 1969, 315, n.64). But this overlooks the role of the Forms in connection with such concepts as 'large' and 'numerous'. It is just because particular things or groups are never 'absolutely' large or numerous, that Forms for those concepts are introduced. The connection between comparative adjectives and Forms is made explicit at 102b−c, where Socrates explicates 'larger' and 'smaller' with reference to the Forms Large and Small. This makes it highly unlikely that Plato has ignored, let alone overlooked, the difference between comparative and simple adjectives. See on 102a10−d4.

At 101a5−b2 and 101b4−7 Socrates expresses 'fears' that throw light on what was wrong with the reason rejected earlier (96d8−e1) for one man or horse being larger than another. There would be two things to fear in giving 'a head' as the reason.

(1) 'If you say that someone is larger and smaller by a head, then, first, the larger will be larger and the smaller smaller by the same thing' (101a6−8). The apodosis of this sentence could mean either

(i) x is larger than y by a head and y is smaller than x by a head, or
(ii) x is larger than y by a head and smaller than z by a head. With
(i), the phrases 'the larger' and 'the smaller' will refer to two different
items, x and y, with the converse relations of 'larger than' and
'smaller than' holding between them. On this view, the supposed
'contradiction' could be formally deduced from 'x is larger than y
by a head', given that:

$$(x, y)\{(x > y \text{ by } h) \equiv (y < x \text{ by } h)\}.$$

With (ii) 'the larger' and 'the smaller' will refer to the same item, x.
which will be 'larger' and 'smaller' in relation to two different things,
y and z. On this view, the 'contradiction' could not be formally
deduced, since from $(x > y \text{ by } h)$ we cannot derive $(\exists z)(x < z \text{ by } h)$.
But (ii) seems to follow more naturally from the antecedent 'if you
say that someone is larger and smaller by a head', which mentions
only a single subject. (ii) would seem a more typically Platonic way
of making the point that particulars may have contrasted predicates
in different relations. And it has the advantage of enabling the later
discussion of 'Simmias is larger than Socrates and smaller than
Phaedo' (102b–d) to be linked directly with the present example.

On either interpretation the essential point is that 'a head' could
just as well be viewed as a reason for 'being smaller' as for 'being
larger', and therefore cannot be what constitutes anything's being
larger. Hence it cannot help to answer the conceptual question 'what
is *larger*?' Evidently, it is here being assumed that if any feature is
constitutive of a characteristic F, that feature will be found in all
and only those things that are F, and not in things that are G. These
lines thus fulfil the promise of 100b3–4 to 'display' the sort of
'reason' with which Socrates is concerned. For they exhibit,
without expressly stating, the requirement that the 'reason' in
question should be both a necessary and sufficient condition of the
concept that has to be explicated. Whatever is the 'reason' for a
thing's being F, or more F, cannot also be the reason either for its or
for anything else's being G, or more G.

Vlastos (loc.cit.) assumes interpretation (i), and objects that the
fact that y is smaller than x by a head would be a spurious reason
for rejecting 'a head' as what makes x larger. For, he urges, x and y
are different items, and 'there is no contradiction in the same cause
producing contrary effects on different things'. On interpretation (ii)
this difficulty does not arise, since only a single item, x, will be
involved. But even on interpretation (i) Vlastos' objection does not
affect Socrates' point. For he is, in effect, here stipulating what shall
count as a 'reason' for any given property, and he is excluding as a
reason for F anything that features in cases of F and G alike. This
point can be made whether the items concerned are the same or not.

See on 96e6–97b7.

(2) The other objection to 'a head' as the reason for one man's being larger than another is (a8–b2) that a head is itself a small thing, and 'it's surely monstrous that anyone should be large by something small'. This displays a further requirement for a 'reason'. Whatever is to be a reason for x's being F must not itself be characterized by F's opposite, G. No adequate 'reason' for a property, that is genuinely constitutive of it, can possess the opposite of that property. So a head, being characterized by smallness, cannot be what constitutes a thing's being larger. The examples at 101b4–7 can be understood similarly. Both the rejected answers, 'two' and 'half of two cubits', are to be thought of as something 'small', and therefore ineligible as 'reasons' for anything's being 'large', or 'larger'.

Here again Vlastos (op.cit. 316, n.64) finds the argument flawed. The fact that a head is a small thing would not, he objects, preclude it from making x *larger*, as distinct from *large*. For x may be a larger man than y, without being a large man. But this objection seems, once again, to miss Socrates' point. The difficulty is: how can something 'small' or (in this case) 'smaller than y' be what *constitutes* x's being 'large' or (in this case) 'larger than y'? How could something 'small' or 'smaller' be the true 'reason' for anything's being 'large' or 'larger'? By calling this supposition 'monstrous' (b1), Socrates exhibits a further condition that a true 'reason' must meet.

His objections to the rejected reasons are here formulated in an eristical manner, no doubt in parody of the contradiction-mongers (101e1–2). But the principles implicit in these objections have a serious role in the coming argument. Putting them together with the one noted earlier (see on 96e6–97b7) the requirements for a 'reason' may be summarized as follows:

(i) No opposite, F, can count as the 'reason' for a thing's having a property, if its opposite, G, can also give rise to that property (97a7–b3).

(ii) Nothing can count as a 'reason' for a thing's having a a property, if its opposite, G, can also give rise to that property (101a6–8).

(iii) A 'reason' for a thing's having a property F, cannot itself be characterized by the opposite of that property, G (101a8–b2).

Requirement (iii) is crucial for what follows. For when Socrates comes, later on, to improve upon the present 'safe' Form-Reason hypothesis with 'a different kind of safeness' (105b8), he does so with examples that are 'safe' from the objection here brought against 'a head'. Fire, fever, and oneness (or a unit) cannot be characterized by the opposites of the properties of which they are 'reasons'. Soul is a 'reason' of the same type. What qualifies it as a 'reason' for something's being alive is precisely what disqualifies 'a head' as a reason for something's being larger. Hence, in this trivial example a major principle underlying the final proof of immortality can be discerned.

The principle in (iii) is, however, highly questionable. It is well discussed by E. L. Burge, *Phronesis* 1971, 5. See also on 105b5–c8 (p.213), 105c9–d12.

101b9–c9. The grounds for rejecting addition and division as reasons for things' coming to be two, or one, were given earlier (97a7–b3). The reason now recommended is that they participate in the Forms Twoness and Oneness. The assimilation of number concepts to others tends to mask the peculiar difficulties to which they give rise (see on 96e6–97b7). Adequate treatment of those problems would call for an inquiry into number concepts such as Plato envisages at *Republic* 525a–526c. But it is not to his purpose to pursue it here.

Plato uses two kinds of words for numbers: (1) the ordinary words for the series of cardinal numbers, and (2) a series of words ending in *-as, (monas, duas, trias,* etc.). It is uncertain whether any consistent distinction is intended between these, and in particular whether members of (2) refer exclusively to Forms, and whether members of (1) never do so. In the present passage members of (2) are used, and the *Forms* Oneness and Twoness are clearly meant. In the next few pages, however, the matter is often more debatable. For this issue, which becomes crucial for the interpretation of the whole argument, see J. Schiller, *Phronesis* 1967, 57–8, and D. O'Brien, *C.Q.* 1967, 217–19. The formal difference between the two series has been marked in translation by adding '-ness' for members of (2): 'oneness', 'twoness', 'threeness', etc., and omitting it for members of (1): 'one', 'two', 'three', etc. The English 'monad', 'dyad', and 'triad' are transliterations of the roots of words in series (2), but their special associations make them unsuitable as translations. The present renderings may, however, wrongly give the impression that the abstract character possessed by, e.g., sets of three things is meant. The Greek words contain no suggestion of this. The termination '-ness' has been used simply to mark the formal difference between these words and members of series (1). In this way no questions of interpretation are begged, or, of course, solved. See on 103e5–104c6, 104d5–e6, 104e7–105b4.

101c9–102a9. Socrates here resumes his comments on hypothetical method, interrupted since 100a. They are now framed as precepts to Cebes, but are presumably to be taken closely with what

Socrates has said that he does himself. At 101d1–2 he says you 'would hang on to that safety of the hypothesis, and answer accordingly', i.e. in the way specified at 101c2–7, by appealing to the relevant Form. The phrase translated 'that safety of the hypothesis' is somewhat awkward. P. Plass (*Phronesis* 1960, 111–12) would translate 'that safe consequent of the hypothesis', supplying 'consequent' from 101d4 below. But this seems neither natural nor necessary, if the 'hypothesis' is not merely that Forms exist, but that things are *F* by participating in the Form *F*, i.e. the Form-Reason hypothesis of 100b5–c8. This answer you would give, Socrates tells Cebes, being 'scared of your own shadow' (c9–d1). Here he alludes to the risk incurred by any departure from the Form-Reason hypothesis. Any other answer to the question 'what makes *F* things *F*?' would be prey to rebuttals of the sort illustrated at 101a–b.

At 101d3–5 he continues: 'But if anyone hung on to the hypothesis itself, you would dismiss him, and you wouldn't answer till you should have examined its consequences to see if, in your view, they are in accord or discord with each other'. It is far from obvious what is supposed to give rise to this examination, or what it consists in. In particular, its intended scope is unclear. Is Socrates giving *general* guidance on hypothetical method? Or is he concerned merely with its use in the quest for 'reasons'? Note that his directions arise out of the example at 101c. 'The hypothesis itself' (d3) must refer back to the hypothesis whose safety is clung to at 101d1–2, viz. that things come to be (are) two (one) for no other reason than that they participate in the relevant Form. This link with the preceding passage suggests that the present lines should not be isolated from their context. Here as at 100a the hypothetical method needs to be understood, initially at least, in application to the Form-Reason hypothesis itself. For the meaning of 'hang on to' at 101d1 and 101d3 see note 67.

What are the 'consequences' of the hypothesis? The words translated 'consequences' (d4, e3) are not the usual technical term for logical conclusions, but are passive forms of the verb Socrates had used at 100a3 to mean 'proceed'. It seems, however, difficult to understand it here in anything but a logical sense. For unless some sort of test for propositional accord or discord is envisaged, no sense can be made of the examination to see if the things in question are 'in accord or discord with each other'. The word has therefore been translated 'consequences'. Cf. R. Robinson, *P.E.D.* 129–31, R. C. Cross, *P.R.* 1956, 406. For a different view, see Bluck, 14, 169.

What could be meant by asking whether the consequences that spring from the Form-Reason hypothesis are 'in accord or discord

with each other'? It has seemed puzzling that Socrates should
envisage testing the consequences of a hypothesis that he has already
adopted as the 'strongest' (100a4), and with which, therefore, he
should have been satisfied already. Moreover, if 'accord' and 'discord'
here mean 'consistency' and 'inconsistency', how could consequences
springing from a single hypothesis fail to be 'in accord' with each
other? For no single proposition can logically entail consequences
that do, in fact, contradict each other. For these difficulties, see
Robinson, op.cit. 131–3. A hypothesis may, as he suggests, be
viewed as having conflicting consequences if it leads to contradiction
when combined with other standing assumptions. It was in just this
way that Simmias' hypothesis that the soul is an attunement was
disproved. (see on 92c11–e3, 93e7–94b3, p.166).
    Could the Form-Reason hypothesis, which Socrates has insisted
is 'safe' (100e1), be thought to give rise to contradictions of that
sort? Its 'consequences', e.g. that x is large because it participates in
the Form Large, and that y is large for the same reason, and likewise
z, would necessarily all 'accord' with each other, and could present
no contradiction. How, then, could the question whether the consequences of that hypothesis were in accord or discord with each
other possibly arise?
    A possible answer is that Socrates here has in mind sophistical
opponents of the Theory of Forms. The Forms, they might object,
are no less vulnerable than particulars to the 'contradictions'
developed at 101a–b. An assault of that sort is mounted against the
Theory in the *Parmenides*, where 'monstrosities' are proved with
respect to the Forms Large and Small (131a–e), that are recognizably
similar to the 'monstrosities' (101b1) that the Theory is here
designed to avoid. The present passage need not, of course, be held
to refer to the particular arguments given in the *Parmenides*. But it
seems natural that Socrates should tell Cebes that he should be ready
to face arguments of this general type. For it would be of special
importance, for anyone whose faith in rational argument rested upon
the Theory (cf.90c9–d1), that it should be immune from the difficulties that gave rise to it. The fact that Socrates ends his present
remarks with a slighting allusion to 'contradiction-mongers' (e2)
suggests that a supporter of the Form-Reason hypothesis would,
indeed, have to defend it against them.
    In this way, perhaps, 101c9–d5 can be related to the hypothesis
at 101c that was its point of departure. But now (d5–e1) Socrates
moves to a new and still more difficult stage: 'and when you had to
give an account of the hypothesis itself, you would give it in the
same way, once again hypothesizing another hypothesis, whichever
should seem best of those above, till you came to something adequate'.

What is meant here by 'giving an account' of the hypothesis itself? For different meanings of 'give an account', see on 76b4–c10. The most natural sense for it to bear here is 'give a proof', i.e. support or justify the initial hypothesis. Socrates seems to be thinking, as Robinson says (op.cit. 136), of the objector who says 'Yes, your conclusion follows from your hypothesis; but how do you know the hypothesis is true?' This new challenge is understandable. For it would not, presumably, be sufficient to adopt a hypothesis *ad hoc*, merely because it would yield one's desired conclusion. There must be some further ground that would recommend it independently. This ground is to be given 'in the same way', i.e. in the same way as the initial hypothesis was put forward. It, in its turn, will be related to a further hypothesis, in the same way as the original conclusion was related to it.

But here a problem arises. Socrates' remarks seem by now to have cut loose from their moorings at 101c. For the original 'safe' hypothesis, to which reference has so far been made, was that F things are F for no other reason than that they participate in the Form F. Yet the relation between this and the things it was introduced to explain is unlike the relation between premiss and conclusion. How, then, could a hypothesis designed to justify the Form-Reason hypothesis be posited 'in the same way' as was that hypothesis itself? If, as Robinson plausibly maintains (op.cit. 137), the words 'whichever should seem best of those above' (d7) are taken to mean that the relation between successive hypotheses is one of entailment, then the Form-Reason hypothesis would have to follow from 'another hypothesis' in the same way as its entailments follow from it. Yet it seems hard to find in the text, or to supply, any 'higher' hypothesis to which the Form-Reason hypothesis is thus related.

There is further obscurity in the clause 'till you came to something adequate' (e1). Does this mean merely 'adequate to satisfy an objector to the first hypothesis'? Or 'adequate to satisfy yourself'? Robinson (op.cit. 137) excludes the latter, on the ground that 'you were already satisfied with the first hypothesis'. But this seems doubtful. For in dialectic the true philosopher will be his own objector. However strong his hypothesis may seem to him, it behoves him to justify it not only to his interlocutors but also to himself. Socrates has to persuade himself as well as others (91a6–b1, cf.100e1–2).

It should also be asked whether 'something adequate' means 'some adequate *hypothesis*', as Robinson supposes, or whether it will consist in something that is no longer hypothetical in character. A mere hypothesis, it might seem, could not be 'adequate', if its sole merit were that no objection to it could be found. A conclusion, however validly derived from a hypothesis, would be no stronger than the hypothesis itself; and if there were no positive reason to adopt the latter, it would afford no adequate ground for the conclusion. The Theory of Forms is a case in point. It will not give adequate ground for believing in immortality, unless there are independent grounds for adopting it. This, no doubt, is what Socrates means later (107b5–8), when he tells his listeners that they must study 'the initial hypotheses' further, even if they find them acceptable, and that they will follow the argument if they analyse them 'adequately'. See on 65d4–e5 (p.97), 107a2–b10.

What might such an analysis consist in? The words 'best of those *above*' (d7) are sometimes taken to suggest an ascent, via successively 'higher' hypotheses, to a 'starting-point' (cf.e2), i.e. to some ultimate certainty that is not itself a hypothesis, but from which the propositions so far hypothesized can be deduced. Such a starting-point would be 'adequate' in the sense that it needed no justification itself, and rendered the system of propositions derived from it not only logically coherent but also true. In the *Republic* (510b7, 511b6) a starting-point of this kind is called 'unhypothetical', and is identified with the Form of the Good. Since Socrates' present account of his method was preceded by the story of his fruitless search for 'the good' (99c6–8), the present move from hypotheses to 'something adequate' has often been thought to anticipate the ascent to a first principle in the *Republic*. Accordingly, some commentators have wished to understand these lines in terms of a hierarchy of teleological propositions, somehow culminating in the Good. See, e.g., R. S. Bluck, *Phronesis* 1957, 21–31. The text, however, gives this no explicit support. No doubt Plato envisaged a system of ordered hypotheses as an ideal, for methodical scientific inquiry and exposition. But we can barely conjecture how, in detail, this ambitious programme was to be carried out. See, further, P. Friedländer, *C.P.* 1945, 256, H. F. Cherniss, *A.J.P.* 1947, 141, M. D. C. Tait, *S.H.G.N.* 110–15.

Socrates ends (101e1–102a1) by telling Cebes that he would not mix things up, like the 'contradiction-mongers', by arguing at the same time both about the starting-point and its consequences. The broad sense of this seems clear: the starting-point of an argument should be examined separately from the propositions derived from it. Aristotle attributes a similar precept to Plato (*E.N.* 1095a32), and it is well suited to the analysis of Platonic arguments generally. There may, however, be a more specific allusion to the contradiction-mongers' technique of confusing propositions about Forms with propositions about the particulars named after them. Such principles as 'it is by the beautiful that beautiful things are beautiful' (100e2–3) would be open to misconstruction, in view of the ambiguity of 'the beautiful'. Just such a confusion in the meaning of 'the larger comes to be from the smaller', or more generally 'opposites come to be from their opposites', occurs later in the discussion (103a4–c2), and has to be disentangled. Cf. *Euthydemus* 300e–304b, where such ambiguities are exploited, and the exploiters castigated in terms similar to those used here–cf.101e5–6 with *Euthydemus* 303c–d. See also on 90b4–91c5. For the phrase 'to discover any of the things that are' (e3) see on 65c2–4.

3.7 The Final Argument (102a10–107b10)

Socrates now advances his final proof that soul is immortal and imperishable. Soul, which brings life to the body, cannot admit death, and is therefore immortal. And since the immortal is imperishable, soul cannot perish, but must withdraw at the onset of death.

102a10–d4. Socrates explicates the statement 'Simmias is larger than Socrates but smaller than Phaedo' in terms of the Theory of Forms. 'Large' and 'small' have been used in translation, rather than 'tall' and 'short'. But since the three men are, presumably, being compared in respect of height, 'overtop' has been used for the verb that expresses the relation between them.

For 'each of the forms *was* something' (b1) as a way of asserting their existence, see on 74a9–b1. At 102b2 the particulars that 'partake' in a Form are said to 'take its name'. For the Forms as 'eponymous' see on 65d4–e5 (p.96), 78d10–e5. Individuals, such as Simmias, are said to 'take the name' of large and small (c10–11). Cf.103b7–8. Note that whether a thing is called 'large' or 'larger', it is regarded as named after one and the same Form, the Form Large. Cf.100e5–6, and see on 100e5–101b8.

Part of Socrates' purpose, evidently, is to distinguish properties that belong to a subject by its nature from those that it merely happens to have, and that it could lack without ceasing to be itself. Simmias does not overtop Socrates 'by nature' (c1), in the way that three and five will later be said to be odd 'by nature' (104a3, a7). He does not overtop Socrates 'by virtue of his being Simmias', but by virtue of the Largeness that he 'happens' to have (c2). This language marks the contrast between what we should call 'essential' and 'accidental' predication, which will be of the first importance in the coming argument.

Beyond this, however, the analysis of comparative statements is problematical.

(1) Why should the statement 'Simmias is larger than Socrates'

be held not to be strictly or literally true (b8–c1), in virtue of its ascribing to Simmias an accidental property? Is it implied that *all* statements of accidental predication, including non-relational ones, need reformulation? And is it further implied that *no* statements of essential predication, not even relational ones, need such recasting, so that not only 'three is odd' but 'three is greater than two' is acceptable as it stands? If this is being suggested, the grounds for requiring a reformulation in one sort of case but not in the other are not explained. But it seems possible, despite the suggestion of 102b8–c1, that the need for reformulation arises more from the relational than from the accidental feature of the example. For it is relational predicates, whether they be accidental or essential, that give rise to the compresence of opposites in a single subject: 'three is greater than two but less than four' is just as true as 'Simmias is larger than Socrates but smaller than Phaedo'. Has Socrates conflated what we should regard as two different distinctions?

O'Brien (*C.Q.* 1967, 200, n.1) says that the relational feature of the example is incidental: 'the colour of an apple, which is an accidental but not a relative attribute, would have served equally well as a contrast to, and as a preparation for, the essential hotness of fire and the essential aliveness of soul'. But the case of an apple's colour would not be a foil to the principle to be maintained at 102d5–103c9, that opposites exclude opposites. For an apple cannot be red and green all over at the same time, as Simmias can be larger than Socrates and smaller than Phaedo at the same time. Yet it is the compresence of opposites in a particular that seems significant. For it will next be argued that Largeness, unlike Simmias, cannot be large and small 'at the same time' (102d7, cf.e8). See next note.

(2) What is gained by interpreting 'Simmias is larger than Socrates but smaller than Phaedo' in terms of Largeness and Smallness being in Simmias (102b5–6)? It may be intended to clarify the notion of largeness, the simple term 'large' being held to be covertly comparative. To say that an individual is large is to say that it is a large member of some class, and therefore larger than most, or than average, members of that class. If so, an account of 'large' will require an account of 'larger'. Yet this will seem unsatisfying, if one expects the simple term to be primary, and the comparative to be explicable in terms of it. The proposed analysis of the comparative statement as 'largeness and smallness are in Simmias' (b5–6) may, therefore, be an attempt to restore primacy to the simple adjective by treating Largeness and Smallness as 'relational properties'. Cf. I. M. Crombie, *E.P.D.* ii. 312.

But the analysis gives rise to a difficulty. (S1) 'Simmias is larger than Socrates' means, we are to understand, (S2) 'Simmias has Largeness in relation to Socrates' Smallness.' And this, apparently, means (S3) 'Simmias' Largeness overtops Socrates' Smallness' (102d1–2). But since 'overtops' is equivalent to 'is larger than', S3 will imply (S4) 'Simmias' Largeness is larger than Socrates' Smallness.' But if so, how is the ascription of 'larger than' to the Form Largeness in S4 to be understood? It looks as if it is 'self-predicative' in the way that was earlier seen to give rise to paradox. Thus, given that:

$(x, y)\{(x$ is larger than $y) \equiv (x$ has Largeness in relation to y's Smallness)$\}$,

then, where x and y are Simmias' Largeness and Socrates' Smallness respectively, S4 will yield (S5) 'Simmias' Largeness has Largeness in relation to Socrates' Smallness.' Here a regress threatens, akin to that of *Parmenides* 132a–b. If, on the other hand, S4 is not self-predicative, it is not clear what it should be taken to mean. It does not seem readily construed as an identity statement, in the manner sometimes proposed for 'the Form Equal is equal' (see on 74d4–8, p.128). How else could the predicate 'larger than' or 'overtops', as applied to the Form Largeness, be understood?

102d5–103a3. It is now argued that opposite Forms cannot be characterized by their opposites. For the translation at 102e5–7, see note 69.

Several problems arise here:

(1) The connection of thought expressed by 'I want you to think as I do' (d5) is not obvious. Why should the foregoing analysis of comparative statements have been given *in order that* Cebes may share Socrates' view on this new point? Perhaps the analysis was meant to dispose of cases in prima facie conflict with the principle being maintained here. The principle that opposites exclude each other might seem to be breached by particulars in which Largeness and Smallness can coexist. But, on the analysis just given, the principle is not really infringed. For the analysis at 102c10–d2, even if it requires 'larger' to be predicated of Largeness, and 'smaller' of Smallness (see previous note), does not require Largeness and Smallness to be ascribed to each other. The question of the relation between Simmias' Largeness and that of Phaedo, or between Simmias' Smallness and that of Socrates, would, no doubt, create embarrassment, given that:

$(x, y) \{(x$ is larger than $y) \equiv (y$ is smaller than $x)\}$.

But the analysis adroitly avoids asserting any relation between the Largenesses or between the Smallnesses of two individuals. The principle that opposites exclude each other therefore remains intact.

(2) Socrates expresses the relations between Forms and their

opposites in a series of 'military metaphors'–'advancing', 'getting out of the way' (i.e. retreat), 'abiding' and 'admitting' hostile forces that 'occupy' a garrison, and 'perishing'. These metaphors will be kept up right through to 106e7. How are they to be applied to Largeness and Smallness? In particular, are 'getting out of the way' and 'perishing' genuine alternatives in this case, and if so, how do they differ?

Hackforth (148, n.3) believes that 'getting out of the way' is brought in here only to provide for the case of soul, the single case in which it is exemplified. This would suggest that the alternative is not meant as a real one in other cases. But in view of the repeated stress upon it, and its wide range of application (e7–a2), it seems better to find distinct interpretations for each option, if possible (see on 103c10–e5, p.198). It is plausible to suppose, with D. O'Brien (*C.Q.* 1967, 204, n.4), that Smallness 'advances' when Simmias is compared with Phaedo, and that his Largeness 'gets out of the way' precisely because, despite the comparison with Phaedo, he remains larger than Socrates. If this is correct, it will be preferable to think of 'perishing' as needing something stronger than mere cessation of the comparison with Socrates. For if Simmias' Largeness in relation to Socrates does not depend upon their actually being compared, it need not 'perish' when the comparison ceases. For 'perishing', then, an actual change of size in one of them will be required. Cf. *Theaetetus* 155b6–c1.

(3) The Forms Large and Small are pointedly distinguished from what Socrates calls 'the largeness in us' (d7) and 'the small that's in us' (e6). The contrast is repeated at 103b5, and must be significant. What is meant by 'the *F* in us', and what is its role in the argument?

Whether Plato distinguished a category of 'immanent Forms', with separate ontological status from the Forms proper, is disputed. The distinction is accepted by Hackforth *passim*, Bluck, 17–18, R. Demos, *P.P.R.* 1947–8, 456–60, R. G. Turnbull, *P.Q.* 1958, 131–43, and G. Vlastos, *P.R.* 1969, 298–301. It is denied by Verdenius (note on 103b5), and by D. O'Brien, *C.Q.* 1967, 201–3.

The phrase 'immanent Form' suggests a more systematic doctrine than the evidence warrants. Certainly, no consistent distinction between 'immanent' and 'transcendent' Forms can be founded upon Plato's terminology (see note 72). He may, more aptly, be said to distinguish here the property Largeness from individual instances of it. Such a distinction arises naturally out of the preceding talk of Simmias' and Phaedo's Largeness (102c4, 102c11). A somewhat similar notion, for the Form Likeness, appears at *Parmenides* 130b3–4. But the scope of the distinction between Forms and their instances 'in us' remains unclear. Is it only for Forms of attributes, such as

Largeness and Smallness, that property-instances are distinguished? Or are there Forms 'in us' for all items for which Forms may be postulated, including such stuffs as fire or snow? Moreover, for those Forms that are explicitly distinguished from their property-instances, what counts as an 'instance' of the Form in question? Is it Simmias himself that instantiates the Form Largeness, or is it only 'the largeness in him' that does so? Or may both be thought of as instantiating the Form in different ways?

Doubt on these points leaves it uncertain what part, if any, 'the largeness in us' plays in the argument. Since the alternatives 'get out of the way' and 'perish' are applied to it, as they will later be to snow and fire, three, and soul, 'the largeness in us' has sometimes been regarded as their precursor in the argument, and they have been construed accordingly as 'immanent Forms' (see on 103c10– e5). But it is not clear that 'the largeness in us' is meant as analogous to the disputed items in the later argument. Note that those items have no counterparts related to Large and Small in the way that they themselves are related to the Forms of Hot and Cold, Oddness, and Life. In terms of Socrates' 'safe' and 'subtle' reasons (105b–c), the only 'reasons' given for things being large or small are 'safe' ones. There is no entity which 'makes' things large or small, in the way that fire or snow, three or soul, (however interpreted), 'makes' them hot or cold, odd or alive. It is far from certain, therefore, that interpretation of the later argument should be controlled by the present distinction.

A possible way of relating the distinction to the argument will, however, be considered below. For this purpose it will be necessary to distinguish between the property-instances of a Form (e.g., Simmias' Largeness) and the individual things that may be thought of as participating in that Form (e.g. Simmias himself). Property-instances, since their designation must include the *name* of the Form in question, will be referred to in what follows as its *N*-instances. The individual *things* participating in the Form will be called its *T*-instances. Thus, 'the largeness in Simmias' will be said to be an *N*-instance of the Form Large, whereas Simmias himself will be called a *T*-instance of it. For the application of this distinction see Version B given in the notes on 104c7–d4 (p.204) and 104d5– e6 (p.207).

103a4–c9. An objection is now raised against the principle that an opposite *F* will never come to be *G*: it appears to conflict with the law of opposites agreed earlier (70e1–71a11). Socrates shows that the objection rests on a misunderstanding, thereby revealing an ambiguity in such expressions as 'the large': they can mean either 'that which is large' or 'the property of largeness' (see on 70e4–71a11, p.108). In the former sense 'the large' can come to be small, in the latter it cannot. Despite this clarification, however, expressions of the form 'the F' will continue to give trouble, notably at 106a–e. See on 105e10–107a1 (p.217).

To draw the distinction between largeness and large things, Socrates has to emphasize the word 'thing' (103b3), that he had used more casually earlier (71a10, b2). It is sometimes remarked, in this connection, that 'things' and their 'attributes' had not, before Plato, been differentiated. Cf., e.g., the use of 'hot', 'cold', 'dry', and 'wet', at 86b8–9. Only later will Plato himself coin a word for 'quality' (*Theaetetus* 182a8). It should be noted that Greek commonly uses unaccompanied plural adjectives, e.g. 'beautifuls', 'larges', 'smalls', to mean 'F things'. Of the adjectives prominent in the *Phaedo* only 'equal' is naturally so used in English.

At 103b5 Socrates distinguishes 'the opposite in us' from 'the opposite in nature'. By 'the opposite in nature' is meant the Form F itself, as distinct from its property-instances 'in us'. For this use of 'nature' in the designation of Forms, cf. *Republic* 597b–598a, *Parmenides* 132d2, *Cratylus* 389a–d. The language at 103b7–c1 again reflects the theory that particulars are 'named after' an eponymous Form. See on 65d4–e5 (p.96), 78d10–e5, 102a10–d4.

At 103a7–8 the law of opposites is recalled in terms of the comparatives 'larger' and 'smaller'. Cf.70e6–71a2. For the shift from 'large' and 'small' at 102d5–103a2 to 'larger' and 'smaller' here, see on 70e4–71a11, 100e5–101b8, 102a10–d4.

103c10–e5. A new phase of the proof begins here. Note the semantic theory underlying the introduction of hot and cold into the argument (c10–11). Socrates asks, literally, 'do you call something hot, and again cold?', i.e. 'is there something designated by each of those names?' At 103e3–4 the Form is said to be 'entitled to its own name for all time'. Once again, the Form F is treated as the prime bearer of the name 'F'. Cf.103b7–c1, and see previous note.

At 103c13–d4 Socrates distinguishes the Hot and the Cold from fire and snow. Are Forms of Fire and Snow meant here, or physical stuffs? Interpretation of the argument hinges largely upon this much vexed point.

The language is non-committal. Socrates uses no Form-referring expressions in connection with 'fire' or 'snow' at any point. It is true that Forms, regarded as bearers of common names, i.e. 'universals' (see on 65d4–e5, p.96), should include Fire and Snow no less than Hot and Cold. A Form of Fire is explicitly mentioned in the *Timaeus* (51b8). Cf. also *Parmenides* 130c1–4. But granted the need for such Forms in Plato's scheme of things, it is a further question whether they are being referred to here.

G. Vlastos (*P.R.* 1969, 318, n.70) and D. Keyt (*Phronesis* 1963, 168, n.2) have wished to understand snow and fire as 'immanent Forms', parallel to the Form of Three at 104d5–7, and have interpreted the whole argument accordingly in terms of entailment relations between Forms. Similarly, Hackforth (156, 162, n.3) thinks that the argument wavers between treating fire as a Form, and taking it as a concrete substance co-ordinate with snow. However, (i) one would expect fire and snow to be co-ordinate throughout. (ii) It seems hard to believe that at 106a3–10 either fire or snow could be anything but physical stuffs. For it could hardly be said of the Form of Snow, not even of an 'immanent' Form of it, that it would go away 'intact and unmelted' (106a5), or of the Form of Fire that it would not be 'put out' (106a9). Nor (iii) can fire be an immanent Form at 106b6, where Socrates speaks of 'the hotness in the fire', unless it be supposed that there can be immanent Forms within immanent Forms. Above all, (iv) on the Vlastos-Keyt view, it seems impossible to interpret 'getting out of the way' and 'perishing' as genuine alternatives. Clearly, Socrates could not be suggesting that the Forms of Snow or Fire might 'perish', since all Forms are imperishable. But if it is 'immanent' Forms, parallel to the Large and Small 'in us' (102d7, e6), that are held to 'get out of the way or perish', how can these alternatives be distinguished in such cases as Snow and Fire? In those cases, it would not be possible, as it was with the Large and Small, to think of 'immanent Forms' as getting out of the way, when the relevant particulars were viewed in a different relation. For 'snow' and 'fire' are non-relational terms. But the alternative is presented as if it were a real one. The contrast that Socrates will draw at 106a–c between snow, fire, and three, on the one hand, and soul on the other, suggests that only in the case of soul is 'getting out of the way' a forced option. In the other cases, both options are expressly left open. Cf. D. O'Brien, *C.Q.* 1967, 204, 208.

On the other hand, if fire and snow are not Forms, but physical stuffs, there need be no difficulty in understanding 'get out of the way' and 'perish' as genuine alternatives: snow can melt, and fire can be put out, or they can be moved. Their 'perishing' by being melted or quenched is expressly suggested at 106a3–10, and the idea of their 'getting out of the way' by being moved, although nowhere mentioned, is not hard to supply. Burnet therefore seems correct in saying (note on 104d1): 'it has not been suggested that fire and snow are Forms, and it seems improbable that they are so regarded.'

At 103e2–5 Socrates generalizes from the snow and fire examples: certain things, although not identical with the Form *F* itself, always possess that Form's character. For the words translated 'form' and 'character' see on 65d4–e5 (p.93) and note 72.

What is meant by qualifying the generalization with the words 'in some cases of this kind' (e2)? Is it that (i) only for some, but not for all, of the opposite *Forms* mentioned, there are things other than those Forms that are always entitled to their name? On this view, it will be implied that for certain Forms, such as Large and Small, there is nothing corresponding to snow and fire, i.e. nothing that is always large, or always small, in the way that snow is always cold, and fire always hot. Alternatively, does Socrates mean that (ii) only some, but not all, stuffs are invariably characterized by one member of a pair of opposites? It will then be implied that certain stuffs, unlike fire and snow, may be characterized by either of a pair of opposites (at different times), and are not invariably characterized by one member of a pair only.

'Some cases of this kind' is more naturally taken, as in (ii) to mean 'such things as fire and snow', than as meaning 'such Forms as Hot and Cold'. But what, on this view, would be ruled out by the reservation? O'Brien (op.cit. 211, n.2) suggests water, which may be either hot or cold, unlike fire, which can only be hot. But water is, arguably, always wet and never dry, and thus stands in the same relation to the Forms of Wet and Dry as does fire to the Forms of Hot and Cold. If the reservation is meant to exclude things that are not invariably characterized by *any* opposite, what would illustrate it? This question calls for further clarification of the concept of an 'opposite'. On a broad interpretation, it might be difficult to find examples of things that are not invariably characterized by some opposite or other. But the reservation would be pointless if its effect were to exclude an empty class.

103e5–104c6. A numerical example is now introduced. Three, while not itself an opposite, must always be characterized by one member of a pair, the Odd, and so must exclude the other, the Even. The argument is sometimes criticized here for assimilating numerical to physical examples. Thus, Hackforth (157) objects that snow's refusal to admit cold is 'a physical fact known through sense perception', whereas the corresponding truths about three and soul are 'statements about the implications of terms'. G. Vlastos (*P.R.* 1969, 321) speaks of 'Plato's reduction of physical to logical necessity in the *Phaedo*'. See also E. L. Burge, *Phronesis* 1971, 11–13. But the passage need not be read as embodying any doctrine about the nature of physical necessity. The fire, snow, and number examples may be taken as entirely subservient to the proof of immortality. For this proof, the vital point is not so much the assimilation of physical to logical necessity as the basing of *meta*physical conclusions upon conceptual argument, the derivation of existential propositions about the soul from consideration of its essential nature. See on 105e10–107a1 (p.217).

It is true, however, that the numerical examples serve to bridge, and even conceal, a serious gap between soul and the physical stuffs with which it has so far been compared. Soul will be thought of as causally affecting bodies (105c–d), as imparting life to the bodies it occupies, just as fire and snow impart heat and cold. But this analogy is weakened by the fact that soul, unlike fire and snow, is not observable (79b7–15). Fire and snow can be recognized and observed independently of the bodies they occupy. Our knowledge that a body has fire or snow in it does not depend upon our finding it to be hot or cold. By contrast, the presence of soul in a body is not observable independently of that body's being alive. The life that we find in a body is our sole warrant for ascribing soul to it at all. Hence the notion of soul's 'bringing life' to body is not truly parallel with the other cases. The transition to it is helped by the example of three. For numbers, like the soul, are not sensible, nor are they observable independently of particular numbered sets.

The status of numbers in Plato is controversial. It is not clear whether he distinguished between the number *n* and the Form *N*-ness. But the following considerations suggest the need for such a distinction: (a) When we speak of, e.g., 'four threes', or 'adding three and three', the threes mentioned can hardly be the Form Threeness, which is unique. (b) Forms are held to be 'incomposite' (78c), whereas numbers might be regarded as consisting of abstract units, and hence 'composite'. (c) Forms cannot 'perish', whereas numbers are conceived as able to do so (104c1–3, 106a1). (d) Numbers, unlike Forms, can have contrasted predicates in different relations, e.g. 'more' and 'less', 'double' and 'half'.

Aristotle ascribes to Plato a doctrine of mathematical entities 'intermediate' between Forms and sensible things. The worth of this evidence is disputed, and the doctrine is, at most, inchoate in the dialogues. But an intermediate status for numbers would suit the present parallel between three and soul, in view of the soul's own intermediate status between the Forms and the sensible world (78c–84b). And the above objections to viewing numbers as (a sub-class of) Forms warrant asking, for each occurrence of 'three' or 'threeness' in the coming argument, whether a Form or a number is meant. See W. D. Ross, *P.T.I.* 65–7, 206–12, A. Wedberg, *P.P.M.*

122–35, J. M. Rist, *Phronesis* 1964, 33–7, I. M. Crombie, *E.P.D.* ii. 440ff.

For the terms 'three' and 'threeness' see on 101b9–c9. Nothing can be inferred from Plato's terminology. Note, especially, the different locutions used for members of the odd and even number series at 104a4–b4. The casual shifting from 'threeness' and 'fiveness' to 'two' and 'four' in parallel contexts suggests that no systematic distinction is intended between the two types of terms. See also on 104d5–e6, 104e7–105b4.

Hackforth (151, n.2, cf.156) argues from the use of 'threeness' at 104c5 that 'three' at 104c1 must mean the immanent Form of Three. But it does not follow from the use of 'twoness' and 'threeness' at 104c5, as Hackforth supposes (151, n.1), that the whole paragraph 104b6–c3 is concerned with Forms. For if 'twoness' and 'threeness' at 104c5 mean the numbers two and three, it could well be the number three of which it is said (c1–3) that it will 'perish' rather than become even. Moreover, the items exemplified by three are said (b9–10) not to admit 'whatever Form may be opposite to the one that's in them'. To speak of a Form's being 'in them' is to suggest that 'they' are not Forms themselves.

Whatever may be meant by 'three' or 'threeness', it is difficult to understand the 'military metaphors' in relation to this example. What is meant by the Form Even's 'attacking' three, and how should three's 'getting out of the way' and 'perishing' be understood? As before, it is preferable to take these as genuine alternatives if possible. See on 103c10–e5 (p.198). Perhaps three's 'getting out of the way' could be understood in a manner analogous to the withdrawal of Simmias' Largeness in face of a comparison with Phaedo instead of Socrates. Three might be thought of as withdrawing from a set, when that set is viewed in terms of a different unit-concept: three 'withdraws' from three musicians when they are viewed as one *ensemble*; by contrast, it 'perishes' when a fourth member is added to their number. Cf. *Parmenides* 129c4–d6.

At 104c5 Socrates says: 'Moreover, twoness isn't opposite to threeness.' Hackforth (151, n.3) thinks that this remark has no relevance by itself, and 'restores logic' by supplying in his translation a counterpart statement about two to the one just made about three, i.e. that two will perish rather than become odd. But this is unnecessary. The point of insisting that three is not an opposite is to show that the refusal to admit opposites may be a feature of things that are not opposites themselves. For this is to be the position with regard to soul: it will be held to exclude an opposite, death, even though it is not an opposite itself. Cf. O'Brien, *C.Q.* 1967, 213–15.

104c7–d4. There are major uncertainties of translation in this passage, which affect the interpretation of the whole argument.

(1) The present version of 104c7–9 leaves it open whether the 'other things' mentioned in the second half of the sentence are Forms. Hackforth, however, translates: 'Hence it is not only two opposite forms that won't endure an onset by one on the other; there are others also that won't endure the onset of opposites.' This makes Socrates claim that not only do Forms of opposites exclude each other, but that certain other Forms likewise exclude one member of such a pair. Accordingly, Hackforth renders the question at 104c11–12: 'Then would you like us, if we can, to specify what sort of forms these are?' However, Forms are not explicitly mentioned in the text, and the question whether the definienda are Forms is prejudged in such a translation. The present version, 'would you like us to define what kinds these are?', leaves the matter open.

(2) At 104d1–3 the translation makes Socrates refer to things that are 'compelled by whatever occupies them' to have not only the occupier's Form, but also that of some opposite. For the grammar and text, see notes 70 and 71. The version adopted follows Tredennick, G. M. A. Grube, *C.P.* 1931, 197–9, and J. Schiller, *Phronesis* 1967, 54–5. This is consistent with the translation of 104c7–9 above. For the 'things' referred to here, like those at 104c8, will not necessarily be Forms, but may be other items, which, on being occupied by a Form, such as Threeness, are thereby compelled to have not only the character of that Form, but also that of some opposite Form, such as Oddness. However, the Greek may be equally well, or better, translated either (i) 'those that compel whatever they occupy to have not only their own (viz. the occupiers') character but the character of some opposite as well', or (ii) 'those which compel the object which they come to occupy to have not only its own (viz. the occupied object's) character, but also the character of a certain opposite'. For (i) see O'Brien, *C.Q.* 1967, 215–16. For (ii) see Hackforth (similarly Bluck). The important difference between both these versions and the translation adopted is that they make Socrates specify as the definienda a class of occupying Forms. For in these versions, the definienda will be identified with the occupiers, and these in turn will be illustrated at 104d5–7 by the Form of Three; whereas on the translation adopted, the definienda will be identified with the things occupied by such Forms, and are therefore unlikely to be Forms themselves.

The present version of 104d1–3 is better suited to the view of the argument preferred in these notes. It enables the disputed items to be taken not as Forms but as physical stuffs or numbers. It is, admittedly, subject to some linguistic difficulty, although in view of the uncertainty of the text at 104d2 this is not decisive (see note 70). In addition, however, one substantive objection to taking 104d1–3 as required by this translation must be acknowledged. It makes Socrates refer to a class of items such that *whatever* occupies them, they are compelled to have not only the Form of that thing, but also the Form of some opposite. And it may be doubted whether there exists a class of items, such that *any* Form occupying them imports the Form of an opposite along with it. It is true that in the case of numbers more than one Form may have this effect. It will be mentioned later (105a6–b1) that not only 'ten' but also 'the double' excludes the Odd. The number ten may thus be thought of as occupied by at least two Forms, those of Ten and Double, that compel it to be even. But it is not clear that *all* Forms have such an effect upon it.

Possibly, therefore, the phrase 'whatever occupies them' refers not to a plurality of Forms occupying one and the same item, such as ten in the above example, but rather to a plurality of Forms severally occupying the different items that Socrates is seeking to define. These include the whole series of natural numbers (104a7–b4). So Plato, with numbers uppermost in mind, could perhaps have written 'whatever occupies them' with reference to the whole series of Forms for numbers, each Form being thought of as occupying a different number, and making it either even or odd.

It may be useful here to set out alternative versions of the whole argument warranted by the translations just considered. Version A is based on the translation adopted. Version B is supported by rendering the definienda at 104c7–13 as Forms, and translating 104d1–3 with Hackforth or O'Brien. Divergent interpretations of certain passages discussed in later notes will be labelled A or B with reference to these versions. For the term '*N*-instance', used in B3 and B8, see on 102d5–103a3 (p.196). For an assessment of the key stages of the argument, on each of these versions, see on 105b5–c8 (p.213) and 105c9–d12 (p.214–15).

Version A	*Version B*
A1. There are items which, although not themselves opposites, will not admit one member of a pair of opposites (104c7–9).	B1. There are certain non-opposite Forms, such that whatever possesses them will not admit one member of a pair of opposite Forms (104c7–9).
A2. These items are such that, if they are occupied by a non-	B2. These non-opposite Forms are such that whatever they

Version A

opposite Form *A*, they must possess an opposite Form *F* (104d1–8).

A3. Such items will never admit the opposite of the Form *F*, i.e. the Form *G*, hence are un-*G* (104d9–e6).

A4. Such items may be defined as things that bring the Form *F* to whatever they enter (105a3–4).

[A3 + A4]:
A5. Items occupied by Form *A* that bring the Form *F* to whatever they enter will never admit the Form *G* (105a4–5).

A6. If a thing (*x*) is such that, whatever *y* it is in, *y* will be *F*, *x* may be said to 'bring' *F* to *y* (supplied).

A7. Soul is such that, whatever body it is in, that body will be living (105c9–d2).

[A6 + A7]:
A8. Soul brings Life to whatever body it occupies (105d3–5).

A9. The opposite of Life is Death (105d6–9).

[A5 + A8]:
A10. Soul will never admit the opposite of what it brings (105-d10–12).

Version B

occupy must have not only them, but an opposite Form as well (104d1–8).

B3. When a non-opposite Form *A* brings an opposite Form *F* to whatever the Form *A* occupies, then an *N*-instance of the Form *A* will never admit *F*'s opposite, the Form *G* (104d9–105a5).

B4. If a non-opposite Form *A* is such that, whatever body (*x*) it is present in, *x* will be *F*, then Form *A* brings *F* to *x* (supplied).

B5. The Form of Soul is a non-opposite Form, such that whatever body it is present in, that body will be living (105c9–d2).

[B4 + B5]:
B6. The Form of Soul brings Life to whatever body it occupies (105d3–5).

B7. The opposite of Life is Death (105d6–9).

[B3 + B6]:
B8. An *N*-instance of the Form of Soul, i.e. an individual soul, will never admit the Form opposite to that which the Form of Soul brings (105d10–12).

Version A	Version B
A11. What will not admit Death is im-mortal (105d13–e3).	B9. What will not admit Death is im-mortal (105d13–e3).
[A8 + A9 + A10]: A12. Soul will not admit Death (105e4–5).	[B6 + B7 + B8]: B10. An individual soul will never admit Death (105e4–5).
[A11 + 12]: A13. Soul is im-mortal (105e6–7).	[B9 + B10]: B11. An individual soul is im-mortal (105e6–7).
A14. What is im-mortal is imperishable (106c9–d9).	B12. What is im-mortal is imperishable (106c9–d9).
[A13 + A14]: A15. Soul is imperishable (106e1–107a1).	[B11 + B12]: B13. An individual soul is imperishable (106e1–107a1).

104d5–e6. Socrates illustrates the suggestion made at 104d1–3 with the example of three. This passage contains the one and only unambiguous mention of a Form, other than Forms of opposites, in the entire argument. Those who believe that the items under discussion are Forms will naturally regard the Form of Three (d5–6) as an instance of the class that Socrates had proposed for definition at 104c11–12. The passage is important, in view of the deliberate parallel between the cases of three and soul, and the similarities of language with 105d3–5. But it does not settle the question whether the definienda are Forms. For, on the translation adopted at 104d1–3, they will be exemplified here not by the Form of Three, but rather by whatever it is supposed to occupy (see previous note). If so, the passage will be identifying the definienda not with Forms that import opposites, but with the items occupied by such Forms. Its argument will then be that those items will not admit the Form opposite to the one imported into them. This will not constitute a 'definition' of the items in question. Indeed, it is not until 105a1–2 that Socrates says 'see if you define them thus'.

Here the problem of interpreting Plato's locutions for numbers again becomes acute. D. O'Brien has argued (*C.Q.* 1967, 216–19) that 'in the elaboration of the numerical example (i.e. from 104b6) there is a consistent distinction between form and particularisation. The form is described as "the Form of Three" or more simply as "threeness". The particularisation is described as "three".' But this alleged distinction is very hard to sustain. Both at 104c5 and 104e5, 'threeness' follows immediately upon occurrences of 'three', where the latter stands, in O'Brien's own view, for the number three. The point of switching from number to Form in these places is difficult to see. Moreover, as O'Brien recognizes (op.cit. 218), 'threeness' is used in parallel with 'two' at 104a4—b2, where 'threeness' and 'five-ness' exemplify the odd series of numbers, and 'two' and 'four' the even. O'Brien suggests that it is natural for Plato's language 'to become firmer with the *elaboration* of his example'. But Plato could quite well have registered this important distinction, had he wished to, from as early as 101c5—6, where the '-ness' terms were used for the Forms of One and Two. Again, if the distinction is supposed to be firmly established from 104b6 onwards, why does Socrates back-slide at 105a6—7? See next note (p.208).

Hackforth (151, n.2, 152, n.1, 156) holds that 'three' and 'three-ness' are used interchangeably to stand for the immanent Form Threeness, and that the meaning of 'three' at 104e1—3 can be fixed from the use of 'threeness' at 104e5. In drawing no distinction between 'three' and 'threeness' he seems correct. But it does not follow that both are used to mean 'immanent Form'. It seems equally possible to hold that (i) neither 'three' nor 'threeness' means a Form of any kind, but that (ii) both alike refer to the number three; and that therefore (iii) the *only* reference to the Form of Three in the whole passage occurs in so many words at 104d5—6.

But even if 'three' and 'threeness' are taken as just suggested, the meaning of 104d5—7 and the point of the succeeding argument are still uncertain. For *what* is it that is supposed to be occupied by the Form of Three and compelled to be not only three but also odd? Is it the number three, or is it sets of three things? O'Brien (op.cit. 212, 217) argues that only the number three could be said to be odd 'by nature' (104a3, a7); a group of oxen, which might change in number, could not. But the claim that whatever the Form of Three occupies must *ipso facto* be odd seems as plausible for sets as for numbers. Cf. *Hippias* I, 302a1—7. O'Brien also appeals to Socrates' later reference to a 'number's' being made to be odd (105c4). But this is not conclusive, since 'number' may mean a numbered set (cf. *Phaedrus* 247a2). It is therefore unclear whether Plato is thinking of the Form of Three as (A) occupying the number three or as (B) occupying a set of three things.

There are, accordingly, two ways of taking the argument of this section. (A) 'Whatever the form of three occupies' refers to the number three, and it is to this that 'a thing of that kind' refers back at 104d9. On this view, the argument runs as follows: (i) whatever the Form of Three occupies will be odd; (ii) the Form of Three occupies the number three; hence (iii) the number three will be odd, and hence (iv) uneven. This interpretation would suit Version A of the argument given in the previous note. Cf. J. Schiller, *Phronesis* 1967, 57−8.

Alternatively, (B) 'whatever the form of three occupies' may be taken as sets of three things, and the argument understood as follows: (i) whatever sets the Form of Three occupies must be odd (d5−8); hence (ii) the number three will have no part in the Form opposite to the Odd, i.e. the Form Even (d9−e4); hence, (iii) the number three will be uneven (e5−6). Here, as in Version A, 'a thing of that kind' (104d9) refers back to the number three. But the number is viewed as an *N*-instance of the Form (see on 102d5−103a3, p.196); and the argument runs from the effect exerted by the Form of Three upon its *T*-instances, triadic *sets*, to the property of the *number* three: the number, or *N*-instance, will have essentially that property which the Form compels the sets to have while it occupies them; it will therefore not admit that property's opposite.

The general principle implied on this interpretation would be that when a non-opposite Form *A* compels its *T*-instances to possess an opposite Form *F*, then an *N*-instance of the Form *A* will never admit the Form *G* (see B3 in the summary of the previous note). This principle would be applied to the soul by treating it as an *N*-instance of the Form of Soul (i.e. as 'the soul in us'), and the bodies it animates as *T*-instances of that Form (i.e. as 'things besouled'). See B6 and B8.

On either of the above versions, the parallel between the number three and the soul is dubious. For it is hard to understand either the Form's occupancy of the number three (Version A), or the treatment of the number three as an *N*-instance of the Form (Version B), if there is only *one* such number. The referent of 'the number three' is naturally taken, in English at least, to be unique, whereas that of 'the soul' need not be: 'the soul' may mean 'our souls' (just as 'the appendix' may mean 'our appendices'), whereas 'the number three' can hardly stand for a plurality. If Plato is taken to have believed in a plurality of threes, as in the doctrine of intermediates referred to on p.200, it would be possible to think of '*a* three' rather than of '*the* number three'. But such expressions as 'a three' or 'threes' are more naturally used in English of sets than of pure numbers. The required parallel between 'three' and 'soul' is therefore peculiarly difficult to express.

104e7−105b4. This difficult passage divides into two parts: (1) At 104e7−105a5 Socrates proposes a definition of the class of entities he had suggested defining at 104c11−12. (2) At 105a5−b3 he gives some further numerical examples.

(1) For the complex grammar of the 'definition' (a2−5) see note

74. It does not, unfortunately, read like a definition at all, but simply enunciates the general principle that whatever A items bring F to something cannot themselves admit G. This is a cardinal principle of the argument, which will be applied directly to the case of soul at 105d10–11. See on 100e5–101b8 and next note. Its meaning, however, turns upon whether the designated A items are Forms, and this still remains unclear.

At 104e8–105a1 they are exemplified by 'threeness', 'twoness' and 'the fire'. The translation 'the fire' keeps the Greek definite article, but should not be read as a definite description, referring to an individual fire. It means either 'fire' in a generic sense, i.e. stuff called 'fire', or the *Form* of Fire. D. O'Brien (*C.Q.* 1967, 220) argues from the numerical locutions 'threeness' and 'twoness' that Plato is probably 'now thinking of fire to some extent as form'. But the numerical language is quite inconclusive (see on 101b9–c9 and previous note). In the further examples (a6–7) of what is, presumably, the same point, Socrates switches to the ordinary terms for the cardinals 'five' and 'ten'. This confirms the view of J. Schiller (*Phronesis* 1967, 57) that Plato shows a 'studied indifference to the locutions by which he refers to numbers'. It cannot, therefore, be argued either, on the strength of 104e8–105a1, that Forms are meant, or, on the strength of 105a6–7, that they are not. Hackforth's translation at 105a3–4 begs the question by importing Forms where there are none in the Greek.

At 104e10 and 105a3–4 Socrates speaks for the first time of the items in question 'bringing' an opposite to something. The same word is used later (105d3–4, d10–11) of soul's 'bringing' life to body, and may be an extension of the military metaphor, referring to the 'bringing up' of reinforcements. However, the meaning of 'bring', and consequently the identity of the 'bringer' and the 'recipient' of an opposite Form, are disputed.

(A) 'Bringing' may be understood as 'causally imparting', and the 'bringer' may be taken not as the *Form A*, but as any x that participates in the Form A, and is therefore F, and by its presence imparts F to another individual, y. On this view, the principle being formulated here will be:

$$(x, y)\,\{Ax.x\,|\,\text{causes}\,y\,\text{to be}\,F) \supset (\sim Gx)\}.$$

If this formula expresses Plato's meaning, its application will be as follows: 'A' will be replaced by 'participates in the Form Soul', and 'G' by 'participates in the Form Death'. x's causing y to be F will represent an individual soul's 'bringing' life to any body that it enters, i.e. 'causing' it to be alive, and it will be from this that soul's refusal to admit death will be inferred. This fits Version A given at 104c7–d4 (p.204).

Alternatively, (B) 'bringing' may be taken to stand for the same relation as was illustrated at 104d by the Forms Three and Odd, i.e. a non-symmetrical relation between two Forms, A and F, such that whatever participates in Form A must also participate in Form F. Cf. G. Vlastos, *P.R.* 1969, 317. On this account, the 'bringer' will be a Form, such as Three, and the 'recipient' will be an individual that participates in that Form. Thus, where A is the 'bringing' Form, F the Form brought, and G the Form opposite to F, the principle being enunciated here would, on this view, be simply:

$$(x)\,(Ax \supset {\sim}Gx).$$

Note, however, that this formula would not fit Version B of the argument, and would not yield the premiss required for proving the soul's immortality. For Socrates will not argue that it refuses to admit Death merely on the ground that it participates in the Form Soul, i.e. that it *is* soul. He argues that it excludes death because it brings life *to the body*. If, therefore, the argument is to be construed in terms of entailment relations between Forms, the more complex pattern of argument given under (B) in the previous note (p.207) will be needed.

(2) The further numerical examples are well explained by D. O'Brien, op.cit. 221–3. See also F. M. Cornford, *C.Q.* 1909, 189–91. The words 'This, of course, is itself also the opposite of something else; nevertheless, it won't admit the form of the odd' (a8–b1) are difficult. They seem meant as an aside about 'the double' as such, and not about ten qua double. Hackforth (153, n.1) translates and interprets the second half of the sentence as if its subject were 'ten'. But it seems better to take the subject as 'the double' throughout. The point will then be that 'double', unlike the numbers two, three, five, and ten, that have been instanced as excluding odd or even, is itself an opposite of something else, namely 'half' (cf. *Republic* 438c1–2, 479b3); nevertheless—i.e. despite its infringing the norm by being an opposite—it still excludes the odd, since no number that is double can, in fact, be odd.

Two series of fractions are instanced (b1–3) as excluding the Form of Wholeness: $\frac{1}{2}, \frac{3}{2}, \frac{5}{2}$, etc., and $\frac{1}{3}, \frac{4}{3}, \frac{7}{3}$, etc. These examples are of no importance for the main argument.

105b5–c8. Socrates now puts forward a new kind of answer which he illustrates with a series of examples, 'fire', 'fever', and 'oneness' (or 'a unit'). The main problems here are: (1) What exactly is the grammar and sense of the lines indicating fire and fever as the reasons for a body's being hot or ailing (b8–c4)? (2) What is the meaning of the numerical example? (3) How is the new type of answer related to the old 'safe' answer in terms of Forms? (4) Why does Socrates see in it 'a different kind of safeness'?

(1) For the grammar and text at 105b8–c4 see note 75. Hackforth translates 105b8–9: 'what must be present in a thing's body to make it hot?' (with parallel renderings of the questions at 105c3–5). But this wrongly suggests that fire and fever are necessary conditions for heat and illness respectively; whereas fever, at least, is clearly not a necessary condition for illness but only a sufficient one (cf. *Alcibiades* II, 139e–140a). Fire, too, is probably not meant as a necessary condition for heat, since it is parallel in the argument to snow, and the latter could not be held a necessary condition for cold (note also 63d7–8). Hackforth (161) regards it as a weakness of the answers 'fire' and 'fever' that they give conditions that are merely sufficient and not also necessary. Of course, if the relevant phrases are translated as if they specified necessary conditions, they will appear to be making a false claim. But they clearly should not be so translated. It is only in the case of soul (105c9–d2) that the new answer gives a condition that is indisputably necessary as well as sufficient. In general, then, the new answers differ from the old ones in being merely sufficient, whereas the old ones were both sufficient and necessary.

(2) The word translated 'oneness' (*monas*) at 105c6 may stand for the Form of One, as it clearly does at 101c6. But it may also be rendered 'a unit'. Hackforth translates it thus, and explains it (158, n.2) as 'the one left over in the middle when an odd number is divided into two equal parts'. This explanation conforms to two definitions of 'odd' criticized by Aristotle in the *Topics*: 'that which is greater by one (*monas*) than an even number' (142b8), and 'a number with a middle' (149a30–31). See also Euclid, *Elements* vii, Def. 7, ed. T. L. Heath, ii. 281, and H. F. Cherniss, *A.C.P.A.* 25, n.19. Hackforth's interpretation gives a clear sense in which the 'odd' or unpaired unit makes a number odd, and is well suited to the root meaning of the Greek word for 'odd'. Cf. also *O.E.D.*, s.v. 'odd'.

Thus understood, 'a unit' would be both a necessary and sufficient condition for three, five, etc. being odd. It would then be out of line with the cases of fire and fever, but in line with that of soul. Hackforth's interpretation, however, seems inconsistent with his further account (162), in which 'Unit' is treated as a Form, importing Oddness. For it is hard to see how 'a unit', as Hackforth explains it, could be thought of as a Form. If a Form is meant, it must be the Form of One, thought of as bringing oneness to any particular 'one' that it occupies, and thereby making it odd. In that case the translation 'oneness' will be required, and the example would be in line with the cases of fire and fever, giving a sufficient, but not a necessary condition for oddness. Cf. O'Brien, *C.Q.* 1967,

224–5.

Would 'a unit' itself be odd? W. D. Ross (ed. Aristotle, *Physics*, 604) says that according to the normal view of Greek mathematicians, two was the first number. On this view, 'a unit' would not, strictly, be a number, but that of which numbers consist, or in terms of which 'number' is defined. See also T. L. Heath, *H.G.M.* i. 69–71, and M. E. Hager, *C.R.* 1962, 1–2. The 'unit' (*monas*) was sometimes called 'even-odd', being thought of as a parent of all numbers. This, if relevant here, would create some difficulty for the principle that a 'reason' must exclude the opposite of that for which it is a reason. But, a different, perhaps more popular, conception of 'one' (*to hen*) is found at *Hippias* I, 302a3–5, where it is explicitly said to be odd. It must be so regarded here on any interpretation of the argument. It remains unclear, however, whether what is made odd is regarded as a pure number or as a single-membered set. This turns on the meaning of 'number' at 105c4. See on 104d5– e6 (p.206).

(3) As noted above, the present series of answers give sufficient, but not necessary conditions. They do not, therefore, satisfy the principle, implicit in the earlier discussion, that no opposite, F, can count as the reason for something, if its opposite, G, can give rise to the same thing (see on 100e5–101b8, p.186). Thus, the answer 'fever' is open to the very objection that Socrates raised against 'addition' at 97a7–b3: illness could be due to the opposite of fever, hypothermia. Evidently, therefore, the present 'reasons' are not meant as *constitutive* of what they explain. They do not aim at answering the conceptual question 'what (logically) makes things F?'

What, then, is their purpose? There are two different ways of interpreting them, according as they are or are not construed as Forms.

(A) If they are not taken as Forms, they will specify reasons that 'make' whatever they are in to be F, in a causal and not merely a logical sense of 'make'. On this account, the new answer does not supersede the old 'safe' one in terms of Forms, but supplements it, by showing how a particular object or number comes to be occupied by the Form in question. Thus, fire makes bodies participate in Hotness. Similarly, fever, regarded as a cause rather than as a symptom of illness, makes them participate in Illness. This account fits the numerical example less well, since the notion of causal 'making' is strictly inapplicable here. But an unpaired unit may be thought of, analogously, as imparting a Form, Oddness, to a number or set that participates in that Form. Soul will be thought of, similarly, as imparting the Form Life to the body that it occupies (105c9–d12). It 'makes' the body to be alive, in no mere logical sense of 'makes', but in the sense that it gives it life, or quickens it. Alternatively, (B) The reasons here specified are *Forms* of Fire, Fever, and Oneness. Thus, with variations, Hackforth, 162, G. Vlastos, *P.R.* 1969, 317–20, D. O'Brien, *C.Q.* 1967, 223–8, E. L. Burge, *Phronesis* 1971, 11–12. Understood thus, the new answers specify, not 'causes' of a thing's being *F*, but logically sufficient conditions from which its *F*-ness may be inferred.

Once again, no conclusions can be drawn from Plato's terminology. There is no explicit reference to Forms in the passage, unless it be held that at 105c6 'oneness' must be meant, in conformity with 101c6. But no decisive inference can be based upon the locutions for numbers (see on 104d5–e6, p.205–6).

If the 'reasons' given here are taken as Forms, the 'bodies' in which they are said to be present cannot, unless Plato's examples are hopelessly disparate, simply be *N*-instances of the Form in question, e.g. a particular fire, thought of as occupied by the Form of Fire. For such an interpretation would not fit the fever example. Socrates could not refer to the presence of the Form Fever in a particular fever as its presence in a 'body' (c3), for a particular fever, unlike a particular fire, is not itself a body. If, therefore, Forms are meant here, the 'bodies' they occupy cannot be fires, but must be things on fire, e.g. sticks. Nor can they be fevers; they must, rather, be things feverish, e.g. human bodies. Similarly, in the case of soul: Socrates could not be referring at 105c9–11 to the Form of Soul's presence in a particular soul. For the soul is not a body. In view of this, the Form interpretation of these lines can be made to fit the case of Soul and Life at 105c9–d12 only with great difficulty. See next note.

(4) Some of the new answers of this passage, such as fire and fever, may seem no less 'mechanistic' than the ones earlier rejected (see C. C. W. Taylor, *Mind* 1969, 52–3). Indeed, by calling them 'subtler' (c2), Socrates links them with the answers that were unacceptable before (cf. 'subtleties' 101c8, and 'those other wise reasons' 100c10). Why, then, are such 'subtleties' now admitted as giving 'a different kind of safeness'? How could they be thought 'safe' from the dangers that had threatened such answers before?

As noted in (1) above, they do not enjoy the complete safeness of the old Form 'reasons', in that they are not necessary conditions for what they explain. But they *do* satisfy Socrates' other requirements for 'reasons'. In particular, and of paramount importance for the argument, they do not admit the opposite of the properties that they impart—e.g. fire cannot itself be cold. This what makes them 'safe' as well as 'subtle'. It is this principle that underlies the proof that soul is immortal: since it is the 'reason' for life, soul cannot itself admit death, and therefore cannot be dead (see also on 100e5–

101b8, p.186–7).

What can be said of this principle? It has some plausibility in such cases as fire and snow, which may be thought of as transmitting their own heat and cold to other bodies. Clearly, they could not do this, if those properties were 'neutralized' by the presence of their opposite. But the principle is less plausible in the other examples. Fever does not transmit illness from itself to the body in which it is present. It is *an* illness, but is not itself ill. Nor could the principle be held to apply to reasons more generally. (i) It would have no application to properties that are not members of a pair of opposites. (ii) Even where the properties to be explained are members of such a pair, it is untrue that a reason for one of them must exclude its opposite. A germ that is a 'reason' for illness in a body may itself be healthy. A saccharine pill that is a 'reason' for sweetness in coffee may itself be bitter. But fundamentally, (iii) in any given case it may be doubtful whether there *is* any 'reason' to be found that satisfies the principle under discussion. There seems nothing analogous, in this respect, to fire and snow that could be called a 'reason' for a thing's being large or small. In the case of life, 'soul' is, of course, taken to be a reason that meets the conditions stipulated. But this simply prejudges the question whether, in fact, life *admits of* explanation in terms of the kind of 'reason' that Socrates has displayed. Unless it does, his final proof of immortality cannot get off the ground. See next note.

105c9–d12. Soul is here specified as the reason for body's being alive (c9–11). Cebes does not balk at this. Presumably, it fits his own conception of soul as 'making' body. See on 87d3–e5.

Burnet's text, which gives 'soul' without the article throughout 105c11–e6, has been followed, although the MSS. vary on this point at 105d3, d10, e4, and e6. 'Soul' without the article may mean 'soul-stuff' rather than individual soul. See on 64e4–65a3 (p.89). Some commentators have wished to understand it, rather, as the *Form* of Soul, as at B6 in Version B given in the note on 104c7–d4 (p.204). The difficulties to which this leads may be illustrated from G. Vlastos's account of the context (*P.R.* 1969, 317–20).

Vlastos interprets the inference pattern established by the preceding examples as: '*x* is *F* because, being *A*, it must participate in the Form *A*; and since the Form *A* entails the Form *F*, *x* must also participate in the Form *F*, and hence *x* must be *F*.' (His variables have been adapted to the conventions followed in these notes, where *F* and *G* are used for the Forms of opposites, and *A* for the Form of a non-opposite). Vlastos does not discuss the application of this formula to the argument for immortality. But it is clear that an argument of the proposed pattern could not prove the immortality of the soul in the way required by the present text. For applying the formula, we should have either:

(1) 'A soul is alive because, being a soul, it must participate in the Form Soul, and since the Form Soul entails the Form Life, a soul must also participate in the Form Life, and hence a soul must be alive.'

or (2) 'A body is alive because, being besouled [or being a soul] it must participate in the Form Soul, and since the Form Soul entails the Form Life, the body must also participate in the Form Life, and so must be alive.'

But neither (1) nor (2) is satisfactory. (1) will not fit the text, for it ignores the soul's relationship to the body, which cannot be eliminated, even if the 'subtle' answers of 105b–d are taken as Forms (see previous note). And (2) clearly does not yield the conclusion for which Socrates wishes to argue. He needs a conclusion not about body but about soul. Moreover, he needs a conclusion not just about the Form of Soul, which is 'immortal' like any other Form, but about a particular soul. Yet if the reference at 105c9–d5 is to the Form of Soul, it is hard to see where or how the transition to particular soul, or soul-stuff, is supposed to occur. In Version B a transition has been effected at 105d10–11, by taking those lines to mean that an individual soul will never admit the opposite of what is imparted by the Form of Soul to the body (step B8). But this reading is factitious, and not warranted by anything in the text.

Note also that the words 'Then soul, whatever it occupies, always comes to that thing bringing life' (d3–4) seem intended as an inference from 105c11–d2. So if the earlier lines refer to the presence of particular soul, or soul-stuff, in the body, it is natural to take 105d3–4 in the same way.

It is therefore preferable to take the whole of the present passage as referring to a particular soul, or soul-stuff, whose presence in a body quickens it, as in Version A. Whether or not Platonic ontology recognizes a Form of Soul, parallel to the Form of Three at 104d5–6, and despite the parallelism of language with that passage, a more coherent argument emerges if such a Form is not read into the present text.

On either of the versions distinguished, the main principle of the argument is vulnerable. On Version A, the critical point is the claim that items 'bringing' an opposite F to whatever they enter will not admit G. Since this principle (A5 in the summary at 104c7–d4) depends upon the 'definition' at A4, the argument is flawed by defining the entities in question as those that 'bring' the Form F to whatever they enter. It may, of course, be simply stipulated that no x shall count as a 'reason' for y's being F unless x is itself un-G. But if this artificial restriction is to be imposed upon the concept of a 'reason', it has to be asked whether there might, for some values of F, simply be no 'reason' for things' being F that meets so stringent a condition. See previous note (p.213).

On Version B, the core of the argument will be (B6–B9) that since any body occupied by the Form Soul must be alive, no individual soul can ever admit death. The mainspring of this inference will be the principle (B3) that N-instances of a Form A will not admit the opposite of a property F imparted by that Form to its T-instances. But this too seems questionable. For N-instances may, perhaps, be qualified by the opposites of the properties their Forms impart. An individual hemlock plant, an N-instance of the Form Hemlock, may be living, even though T-instances occupied by the Form of Hemlock (i.e. bodies sufficiently dosed with hemlock) must be dead. This example may seem contrived. But the conception of the Form of Soul's occupancy of a body (B6) is itself both artificial and opaque.

105d13–e9. It is now argued that since soul will never admit the opposite of the Form that it brings, i.e. the Form of Life, it will not admit death, and must therefore be 'im-mortal'.

At 105d16–e1 the words rendered by their derivatives, 'musical' and 'un-musical', have the broader sense of 'cultured' and 'uncultured' (see on 60c8–61c1). 'Un-musical' and 'un-just' are used, like 'un-even' (d15), for verbal symmetry with 'im-mortal'. Similarly, at 106a3–10 'un-hot' and 'un-coolable' translate words coined by Plato to parallel 'im-mortal'. It is important to take these predicates as meaning not merely 'not being G' but 'never being G' or 'incapable of being G'. This is the point of inferring 'is un-G' from 'does not admit the Form G'.

Failure to take note of this has sometimes led to charges of equivocation upon the word for 'immortal'. Thus, D. Keyt has argued (*Phronesis* 1963, 170–1) that in the present passage it means merely 'not dead', or 'alive', whereas by 106e5–6 it has come to mean 'never dying'. But this disregards the force of 'doesn't admit death', from which 'im-mortal' is derived at 105e2–3. To say that a thing does not 'admit' G means that it will never, while remaining itself, participate in that Form. Cf.102e, 103d, 104b–c, 105a, and note the emphatic construction translated 'will absolutely never admit', at 105d10–11. It follows that the predicate 'im-mortal' means not merely 'is not dead' but 'will never be dead'. There is, therefore, no shift in the meaning of 'immortal'. It means consistently 'never dying' or 'incapable of dying'. See also on 64c2–9 (p.87), 72e7–73a3 and 95b5–e6.

Keyt interprets 'soul doesn't admit death' at 105e4 as 'nothing can at one time possess a soul and be dead', and then objects (op.cit. 171) that in order to get his desired conclusion Plato must sub-sequently shift the predicate 'immortal' from that which has soul to soul itself. But this reading of 'soul doesn't admit death', which stems from construing 'soul' at 105d3–5 as an 'immanent Form', is unnatural. If 'soul' is not taken as immanent Form, but as particular soul, or soul-stuff, then the predicate 'immortal' can readily attach to soul itself at 105e6, and no shift of subject need be supposed.

The charge of equivocation upon 'immortal' is related to another, often repeated criticism. The argument proves, it has been objected, only that soul is not dead 'whenever it exists' or 'while it is still soul' or 'so long as it is': it does not prove that soul is not at any time dead, and so not-dead or 'immortal' in the required sense. D. O'Brien (*C.Q.* 1967, 229–31) suggests that Plato may think he is entitled to omit the qualification 'whenever it exists', in virtue of his contention that soul is 'always', i.e. necessarily or essentially, alive. But it seems more likely that he was aware of the need for proof of the existence of a subject of the required type, and that this is precisely what gives rise to the attempted proof of soul's 'imperishability' at 106a–e. See next note (p.217). At *Euthydemus* 296a–d it is noticed that 'always' is logically treacherous, and that 'whenever' clauses may not safely be dropped after its occurrence.

The concept of immortality is not, however, without difficulty. For what is meant by the 'death' which soul will not admit? It cannot here mean 'separation from the body', for soul *will* admit 'death' in this sense (see on 64c2–9, p.87). Could it mean 'perishing'? This is also difficult, for two reasons. (i) Death has just been said to be the opposite of Life (d6–9), and must therefore be thought of here as a state rather than as an event, whereas 'perishing' is an event. (ii) If 'death' means 'perishing', what is to be made of the claim that soul is immortal *and* imperishable, and of the coming argument for the latter predicate? It is, in fact, hard to understand 'death', and 'immortal', in such a way that the final page of the proof is neither otiose nor question-begging. Related difficulties about the meaning of 'death' will arise at 106b1–4 and 106e5–7.

105e10–107a1. This section contains the final phase of the argument. Its purpose is to distinguish the case of soul from those of snow, fire, and three, to which it has so far been assimilated. In those cases, the possibility of 'perishing', in face of an attack by the excluded opposite, remained open. But in the case of soul, this possibility is to be ruled out; soul is not only immortal, it is also imperishable.

The point of contrasting soul with the other cases is to fill a gap in the proof of immortality expressed by Hackforth as follows (163): 'what has been shown is that the predicate "deathless" is contained in the meaning of the subject, soul; whenever, therefore, this subject exists, it has this predicate: but to show that the subject always does exist is quite another matter.' See the criticism of Strato of Lampsacus, given by Hackforth, 196 (g) and (m), and previous note. The present phase of the proof is meant to forestall such criticism. It tries to move beyond the tautology 'as long as a soul exists, it is not dead' to the claim that soul does, indeed, always exist. Like the Ontological Argument, it seeks to conjure an existential proposition out of a conceptual analysis. This is the reason for insisting upon 'imperishable' as an additional predicate (cf.88b6, 95c1, and see on 88a1–b8, 95b5–e6).

In outline the argument runs as follows:

I. If the immortal is imperishable, soul will be imperishable (c9–d1).

II. The immortal is imperishable (d2–9).

So

III. Soul is imperishable (e1–107a1).

There are uncertainties of interpretation at each of these stages.

I.(1) Does 'the immortal' mean (i) 'that which is immortal', or (ii) 'the property of being immortal'? For (i) see D. O'Brien, *C.Q.* 1967, 207. For (ii) see D. S. Scarrow, *P.R.* 1961, 245–52. With (i) the argument will be that since whatever is immortal is imperishable, the soul, being immortal, must be imperishable as well. With (ii) the argument will be that since the property of being immortal is imperishable, its bearer must be imperishable as well.

(ii) is a possible reading, if 'the immortal' is construed as parallel with 'the odd'. For 'the odd' is used at 106b5–6 in a manner parallel to 'the hotness in the fire' (b6–7). At 106b7–8 also it means 'oddness' rather than 'that which is odd', for at 106c5, which looks back to 106b7–8, the meaning must be 'oddness and three depart and go away'. But against this reading of 'the immortal': (a) It is far from clear that 'the im-mortal' is being used in a manner parallel to 'the odd'. Formally, it is parallel, rather, to 'the un-even', the 'un-hot' and 'the un-coolable'. These probably mean 'that which is un-*G*' rather than the property 'un-*G*ness'. (b) 'The immortal is also imperishable' at 106b2 and 106c10 (cf.e1) seems more likely to mean 'that which is immortal is also imperishable'. For on this view, the point of 'also' will be that the subject is imperishable *as well as* immortal, whereas on the alternative view 'also' has no clear function at all. (c) At 106e6 the phrase translated 'the immortal part' must mean 'that which is immortal', since it alludes directly to the soul. Scarrow's reading would therefore involve a shift at some point in the meaning of 'the immortal'. And (d) the allusion to God and the Form of Life (d5–9) would remain, on this view, as a rather lame pendant to the argument.

(2) The references to 'death' at 106b3 (cf.e5) raise several problems: (a) 'Death' can hardly be understood here either as (i) 'separation of soul from body' (64c2–9), or as (ii) 'perishing of soul' (91d6–7). Clearly, in the words 'it won't admit death nor will it be dead', 'death' cannot be understood in sense (i). For the soul *does* 'admit death' in that sense of 'death', when it is separated from the body (see III below). O'Brien (*C.Q.* 1968, 101, n.2) suggests that (ii), which he takes to be a redefinition of 'death', enables 'nor will it be dead' (b4) to mean 'nor will it cease to exist'. But this is not satisfactory either. For Socrates is here recalling the conclusion of 105e2–7, that soul is immortal. Since this conclusion is a premiss in his present argument for its imperishability, he could not use the words 'nor will it be dead' to *mean* 'nor will it cease to exist', without assuming exactly what he is trying to prove.

(b) Both here and at 106e5–7 it is difficult to interpret the notion of death's 'attack'. Note the difference between this and the impact of hot and cold upon snow and fire at 106a. It is not the opposites themselves, hot and cold, that are said to attack snow and fire, but something characterized by those opposites. But there is no embodiment of death in something that is 'applied' to the soul, or to the man, as something hot or cold is physically applied to snow or fire (106a4, a9).

(c) Did Plato postulate a Form of Death? Although such a Form seems required by the framework established for the argument, Socrates nowhere speaks of one in so many words. A Form of Death, unfortunately, generates an awkward paradox. If included in the Form-world as characterized earlier (79d2, 80b1, 81a5), it would have to be immortal or 'deathless'. But a deathless Form of Death would seem to infringe the basic principle of the present argument, that no Form will admit its own opposite.

(3) At 106b7–c1 Bluck translates: 'what is there to prevent it (sc. the odd) from *perishing* and *in that way* ceasing to be odd, and becoming even?' (his italics). But this would involve the paradox of saying that the odd, having perished, acquires the fresh property 'even'. This recalls the earlier problem of finding a subject for 'comes to be *G*' where *G* is a numerical predicate. See on 96e6–97b7 and notes 58 and 65. It is easier to take 'even' at 106c1 as the subject

of 'coming to be', or, as in the translation, to render the phrase impersonally. Cf. O'Brien, op.cit. 95, n.3.

II. It is natural to take 106d2–9 as a proof that 'the immortal is imperishable'. For the meaning of 'the immortal', see I (1) above. One way of taking the proof is as follows:

(1) If the immortal, being everlasting, admits perishing, then there could hardly be anything that does not admit it (d2–4). But

(2) There are things that are imperishable, viz. God and the Form of Life, and anything else immortal there may be (d5–7). So

(3) The immortal is imperishable.

On this view, the function of (2) is to deny the consequent in (1) by affirming the existence of some imperishable things. This would enable the antecedent in (1) to be denied by contraposition. And this denial would be equivalent to (3). But on this reading, the words 'anything else immortal there may be' in (2) would be question-begging. For it would be illegitimate to adduce 'anything else immortal there may be' as cases of immortal things that are imperishable, in order to *prove* that immortal things are, as such, imperishable.

But it is also possible that (1) and (2) should be taken separately, rather than as premises in a single argument. On this view, the real argument resides in (1). Cebes is there implying that the immortal must be regarded as imperishable, inasmuch as it is everlasting. He is assuming, without argument, that there are, indeed, imperishable things. Socrates then endorses his point by mentioning items that are, in fact, both immortal and imperishable, viz. God and the Form of Life.

But if (1) is read in this way, the phrase 'being everlasting' seems to beg the question. For whether the immortal is, indeed, 'everlasting' is precisely what is at issue. Moreover, the words 'anything else immortal there may be' are still difficult. For what could they refer to? Individual souls could hardly be meant, for Socrates would then be anticipating the conclusion drawn at 107a1. On the other hand, if Forms, other than the Form of Life, are meant, why is the Form of Life itself singled out for special mention? Are not all Forms equally imperishable?

For the argument to work at all, it must be supposed that there are at least some things that do not admit perishing. What basis is there for this supposition? It is sometimes suggested that Plato is here relying upon the unstated assumption that 'nothing can come from nothing or disappear into nothing'. See, e.g., Archer-Hind, 119, n.1. The possibility of everything's perishing and nothing's existing is, on this view, being implicitly ruled out. The postulate that there must always exist something is being taken as fundamental, like the earlier, undefended assumption that not everything could finish up dead (72c5–d3).

But such a postulate would seem inadequate for the purposes of the argument. For the supposition (S1) that there must always exist something should be distinguished from the supposition (S2) that there must be something that always exists. The postulate just mentioned asserts only S1. Yet it is S2 that is required. Even if S1 were granted, would it afford any support for S2? And would S2 be effectively supported by invoking God and the Form of Life?

Some commentators have supposed that Plato here falls back upon an appeal to religious faith. Thus Hackforth writes (164): 'it is only if we allow that the appeal is to faith that we can avoid a feeling of deep disappointment in this matter, inasmuch as from the standpoint of logic the argument has petered out into futility.' But the bathos of an appeal to religious faith at the climax of a philosophically sophisticated argument would only deepen the disappointment. A lame appeal to 'divine doctrine' is the last thing we should expect in the light of 85d2–4. Moreover, when Cebes says (d8–9) that the imperishability of God and the Form of Life would be admitted 'by all men', he cannot be serious. God's imperishability would not be admitted 'by all men'. A sceptic would object that it is at least as much in need of proof as the immortality of the soul. The 'religious faith' interpretation simply undercuts the central enterprise of the dialogue.

It is, however, possible to understand the allusion to God and the Form of Life differently. For these two entities are precisely the ones required, in terms of the kinds of 'reason' that Socrates has displayed, as 'reasons' for the existence of the universe as a whole. In the case of living things, 'life' and 'existence' are plausibly identified (see on 95e7–96a5, p.171); and the universe as a whole is viewed by Plato as a living thing (see on 72a11–d5, p.113). The 'safe' reason for a thing's being alive is that it participates in the Form of Life. And the corresponding 'subtle' reason is that something else has brought Life to it. At the level of individual organisms, this will be soul. And at the cosmic level, it will be God.

A possible role for God and the Form of Life, within the framework of the foregoing argument, thus suggests itself. They supply, respectively, the subtle and safe reasons needed to explain the existence of a living universe. In this role, God constitutes the cosmic 'reason' for which Socrates has searched (99c6–8). Such a 'reason' answers, in metaphysical terms, his initial question (96b2–3) about the source of life. It fits the allusions to God's designing intelligence in his criticism of Anaxagoras (see on 97b8–98b6), and anticipates the theistic account of the universe in the *Timaeus*.

If this is correct, the allusion to God is no mere *deus ex machina*, but an application to the universe as a whole of the pattern of explanation implicit in Socrates' earlier examples. It may even be said to point to a quasi-causal argument for the existence of an eternal being. The pivotal principle of such an argument would be, once again, that a true 'reason' cannot admit the opposite of that for which it is the reason (see on 100e5–101b8, p.186, and 105b5–c8, p.212). If the living universe demands an explanation of that sort, then there must be something that cannot admit the opposites of life and existence, and can therefore neither die nor perish. Such a reason is God, the true 'reason', perhaps, that Socrates has said he will 'display' (100b8). In this way his 'second voyage' turns out, after all, to lead to the kind of 'reason' he had hoped to discover. And the scholastic arguments for a necessary and eternal being can be seen as 'footnotes' to Plato's text.

III. At 106e5–107a1 the argument is clinched: 'when death attacks a man, his mortal part, it seems, dies; whereas the immortal part gets out of the way of death, departs and goes away intact and undestroyed.' Here, as at 106b1–4, there is difficulty in interpreting 'death'. It cannot be equated either with (i) 'separation of soul from body' (64c2–9) or with (ii) 'perishing of soul' (91d6–7). Substitution of (ii) for 'death' leads to confusion. 'Perishing of soul' could not explain the word 'dies', which is applied at 106e6 to 'his mortal part', i.e. the body; nor could soul intelligibly be said to get out of the way of 'perishing of soul', i.e. its own perishing.

O'Brien (op.cit. 102) says that death is here thought of in sense (i): 'This death is obviously death in the old sense, the death that forces the separation of the soul from the body'. But the old sense of 'death' seems inapplicable here. For in that sense the soul could just as well be said to 'die' as could the body. There would be no case for suggesting that the body 'dies' in that sense, but the soul does not. Nor, in the old sense of 'death', could the soul readily be said to 'get out of its way' (e7).

The difficulty here stems partly from the fact that the original definition of death (64c) had left it unclear what the proper subject of 'die' and 'be dead' is supposed to be (see on 64c2–9, p.86). Is it the whole man, the composite of body and soul, that is to be called 'dead', when its elements are separated from each other? Or may these elements themselves be said to 'die'? Death is almost invariably attributed either to the man (e.g. 70a3–4, b3, 80c2), or to a personal subject (as at 59a7, 87a4, 115d9), or to animate things (72c5–d3). 'Die' is occasionally used of the soul alone (77d3–4, 84b2, 88a6, 88d8). Only here is it used of the body, and Socrates avoids saying that the body 'dies' by referring to it as 'the mortal part'.

At 106e9–107a1 Socrates moves from the claim that 'soul' is immortal and imperishable to the claim that 'our souls' are in Hades. Once again the conclusion is drawn in terms of individual souls (see on 70c8–d6). Whether the shift from 'soul' to 'our souls' is justified will depend upon how the former is interpreted (see on 105c9–d12). At some point in the argument it must be supposed that Socrates is talking of soul as a particular, not merely a Form. But if 'soul' means merely 'soul-stuff', the transition to 'our souls' might be questioned (see on 64e4–65a3, p.90).

107a2–b10. What are 'the initial hypotheses' (b5), that Socrates tells his listeners they must explore further? It can hardly be doubted that they consist in, or at least include, the Theory of Forms. 'Hypotheses' (plural) could refer to the Theory alone, the positing of each Form being thought of as a separate hypothesis. In referring to them here, Socrates is recognizing that the whole case for immortality has rested upon postulates that are in need of further support. See on 65d4–e5 (p.97) and 101c9–102a9 (p.191).

The words 'you will, I believe, follow the argument to the furthest point to which man can follow it up' (b7–8) mean that the listeners will follow 'as far as is humanly possible'. They do not imply any reservations on Socrates' part as to the soundness of the argument, but simply echo Simmias' sentiments about 'human weakness' (b1). These are in keeping with his remarks at 85c–d about the limits of human reason. Cf. also 66e–67a.

4. MYTH
(107c1–115a8)

The myth that now follows gives a speculative picture of the afterlife and judgement of departed souls. It includes a scientific theory as to the nature of the earth. And, by contrasting our earth with 'the true earth' above, it symbolizes the distinction between the sensible world and the world of Forms.

107c1–d2. Socrates here stresses the special need for 'care of the soul' in view of its immortality. K. Dorter (*Dialogue* 1970, 574) takes the passage to mean that Socrates, by giving his listeners faith in immortality, deters them from 'nihilistic immorality'. But

Socrates does not say at 107c6–8 that if there were no afterlife, everything in this life would be permitted. He says that if death were the end, it would be a godsend for the wicked, since it would rid them of their wickedness. Far from suggesting that reward, or avoidance of punishment, in the next life is the reason for being good in this one, he implies that wickedness is burdensome in itself, whatever may happen after death. This is consistent with Plato's defence of justice in *Republic* ii–ix, which is independent of eternal rewards and punishments. See on 69a6–c3 (p.103), 81d6–82d8.

At 107c3 the phrase 'what we call "life"' implies that ordinary usage wrongly restricts 'life' to the period of incarnation, whereas the soul 'lives', properly speaking, for ever. Plato often suggests that words are systematically misapplied and ordinary ways of speaking can mislead us. See 115e4–6. For other examples, cf.60b4, 64d3, 68c5–9, 71b7–8, 73b5, 75e5, 76a6–7, 82b1, 86d3, 95d4, 96a7–8, 99b2–6, 112c2. See also *Symposium* 205b–d, *Republic* 493a–c.

108c5–109a8. The geophysical theories that follow include an account of the shape, position, surface, and inner structure of the earth, and a description of its seas, rivers, and volcanoes. Some of these subjects had been touched on by Socrates earlier (97d–98a, 99b–c). Here he shows more knowledge of them than his professed ineptitude for natural science might have suggested.

The identity of 'Glaucus' (108d4) is uncertain. But 'the skill of Glaucus' seems to have been proverbial for 'a great scientist' (Hackforth).

At 108e5 the translation 'round', rather than 'spherical', avoids prejudging the question whether the earth is, in fact, thought of as spherical. For the traditional interpretation see Bluck, 135, 200–1. For the alternatives see J. S. Morrison, *Phronesis* 1959, 101–19 (hemi-spherical), and T. G. Rosenmeyer, *C.Q.* 1956, 193–7, *Phronesis* 1959, 71–2 (disk-shaped), opposed by W. M. Calder, *Phronesis* 1958, 121–5.

113d1–114c8. Punishments in the afterlife are represented as purgatorial (d7–8), not vindictive (cf. E. R. Dodds, ed. *Gorgias* 525b1–526d2). Only incurable malefactors are consigned to Tartarus for ever (e1–6). Their punishment is a deterrent to other souls (cf. *Republic* 615c–616a), a belief which, as Dodds points out, makes sense only if the doctrine of rebirth is presupposed.

At 114a8–b5 souls are depicted as begging forgiveness for earthly misdeeds, which they must, presumably, remember having committed. Personal survival is, indeed, often held to entail the persistence of at least some memories from the life before death. But there has been nothing in the foregoing arguments for immortality to suggest that the discarnate soul remembers anything from its former life, or that it is capable of such states as penitence (a1). See on 64e4—65a3 (p.90).

The idea that fully purified souls will live 'bodiless' (c3—4) for the rest of time has appeared before (81a9), and implies that these souls will be altogether immune from rebirth. Strictly, this is incompatible with the conception of the soul's endless alternation between incarnate and discarnate states, which was posited at 77d4. For 'bodiless' existence cf.76c12 and see on 76c11—13.

114d1—115a3. The status of the myth is indicated at 114d1—6: exact knowledge of the afterlife is disclaimed, but belief in 'either this or something like it' is said to be 'a noble risk'. Such myths are, as E. R. Dodds has said (ed. *Gorgias* 523a2), 'a prolongation into the unknown of the lines established by philosophical argument'. They go far beyond anything the argument has suggested regarding the experience of the discarnate soul, and do not lend themselves to logical analysis.

'One should repeat such things to oneself like a spell' (d6—7). This recalls Socrates' earlier injunction to 'sing spells' to charm away the fear of death (77e8—9). But the myth just concluded would be more likely, one would think, to have the opposite effect on anyone who repeated it to himself, unless his conscience was unusually clear. Cf. *Republic* 330d4—331a1.

114d8—115a1 should not be taken to imply that reward after death is the sole reason for practising the virtues mentioned here. See on 69a6—c3 (p.103), 81d6—82d8, 107c1—d2.

5. SOCRATES' DEATH
(115b1—118a17)

Socrates gives final directions to his friends, and drinks the poison. His death follows.

115b1—116a1. This passage contains some striking expressions of the idea that the soul is the 'true self'. See on 64e4—65a3 (p.88).

117e3—118a4. For the action of the poison see Burnet, 149—50, and C. Gill, *C.Q.* 1973, 25—8. Gill argues that Plato's description of the symptoms is highly selective, and that the whole account is designed to represent the conception of soul that has been advocated in the discussion.

118a7–8. The offering of a cock to Asclepius is sometimes supposed to be for healing Socrates of the sickness of human life. He might refer to himself in the plural—cf.116d4. But the idea that life is a sickness, although once attributed to Cebes as part of an objection (95d1–4), is nowhere espoused by Socrates, and is hardly compatible with 90e2–91a1. It is simpler to take the words as referring to an actual debt, incurred in some connection unknown. They are in keeping with the tribute to Socrates in the closing lines.

NOTES ON THE TEXT
AND TRANSLATION

1. The translation 'prison' at 62b4 fits the theme of the soul's imprisonment in the body, which runs all through the dialogue (cf., e.g., 67d1–2, 82e–83a), and which is symbolized in its dramatic setting. If the meaning is 'guard' or 'garrison', the incarnate soul will be thought of as engaged in a military 'watch'. For a thorough discussion see Loriaux's note, and J. C. G. Strachan, *C.Q.* 1970, 216–20.

2. At 62c1, and occasionally elsewhere, οὐκοῦν has been translated as if accented οὔκουν. Cf., e.g., 71e4, 81a4, 83d1, and see J. D. Denniston, *G.P.* 432.

3. Or, taking μᾶλλον with θερμαίνεσθαι (63d7–8), 'people get overheated through talking'.

4. At 64a6, and generally, τεθνάναι has been translated 'be dead', despite Burnet's view, endorsed by Loriaux (50), that it may properly be translated 'die'. Burnet says (note on 62a5) that ἀποθνῄσκειν lays stress on the process of dying, of which τεθνάναι is the completion. However, ἀποθνῄσκειν will later be used (71c–e) to stress the process of dying, by contrast, rather, with the *state* of being dead. 'Die' is, no doubt, required in some of the passages cited by Burnet. In the *Phaedo*, however, it seems needed only at 62c3 and 81a1. 'Be dead' is preferable at 62a5, 64c5 (in view of εἶναι at 64c8), 67e2 and 67e5, as well as in the present passage. It is clearly required for the opposition between τὸ τεθνάναι and τὸ ζῆν at 71c1–5 and in the ensuing argument. Cf.77d3, and see on 71d5–e3.

5. The translation italicizes 'just' at 65d4 (and 'beautiful' and 'good' at 65d7) instead of translating αὐτό, whose function is to mark a Form-referring use of the adjective. It is not clear whether δίκαιον αὐτό should be taken as complement of εἶναι, as in the translation, or as subject: 'do we say that *just* is something, or (that it is) nothing?' (cf.64c2, 102b1). See also on 74a9–b1 and 100b1–c8.

6. Loriaux (85, 204) interprets 65d11–12 as if it meant 'Did you lay hold of them by some perception other than those that come by way of the body?' Read thus, the question would be properly answered 'Yes', and apprehension of the Forms would be viewed as a kind of intellectual 'perception'. However, if, as Loriaux also says

(note on τὴν ὄψιν, p.87), ἄλλῃ τινὶ αἰσθήσει is echoed by ἄλλην αἴσθησιν at 65e8–66a1, this interpretation is impossible. Moreover, ἆρα . . . θεωρεῖται (65e1–2) seems to be a reformulation of the question being asked here, which must be parallel to that already asked at 65d9 for the eyes, and expecting the answer 'No'. For the meaning of αἰσθήσει on this view, see on 65b1–7.

7. More literally (65d13–e1): 'that which each one happens to be', taking ὅ as complement of ὄν, and the whole clause as object of λέγω. Note that the meaning of 'be', since the use is 'incomplete', cannot be existential here. This supports the interpretation of similar phrases adopted at 78d4–5. See note 31. οὐσία is used here with reference to the 'being' of individual Forms–cf.101c3. Elsewhere (76d9, 77a2, 78d1, 92d9) it is used more broadly for the whole domain of Forms. See C. H. Kahn, *V.B.A.G.* 460.

8. What does αὐτῶν τὸ ἀληθέστατον at 65e1–2 mean? Hackforth translates 'the full truth of them', and Bluck 'the truth about them'. It is not easy to get these meanings from the Greek. But to take αὐτῶν as a partitive genitive would give an unsuitable sense, since (i) there can be no intention to limit the question being asked to 'the most real of the Forms', and (ii) there is no suggestion in the *Phaedo* that any one Form is more real than the others.

9. The translation retains τήν at 65e7 and τινά at 65e8. Burnet's proposal to read τιν' at 65e7, and delete τινά at 65e8, seems neither necessary nor even likely, if ὄψιν and ἄλλην αἴσθησιν echo τοῖς ὀφθαλμοῖς (65d9) and ἄλλῃ τινὶ αἰσθήσει (65d11) respectively. The meaning of ὄψιν will depend upon the reading: τὴν ὄψιν would be more naturally taken as 'the sense of sight', whereas τιν' ὄψιν could only mean 'any visual experience'. ἄλλην αἴσθησιν could mean, whether or not τινά is retained, 'another sense experience' or 'another sense': either of these might be said to be 'dragged in'.

10. The translation retains μετὰ . . . σκέψει at 66b3–4, and takes ἐκφέρειν with J. E. Harry (*C.R.* 1909, 218–21) to mean 'lead astray', understanding the path in question to be the body. Philosophers will then be said to recognize that it *side-tracks* them in their quest for truth, and will thus be answering the question posed at 65a9–b1 in the light of the intervening argument.

11. The translation at 67c5–6 follows J. V. Luce (*C.R.* 1951, 66–7), Hackforth, and Verdenius, in taking the reference to be simply to the earlier discussion, and not to any ancient religious doctrine. For the alternative view, see Burnet, Bluck, and Loriaux.

12. The text at 68a4 is not quite certain, and there is much to be said for bracketing καὶ γυναικῶν καὶ ὑέων with Verdenius. The language suggests an antithesis between παιδικά and φρόνησις, to which wives and sons would be irrelevant. Cf. *Gorgias* 482a4.

13. For the text of 69a6–c3 see Bluck, 154–6, J. V. Luce, *C.Q.* 1944, 60–4, and notes by Verdenius and Loriaux. The translation retains καὶ τούτου μὲν πάντα and ὠνούμενά τε καὶ πιπρασκόμενα, and καί in 69b6. With Burnet's text the reference to 'buying and selling all things for this' will be omitted. Burnet gives the meaning of 69b1–3 as 'when accompanied by this [i.e. wisdom] our goodness really is goodness', μετὰ φρονήσεως (b3) picking up μετὰ τούτου (b1).

14. Burnet and Loriaux hold that at 70b4 and 76c12 φρόνησις is used in a popular sense, meaning 'intelligence' or 'wits'. But the word has been translated 'wisdom', here as elsewhere (see on 69a6–c3), for the sake of the coming argument. For if the φρόνησις possessed by the soul in its previous existence were different from that which philosophers hope to attain in the afterlife (66e–67a, 68a–b), the Cyclical and Recollection Arguments would support that hope by mere equivocation.

15. Literally (70b6), 'tell a tale'. Cf.61e2. Socrates has earlier remarked that he is no tale-teller himself (61b). The ensuing proofs of immortality are not, of course, 'tales' like that of the afterlife in 107c–114c. But the argument from opposites that now follows contains a striking fusion of myth with logic, and the verb διαμυθολογεῖν may possibly be used with this in mind (though it need mean no more than 'converse', as at *Apology* 39e5).

16. μεμνήμεθα (70c6) has been taken to mean 'we've recalled'. With this meaning, Socrates will be glancing back to his earlier references (63c5, 69c7) to religious teachings about the afterlife. The meaning may, however, simply be 'we recall' ('comes into my mind', Hackforth). ἀφικόμεναι has been taken in apposition to the subject of εἰσίν, and εἰσίν as 'they do exist', rather than 'they are there'. See Loriaux.

17. Placing a semicolon at 70d2 after οὖσαι and taking καί, as often, with concluding force (Verdenius).

18. It seems preferable to place a full stop after ἕτερον at 71b2 and to read γάρ with T. Thus Robin.

19. The translation at 73a7 takes ἑνί in its ordinary sense of 'one', and follows Verdenius in taking ἔπειτα to mean 'for example'. 73b1–2 will then be an application of the questioning procedure

Socrates has mentioned in 73a7–9 and not a new way of proving his point, as the translation 'secondly' (Burnet, Hackforth) would require.

20. Reading λέγω δέ τινα τρόπον τόνδε, with Verdenius, at 73c5–6.

21. Taking αὐτό both as object of ἐπιστάμεθα and with ἐστιν at 74b2. L.S.J. s.v. ὅς give several examples of ὅς, though not of ὅ, introducing an indirect question. See note 26.

22. The translation follows Burnet's text at 74b8–9, reading τῷ μέν ... τῷ δ', and preserves the ambiguity of the contrast. If the articles are masculine, they must be taken with φαίνεται, in sense (a) discussed in the Notes—see on 74b7–c6 (p.122). If they are neuter, they will be governed by ἴσα, and will bear sense (b). For sense (c) one would expect, rather, τῇ μέν ... τῇ δ'. R. P. Haynes (*Phronesis* 1964, 20–1) suggests that τῳ could give this sense if taken as dative of the indefinite pronoun. But there seems no parallel for τῳ μέν ... τῳ δέ being used in this way. Reading τότε μέν ... τότε δ' with TW, the meaning will be as in sense (d).

23. It seems necessary to read ὡς ἐάν for the MSS. ἕως ἄν at 74c13 to obtain the sense 'so long as', 'provided that'. See Hackforth, 193.

24. The translation 'what it is itself' follows Burnet's text at 74d6 and takes the use of ἐστιν as incomplete. But the meaning may be '*that which is*, itself'. See also notes 25 and 28, and on 75c7–d6 (p.130). The text is very uncertain. But on any reading or interpretation it seems that ἐστιν ἴσον has to be understood as completing the ὥσπερ clause.

25. For the translation 'what equal is' at 75b1–2 see on 75c7–d6 (p.131). Taking ἴσον as subject brings the grammar close to that suggested for 74b2—see note 21. The interpretation 'the equal which is' seems ruled out by the fact that τοῦ is in a different case from ἴσον. But the meaning might be 'that which is equal.'

26. ὅτι ἐστιν, which Hackforth leaves untranslated at 75b6, must refer to the nature, not the existence, of the equal. Hence ἐστιν should be taken as incomplete, and ὅτι as an interrogative 'what'. Cf.74b2, and note 21.

27. The translation follows Burnet and Hackforth in taking ἐκεῖσε ἀνοίσειν at 75b7 as equivalent to ἐκεῖσε ἀνεφέροντες ἐννοήσειν. But this is very awkward, and there is much to be said for supplying καὶ ἐννοήσειν after ἀνοίσειν, or deleting ὅτι ... φαυλότερα, with

Archer-Hind, as a gloss.

28.   Reading τοῦτο, ὅ ἐστι at 75d2 with BTW, and taking ἐστι as incomplete. There seems no justification for Burnet's departure from the united MSS.' reading, since ὅ ἐστι may occur without αὐτό—cf. 92d9. But the original reading may have been τοῦτο, τὸ ὅ ἐστι, the article marking the use of ὅ ἐστι as a name, as at 92d9, but omitted by haplography. For the translation 'what it is' see on 75c7—d6 (p.130), and notes 24—6.

29.   The single word ἐπιστήμας (75d4) has to be translated 'pieces of knowledge', since 'knowledge' has no plural. Cf.75e4 and 76c15.

30.   Or perhaps, taking φύσει with προσήκει (78c1—2), 'then is it true that what has been put together and is composite is naturally liable to undergo this'. With the translation adopted, some contrast may, as Burnet suggests, be intended between artificial and natural compounds. But nothing in the argument turns on the distinction.

31.   Literally 'each thing, what it is itself' (78d3—4), 'each of them, what it is' (d5), taking ἐστι as incomplete. See on 75c7—d6 (p.131) and notes 24—6. Cf. also 65d13—e1 and note 7.

32.   τὸ ὄν (78d4) has been taken as referring back to αὐτὴ ἡ οὐσία (78d1) with Verdenius and Loriaux, and not closely with αὐτὸ ἕκαστον ὅ ἐστιν - 'the being itself whatever it may be' (Hackforth).

33.   It seems necessary to bracket καλῶν either in 78d10 or in 78e1. The translation follows Burnet, bracketing ἢ καλῶν in 78e1. If καλῶν is bracketed in 78d10, the meaning will be: 'But what about the many things, such as men or horses or cloaks or anything else at all of that kind? Equal things or beautiful things or all things that bear the same name as those objects?'

34.   τῶν ὄντων is used at 79a6 broadly to include the seen as well as the unseen world. See on 65c2—4.

35.   The translation follows Verdenius' and Loriaux's account of 80c5—7. χαριέντως has been translated 'in beautiful condition', rather than 'in favourable condition (sc. to preservation)' (Hackforth). The ἐάν clause need not be taken to specify favourable conditions. It is better translated 'even if', and understood to specify relatively unfavourable ones, the thought being that 'a healthy body decomposes more rapidly than an old and withered one' (Burnet). If so, καὶ πάνυ μάλα will not contrast sharply with ἐπιεικῶς συχνὸν χρόνον, but will represent a rather weak case, in contrast with the stronger ones which follow. ἐν τοιαύτῃ ὥρᾳ has been translated 'in the flower of youth', rather than 'at a fine season of the year'

(Burnet, Bluck). Burnet says that if ὥρᾳ meant 'flower of youth', τοιαύτη would be otiose, and that when mentioned in connection with death it means 'a ripe old age'. However, as Verdenius says, these objections neutralize each other, since τοιαύτη may be added to avoid a misunderstanding of ὥρᾳ.

36.   Reading σῶμα at 82d3, as Verdenius suggests. Cf. *Timaeus* 88c3.

37.   Hackforth (92, n.1) translates (82e5–83a1): 'the way in which the prisoner would be most likely to cooperate in his own incarceration is through his desire', taking the ὡς clause as subject of ἐστίν. This is very awkward and takes μάλιστα out of order. Verdenius would take εἰργμοῦ to mean 'imprisonment'. However, it cannot mean that at 82e3, and if it is taken in that way at 82e5 there will be an awkward shift of sense.

38.   Bracketing καὶ φόβων (83b7) with Burnet, but retaining ἢ λυπηθῇ (83b8–9) with Verdenius and Loriaux.

39.   Omitting φασιν (83e6) with the Arsinoë papyrus for the reasons given by Hackforth. With φασιν the meaning will be: 'it is not for the reasons given by most people'.

40.   The translation at 84a5–6 follows Burnet's text and Loriaux's explanation. ἐναντίως is taken to mean 'in reverse' (to Penelope) rather than 'undoing her web' (Hackforth, Bluck). Penelope unpicked at night what she had woven during the day. The soul is thought of as reweaving at night, through sensual indulgence, the 'web' (τινὰ ... ἱστόν) that philosophy has unravelled during the day.

41.   Hackforth translates 84c4 'were having a few words'. See, however, *Lysis* 211a and other passages cited by W. L. Lorimer, *C.R.* 1960, 7–8, supporting 'were talking in a low voice' (Burnet, Bluck).

42.   Understanding the subject of λεχθῆναι (84d1) as τὰ λεχθέντα from 84c5. This seems preferable to 'if you think it would be better that it should be stated' (Bluck).

43.   The translation follows Burnet's text at 88a2, which involves taking 'you' here to refer to Cebes himself. He is voicing the argument of an imaginary objector, who is prepared to grant 'the speaker', i.e. the proponent of immortality, 'even more than what you say': even more, that is, than Cebes has himself conceded (87a1–4)—that the soul's prenatal existence has been adequately proved. It is, however, difficult to take σύ to refer to Cebes himself, when the objection has been presented in *oratio obliqua*;

and it is awkward to understand τῷ λέγοντι as meaning, without further explanation, the proponent of immortality. Some editors therefore bracket ἤ at 88a2: 'If one were to grant even more to someone who says what you (sc. Socrates) say'. On either reading, however, Cebes will be making the same concession to the same viewpoint. See Bluck, 157–9 for further difficulties. The passage may, as Hackforth suggests, be incapable of strict grammatical analysis.

44.   Or perhaps (89b3–4) 'it was his way sometimes to play with my hair' (Bluck). If παίζειν means 'make fun of', Socrates may, as Robin suggests, be making fun of Phaedo for wearing his hair long, though he was past the age at which it was customary at Athens to do so.

45.   λευκὸν ἤ μέλανα (90a7) is usually translated 'white or black'. The words can, however, mean 'pale' and 'dark' (cf., e.g., Republic 474e1–2), and this seems better suited to the notion of a range.

46.   τῶν ὄντων (90d6) has been taken as if governed by the whole phrase τῆς ἀληθείας τε καὶ ἐπιστήμης. If it is governed only by τῆς ἀληθείας (cf.99e6), the meaning will be 'deprived of the truth of the things that are and of knowledge'. For τῶν ὄντων see on 65c2–4.

47.   Reading ἄνοια at 91b5 with Burnet, and translating 'ignorance' rather than 'folly' (Bluck). Socrates' ignorance will consist in his mistaken belief in the afterlife. With the reading διάνοια the meaning will be 'this opinion of mine will not persist'.

48.   εἰκότος (92d1) has been translated 'likelihood' rather than 'analogy' (Burnet). Burnet cites Theaetetus 162e5 and Euthydemus 305e1, but as Hackforth says, those passages tell strongly in favour of 'likelihood'.

49.   L. Lorimer's proposal (C.R. 1938, 165–6) to read (92d2) δοκεῖ <ἃ δοκεῖ> ἀνθρώποις would give the sense 'whence most people derive the opinions they hold'. However, what is at issue is not most people's opinions in general, but only their belief in the attunement hypothesis. For a convincing defence of Burnet's text, see J. Tate, C.R. 1939, 2–3.

50.   Placing a colon at the end of 92d9, and keeping the MSS. αὐτῆς with Burnet. 'Being' belongs to the soul, is 'of it' (αὐτῆς), in the sense that it is the object of the soul's apprehension. Cf.76e1, 'finding again what was formerly ours', and 75e5, 'knowledge belonging to us'. If, however, Mudge's αὐτή is adopted, the

meaning will be: 'just as surely as the Being itself exists'. The soul's pre-existence will then be related only to the existence of the Forms, and not to its apprehension of them. Cf.76e2–4. For οὐσία see note 7. ὅ ἐστιν has been translated 'what it is' in conformity with its interpretation elsewhere. See on 75c7–d6 (p.130), and notes 21, 24–6, 28, and 31.

51. The difference, if any, at 93a14–b2 between μᾶλλον and ἐπὶ πλέον, and between ἧττον and ἐπ' ἔλαττον is uncertain. Hackforth thinks there is no difference. Olympiodorus took the first member of each pair to refer to pitch and the second to intervals (see Burnet's note on 93a14). Verdenius plausibly takes ἐπὶ πλέον to mean 'extending over a greater part', i.e. covering a greater number of strings.

52. Verdenius says that the εἴπερ clause (93b1) should be taken with ἐπὶ πλέον only, and expresses the fact that ἐπὶ πλέον (in the sense explained in note 51) is a rather theoretical case, since in practice all strings will have been tuned. But it is hard to understand how an attunement, as opposed to an instrument, could be tuned ἐπὶ πλέον in this sense.

53. The translation follows Burnet's text at 93d4, but not his version of 93d2–3, 'this is just our admission'. The clause μηδὲν . . . εἶναι (d3–4) has been taken as dependent upon τὸ ὁμολόγημα: 'this is the admission that . . .' Hackforth (115–16, n.4) and others, finding contradiction between these lines and 93a14–b6, have bracketed ἁρμονίας in 93d4, taking ἁρμονίαν in the same line as complement, and ἑτέραν . . . ἑτέρας to refer to one *soul* as compared with another: 'one soul cannot be more or to a greater extent, or again less or to a smaller extent, an attunement than another'. With this reading, τὴν δέ (93d6) and ἡ δέ (93d9) will refer to *the soul* and not to attunement, as they do in the translation adopted. However, there is no MS. support for the change, and it destroys what looks like a deliberate parallelism of language at 93d2 and 94d4. It also entails taking 93d6–7 in such a way as to anticipate the reasoning of 93d12–e2.

54. Or perhaps (94b4–5) 'Is it a man's soul that controls every part of him?' (Hackforth).

55. φθορά (95e9, 96b9) has been translated 'destruction', and ὄλεθρος (e.g., 95d2) 'perishing'. The cognate verbs have been translated correspondingly throughout. There seems no significant difference between them, both being used as general terms for 'ceasing to exist'. At 106e ἀδιάφθορος will be used as a variant for ἀνώλεθρος.

56.   The ancient sense of φύσεως ἱστορία (96a8) is preserved, as Burnet says, in 'natural history', but this term is too narrow for the range of inquiries Socrates mentions.

57.   Or perhaps (96d5) 'and so the little child had become a big man' (Hackforth). But τὸν σμικρὸν ἄνθρωπον is naturally taken as one phrase.

58.   At 96e9 and throughout 97a–b δύο has been translated as complement of γίγνεσθαι. Up to 97a1 this is clearly correct. From 97a4 onwards, however, it is uncertain whether Socrates is talking about 'the coming into being of two' (Hackforth) or about 'one' (or each of a pair of 'ones') 'becoming two' (Tredennick). See on 70c4–8 (p.104) for the relation between a thing's coming to be *F*, and *F*'s coming to be. If δύο is a complement at 97b1, what should be understood as subject of γίγνεσθαι? *What* exactly has 'come to be two'? For this puzzle see on 96e6–97b7. The translation at 97b4, 'why it is that one comes to be', follows Burnet, Hackforth, and Bluck in taking ἕν as subject. It could be taken as complement by supplying 'things' as its subject—'how it is that things become one' (Tredennick), or by understanding γίγνεται impersonally—'how there comes to be one'. See also 101b9–c5 and note 65.

59.   More literally (97d1), 'in any other way'. But the implication that a thing's existence is also to be thought of as a way of 'acting or being acted upon' seems unnatural.

60.   Literally (98e5), 'by the dog'. For this favourite Socratic oath see E. R. Dodds, ed. *Gorgias* 482b5.

61.   More literally (99b4–5): 'most people, groping, as it were, in the dark' (Bluck). The translation follows an explanation of these lines, cited by Verdenius, as an allusion to blind man's buff. The blindfold player, after catching one of the others, has to 'paw him over' (ψηλαφᾶν) and try to guess his name correctly. It is with him that most people are being compared in their mistaken assignment of the term αἰτία.

62.   The translation 'kneading-trough' follows the reading καρδόπῳ in Burnet's text at 99b8. In his note he prefers καρδοπίῳ, 'the lid of a kneading-trough'. This would fit Aristotle's account of the theory (*De Caelo* 294b15). However, the kneading-trough itself, as a round, flat object, would illustrate the theory well enough.

63.   προσγενομένη may be retained at 100d6, if it is supposed that it has been assimilated to the preceding substantives (Bluck). The alternatives are to accept Wyttenbach's προσαγορευομένη (defended

by Burnet), to read προσγενομένου (Hackforth), or to omit the word altogether (Archer-Hind). With Wyttenbach's conjecture, the question left open will be what the relation between Forms and particulars should be *called.* With any other reading the sense will be as given in the translation.

64. ἐναντίος λόγος (101a6) has been translated 'contradiction'. It may mean simply 'an opposing statement', i.e. a *denial* that *A* is larger than *B* by a head. Or it may mean the *paradox* generated (101a6–b2) by saying that *A* is larger than *B* by a head.

65. ἕν and δύο are clearly complements of ἔσεσθαι at 101c6–7. δύο has also been taken as complement of γενέσθαι at 101c1 and 101c5. But 'reason for the coming into being of two' or 'reason for there coming to be two' also seem possible in these lines. Cf.97a–b and note 58.

66. For οὐσία (101c3) see note 7.

67. ἔχεσθαι has been translated 'hang on to' at 101d1 and 101d3. As usually interpreted, it undergoes an abrupt shift of sense from 'hold firmly on to' to 'take issue with'. P. M. Huby (*Phronesis* 1959, 14. n.1) has suggested reading ὀχούμενος ἐπί for ἐχόμενος in 101d1–'riding upon the safety of the hypothesis'–comparing 85d1. But ἐχόμενος has occurred at 100d9 in precisely the sense required at 101d1, whereas L.S.J. give no parallel for that required at 101d3. If the text is to be emended, therefore, alteration of the latter passage, such as Madvig's ἔφοιτο, seems preferable.

68. The meaning at 102d3 is uncertain. Socrates may be comparing his cumbersome style with that of a legal document (Archer-Hind), or with artificially balanced prose-writing (Burnet), or 'talking like a professor' (Bluck).

69. ἐκεῖνο (102e5) has been expanded in translation to 'the large in us'. Hackforth translates: 'the Form that is tall can never bring itself to be short: and similarly shortness, *even the shortness in us*, can never consent to be or become tall' (emphasis added). The words italicized give the impression that the Forms Large and Small *as well as* 'the large and small in us' are being referred to. Yet these lines can be concerned only with the latter, since the suggestion at 103a1 that opposites must either withdraw *or perish* could not apply to the Forms themselves.

70. Much hinges on the grammar and text at 104d1–3. The translation takes ὅτι as subject of κατάσχῃ, ὅτι ἂν κατάσχῃ as subject of ἀναγκάζει, ἅ as object of ἀναγκάζει, and αὐτοῦ as referring to ὅτι. The alternative is to take ὅτι as object of κατάσχῃ,

ἅ as subject of ἀναγκάζει, and ὅτι ἂν κατάσχῃ as object of ἀναγκάζει. αὐτοῦ will then refer either to ὅτι (Hackforth) or to ἅ (D. O'Brien, *C.Q.* 1967, 215–6). For the shift from plural to singular on the latter view cf.70e5, and see Burnet on 104d2. On the translation adopted αὐτό is very hard to explain, and would be better emended to αὐτά. If the original reading was αὐτά, an attempt to correct it by a copyist who had misunderstood ἅ . . . ἀναγκάζει could explain the readings αὐτό in BT and αὐτοῖς in W. αὐτό may, however, be correct, and αὐτοῖς due simply to dittography before ἴσχεων. If so, O'Brien's or Hackforth's version of the sentence will be preferable. For the effect of these alternatives upon the argument see on 104c7–d4.

71. The MSS.' reading αὐτῷ at 104d3, retained by Burnet, is very difficult on any interpretation. It seems best either to omit it, as in the translation, or, if ἐναντίον must have a dative, to read τῷ with Robin or αὖ τῷ with Bluck.

72. No clear distinctions seem marked by Plato's usage of εἶδος, ἰδέα, and μορφή. At 104d9, as at 104b9, 104d2, 104d6, and 105d13, ἰδέα appears to be used as a variant for εἶδος as used at 104c7. Bluck (17, n.7) and Hackforth (150, n.1), both with reservations, suggest that εἶδος on the one hand, and ἰδέα and μορφή on the other, may be aligned with 'transcendent' and 'immanent' Forms respectively. But no safe inferences can, in fact, be drawn from the use of any one of these expressions.

73. The translation follows Burnet's text at 104e8, retaining τὸ ἐναντίον. Hackforth and Verdenius would bracket it, as a misguided gloss upon αὐτό. See, however, D. O'Brien, *C.Q.* 1967, 216.

74. The translation retains αὐτὸ τὸ ἐπιφέρον at 105a4, though it may be merely a correct gloss upon ἐκεῖνο. τὴν ἐναντιότητα (a4–5), translated 'the quality opposed', seems a variant for ἡ ἐναντία ἰδέα (104d9). ἐπιέναι, though elsewhere rendered 'attack', has been translated 'enters' at 105a3–4, since in this context its subject seems not to be thought of as hostile to what it visits—cf. ἥκεων ἐπί at 105d3. The reference of the pronouns is very obscure. At 105a3, despite Burnet's note, ἐκεῖνο has been taken as subject of δέξασθαι, and antecedent of ὃ ἂν ἐπιφέρῃ, and ἐκείνῳ with ἐπιφέρῃ (Verdenius). Thus, apparently, D. O'Brien (*C.Q.* 1967, 214) and see J. Schiller, *Phronesis* 1967, 56. Bluck, however, would take ἐκείνῳ with ἐναντίον: 'anything which brings with itself something opposite to that which it attacks never itself admits the opposite of what is thus brought'. But this interpretation would require that the referent of ἐφ' ὅτι ἂν αὐτὸ ἴῃ be itself an opposite, which—on any

interpretation of the argument—seems incorrect. For whether ὃ ἂν ἐπιφέρῃ be construed as a Form or a particular, and whatever the meaning of ἐπιφέρειν, the item visited will itself be a particular, and not the Form of an opposite.

75. The translation follows Stephanus in deleting ἐν τῷ at 105b9. This simplifies the Greek and brings it more closely into line with the examples in 105c3–6. Retaining ἐν τῷ, the literal meaning is: 'What is it that, whatever thing it comes to be present in, in its body, that thing will be hot?' The interrogative τί is placed inside the subordinary clause, and θερμόν agrees with σώματι, just as περιττός at 105c5 agrees with the masculine ἀριθμῷ. Thus the question asks for the specification of an x, such that (x, y) {(x is in y's body) ⊃ (Fy)}. If περιττόν is read at 105c5 with the first hand in T, it would have to agree with τί at 105c3, and θερμόν would agree with τί at 105b9. This would invite the specification of an x, such that (x, y) {(x is in y) ⊃ (Fx)}. D. O'Brien (C.Q. 1967, 224) rightly rejects this: what is being sought here is a reason for something's being F, not a reason that is itself F. Moreover, the verb νοσήσει (105c3) would be far less naturally predicated of a fever than of a body.

76. ἀδιάφθορος, translated 'indestructible' at 106e1, seems only a variant for ἀνώλεθρος, 'imperishable'. See note 55. But at 106e7 it seems preferable to translate it 'undestroyed'.

77. At 107b9 the exact referent of τοῦτο αὐτό is uncertain. Is the meaning 'if you make sure that you have followed up the argument as far as is humanly possible' (Burnet), or 'if you secure the hypotheses and the deductions from them' (Archer-Hind)? Perhaps Socrates means that an adequate analysis of the hypotheses would necessarily secure their truth. If so, the two alternatives would, in practice, come to the same thing.

78. Reading ὁσίων (108a5), a more general word than θυσιῶν, which it includes in its meaning (Verdenius).

79. Or perhaps (108a7–b1) 'after its long period of passionate excitement concerning the body and the visible region' (Bluck). See 68c9 for this sense of ἐπτοῆσθαι περί. The allusion may, however, be to 81c9–d1, in which case the phrase should be taken as in the translation.

80. Or perhaps (108d2–3) 'but not these things of which he (sc. the theorist alluded to in 108c8) convinces you'. See J. S. Morrison, Phronesis 1959, 105, n.2.

81. The force of κατά (111c5), and the relationship of the

hollows to the regions now to be described, are unclear. Hackforth translates: 'but all round about it there are many places where it is hollowed out'. Bluck: 'and in the earth, in the cavities all over its surface, are many regions'.

82.   Retaining διά (112c3), and interpreting τοῖς κατ᾽ ἐκεῖνα τὰ ῥεύματα with Hackforth, despite the awkwardness of τοῖς governed by εἰσρεῖ. Verdenius suggests 'it flows into the regions which are reached along those streams'. Burnet's text could be translated: 'it flows into the regions of the land along those streams'. But τοῖς remains difficult.

83.   Omitting ἥν at 113c1 with BTW.

84.   Retaining ὡς πορευσόμενος ὅταν ἡ εἱμαρμένη καλῇ at 115a2–3.

85.   Verdenius explains αὐτός at 118a3 as simply marking the fact that the subject of ἥπτετο and εἶπεν is not the same as that of ψύχοιτο and πήγνυτο in the previous sentence. There is thus no need to suppose, with Burnet, that others had touched Socrates by the executioner's direction, or, with Hackforth, to accept Forster's emendation αὖθις.

SELECT BIBLIOGRAPHY

TRANSLATIONS

H. Tredennick, *The Last Days of Socrates*, Harmondsworth, 1954.
W. D. Woodhead, *Plato, Socratic Dialogues*, London, 1953.

EDITIONS, COMMENTARIES ETC.

R. D. Archer-Hind, *The Phaedo of Plato*, (2nd ed.), London, 1894, New York, 1973.
R. S. Bluck, *Plato's Phaedo*, London, 1955.
J. Burnet, *Plato's Phaedo*, Oxford, 1911.
W. D. Geddes, *The Phaedo of Plato*, London, 1863.
R. Hackforth, *Plato's Phaedo*, Cambridge, 1955.
R. Loriaux, *Le Phédon de Platon* (*57a–84b*), Namur, 1969.
L. Robin, *Platon, Phédon*, Paris, 1926.
W. J. Verdenius, *Notes on Plato's Phaedo*, in *Mnemosyne* 1958, 133–243.
H. Williamson, *The Phaedo of Plato*, London, 1915.

OTHER BOOKS

I. M. Crombie, *An Examination of Plato's Doctrines*, London, 1963, i. 303–24, ii. 141–4, 156–71, 295–303, 310–19, 529–31, 539–48.
R. Robinson, *Plato's Earlier Dialectic*, Oxford, 1953, Chs. 7, 9.
T. M. Robinson, *Plato's Psychology*, Toronto, 1970, Ch. 2.
W. D. Ross, *Plato's Theory of Ideas*, Oxford, 1951, Ch. 3.
A. E. Taylor, *Plato, the Man and his Work*, London, 1929, Ch. 8.

ARTICLES

J. L. Ackrill, '*Anamnēsis* in the *Phaedo:* Remarks on 73c–75c', *Exegesis and Argument*, 177–95.
R. S. Bluck, '$\dot{\upsilon}\pi o\theta\acute{\epsilon}\sigma\epsilon\iota\varsigma$ in the *Phaedo* and Platonic Dialectic', *Phronesis* 1957, 21–31.
———, 'Plato's Form of Equal', *Phronesis* 1959, 5–11.
E. L. Burge, 'The Ideas as *Aitiai* in the *Phaedo*', *Phronesis* 1971, 1–13.

J. Gosling, 'Similarity in *Phaedo* 73 seq.', *Phronesis* 1965, 151–61.

H. B. Gottschalk, 'Soul as *Harmonia*', *Phronesis* 1971, 179–98.

R. P. Haynes, 'The form equality as a set of equals: *Phaedo* 74b–c', *Phronesis* 1964, 17–26.

W. F. Hicken, '*Phaedo* 93a11–94b3', *Classical Quarterly* 1954, 16–22.

D. Keyt, 'The Fallacies in *Phaedo* 102a–107b', *Phronesis* 1963, 167–72.

K. W. Mills, 'Plato's *Phaedo* 74b7–c6', *Phronesis* 1957, 128–47, 1958, 40–58.

D. O'Brien, 'The Last Argument of Plato's *Phaedo*', *Classical Quarterly* 1967, 198–231, 1968, 95–106.

G. E. L. Owen, 'A Proof in the περὶ ἰδεῶν', *Journal of Hellenic Studies*, 1957, Part I, 103–11.

P. Plass, 'Socrates' Method of Hypothesis in the *Phaedo*', *Phronesis* 1960, 103–14.

J. M. Rist, 'Equals and Intermediates in Plato', *Phronesis* 1964, 27–37.

D. S. Scarrow, '*Phaedo* 106a–106e', *Philosophical Review* 1961, 245–53.

J. Schiller, '*Phaedo* 104–5: Is the Soul a Form?', *Phronesis* 1967, 50–8.

C. C. W. Taylor, 'Forms as Causes in the *Phaedo*', *Mind* 1969, 45–59.

G. Vlastos, 'Reasons and Causes in the *Phaedo*', *Philosophical Review* 1969, 291–325.

C. J. F. Williams, 'On Dying', *Philosophy* 1969, 217–30.

WORKS AND PERIODICALS
CITED BY ABBREVIATION

A.C.P.A.   *Aristotle's Criticism of Plato and the Academy*, i, H. Cherniss, Baltimore, 1944.

A.D.   *Aristotle on Dialectic: the Topics*, ed. G. E. L. Owen, Oxford, 1963.

A.G.P.   *Archiv für Geschichte der Philosophie.*

A.J.P.   *American Journal of Philology.*

A.P.A.   *American Philosophical Association, Proceedings and Addresses.*

C.P.   *Classical Philology.*

C.Q.   *Classical Quarterly.*

C.R.   *Classical Review.*

DK   *Die Fragmente der Vorsokratiker*, eds. H. Diels and W. Kranz, Berlin, 1951–4.

E.A.   *Exegesis and Argument*, eds. E. N. Lee, A. P. D. Mourelatos, and R. Rorty, Assen, 1974.

E.A.G.P.   *Essays in Ancient Greek Philosophy*, eds. J. P. Anton and G. L. Kustas, Albany, 1971.

E.F.P.   *L'Etre et la Forme selon Platon*, R. Loriaux, Bruges, 1955.

E.P.D.   *An Examination of Plato's Doctrines*, I. M. Crombie, 2 vols., London, 1963.

G.I.   *The Greeks and the Irrational*, E. R. Dodds, Berkeley and Los Angeles, 1951.

G.P.   *The Greek Particles*, J. D. Denniston, Oxford, 1954.

H.G.M.   *A History of Greek Mathematics*, T. L. Heath, 2 vols., Oxford, 1921.

H.S.C.P.   *Harvard Studies in Classical Philology.*

I.A.C.P.   *7th Inter-American Congress of Philosophy, Proceedings*, 2 vols., Quebec, 1967.

I.P.R.	*The Interpretation of Plato's Republic*, N. R. Murphy, Oxford, 1951.
J.H.P.	*Journal of the History of Philosophy.*
L.S.J.	H. G. Liddell and R. Scott's *Greek Lexicon*, revised edition by H. Stuart-Jones, Oxford, 1968.
N.E.P.A.	*New Essays in Plato and Aristotle*, ed. R. Bambrough, London, 1965.
O.E.D.	*The Oxford English Dictionary.*
P.A.M.	*Plato's Analytical Method*, K. Sayre, Chicago and London, 1969.
P.E.D.	*Plato's Earlier Dialectic*, R. Robinson, Oxford, 1953.
P.M.W.	*Plato, the Man and his Work*, A. E. Taylor, London, 1929.
P.P.	*Plato's Psychology*, T. M. Robinson, Toronto, 1970.
P.P.L.	*Philosophical Papers and Letters*, G. W. Leibniz, ed. L. E. Loemker, 2 vols., Chicago, 1956.
P.P.M.	*Plato's Philosophy of Mathematics*, A. Wedberg, Stockholm, 1955.
P.P.R.	*Philosophy and Phenomenological Research.*
P.Q.	*Philosophical Quarterly.*
P.R.	*Philosophical Review.*
P.T.I.	*Plato's Theory of Ideas*, W. D. Ross, Oxford, 1951.
R.M.	*Review of Metaphysics.*
S.H.G.N.	*Studies in Honour of Gilbert Norwood*, ed. M. E. White, Toronto, 1952.
S.P.M.	*Studies in Plato's Metaphysics*, ed. R. E. Allen, London, 1965.
V.B.A.G.	*The Verb 'Be' in Ancient Greek*, C. H. Kahn, Foundations of Language, Supplementary Series, vol. 16, Dordrecht, 1973.

INDEX

The figures in bold type refer to the text

243